Sexting and Young People

Sexting and Young People

Thomas Crofts
University of Sydney, Australia

Murray Lee
University of Sydney, Australia

Alyce McGovern
University of New South Wales, Australia

and

Sanja Milivojevic
University of New South Wales, Australia

palgrave
macmillan

First published 2015 by
PALGRAVE MACMILLAN

Palgrave Macmillan in the UK is an imprint of Macmillan Publishers Limited, registered in England, company number 785998, of Houndmills, Basingstoke, Hampshire RG21 6XS.

Palgrave Macmillan in the US is a division of St Martin's Press LLC, 175 Fifth Avenue, New York, NY 10010.

Palgrave Macmillan is the global academic imprint of the above companies and has companies and representatives throughout the world.

Palgrave® and Macmillan® are registered trademarks in the United States, the United Kingdom, Europe and other countries.

ISBN: 978–1–137–39280–0

This book is printed on paper suitable for recycling and made from fully managed and sustained forest sources. Logging, pulping and manufacturing processes are expected to conform to the environmental regulations of the country of origin.

A catalogue record for this book is available from the British Library.

Library of Congress Cataloging-in-Publication Data

Crofts, Thomas (Wayne Thomas), author.
    Sexting and young people / Thomas Crofts, University of Sydney, Australia; Murray Lee, University of Sydney, Australia; Alyce McGovern, University of New South Wales, Australia; Sanja Milivojevic, University of New South Wales, Australia.
        pages cm
        ISBN 978–1–137–39280–0 (hardback)
        1. Sexting – Law and legislation. 2. Teenage sex offenders – Legal status, laws, etc.. 3. Social media – Law and legislation. 4. Sexting – Social aspects. 5. Sexting – Australia. I. Crofts, Thomas, author. II. Lee, Murray, author. III. McGovern, Alyce, author. IV. Milivojevic, Sanja, author. V. Title.
K5194.C76 2015
344.05′4702854678—dc23   2015012352

Contents

List of Illustrations

Figure

Tables

Foreword

When is a nude picture a 'gift'?

The 'sexting problem' is frequently raised with me by adults and young people in my role as National Children's Commissioner. Adults are worried about the risks associated with children's exploitation and exposure to explicit images in the context of an unregulated digital world. Young people are concerned that what they understand to be private choices and associations are over-policed. It is clear that there is a big disconnect between adults' and young people's perspectives in this space.

This watershed book by Thomas Crofts, Murray Lee, Alyce McGovern and Sanja Milivojevic – *Understanding Sexting by Young People* – provides a rare window into the hearts and minds of young people and their use of technology in their relationships with each other. By conducting a series of focus groups and a survey of over 1400 young people, the authors have gathered new information about sexting behaviour and attitudes to it from both young receivers and senders of 'sexts'. The information generously given by young people for the study is eye opening. Hearing directly from young people about their own interactions and relationships is a powerful reference point from which to gain a deeper understanding of their experiences and perspectives, and, in turn, enables us to rethink our policy and educative interventions.

The authors also set the context within which sexting acts are currently considered, through exploring: the impact of media commentary; the legal frameworks that capture 'sexting' as child pornography; and current educational responses to sexting which tend to perpetuate gender stereotyping and victim blaming.

In analysing the survey results, the authors conceptualise sexting between young people as part of 'a gift economy'. Sexting, it is argued, generally constitutes a 'gift' and the way in which this gift is received depends on the relationship to the sender. A receiver may feel compelled to reciprocate the gift or to send the gift on as a gift to someone else. Of course, taking this latter path usually undermines the position and trust of the original sender.

Despite perceptions in the media and in the community, most sexting participants did not feel coerced or pressured into sending images. Most young males and females in the study reported that they send images 'as a sexy present' or to be 'fun and flirtatious', and, for some participants, sexting was also experienced as a safe way to explore sexuality without physical sexual contact. That said, some participants did accede that there are situations where they might experience pressure to send or send on an image, for example, to keep a relationship, or to look popular.

The negative risks associated with sexting have been well documented. However, for the growing teen, we need to remember that taking risks is a fundamental part of their development and often experienced positively.

Further, the survey results show that sexting generally occurs within a relationship. While many young people report sexting sexual images, they also report not doing it very often, and usually with only one partner.

The authors point to the urgent need to address the criminalisation of sexting among children and young people, even if it is consensual, under a range of current child pornography and child abuse laws. They suggest that new laws covering non-consensual sexting by young people may partly be the answer. However, they warn that care must be taken to ensure that any reform does not end up being a net widening exercise that sees more young people charged with offences.

When we think about our commitment to uphold the rights of children and young people, we are obliged to consider the balance between keeping children safe and their rights to free expression, association and privacy – all so important for their healthy development and identity as active citizens. These human rights are not divisible and need to be able to coexist. While laws can play a part in regulating risky or harmful behaviour, education about the sexual ethics around sexting is more likely to be the solution.

Understanding Sexting by Young People presents a comprehensive and insightful analysis of the issues surrounding the contemporary phenomena of 'sexting' by young people, and the behaviours and perceptions of young people about their motivations in relation to sexting makes for compelling reading.

Megan Mitchell
Australian National Children's Commissioner

Acknowledgements

The authors would like to acknowledge the generous support of a Criminology Research Grant from the Australian Institute of Criminology without which the research that inform this book would not have been possible. Gratitude also goes to the NSW Commission for Children and Young People and the Law School at the University of Sydney for co-funding this project. The team also wishes to thank the NSW Commission for Children and Young People's Youth Advisory Committee for their input into the construction of the survey instrument, and the University of Sydney's Law School and the School of Social Sciences at the University of NSW for ongoing support for research endeavours. Chapter 11 of this book draws on Lee, M. & Crofts, T. (2015). Gender, Pressure, Coercion and Pleasure: Untangling Motivations For Sexting Between Young People. The British Journal of Criminology, 55(3), 454–73 and is reproduced with permission.

This book would not have been possible without the research support of Jarrad Elsmore, Sarah Ienna, Laura McDonald, Dr Lauren Monds, Sally Richards, Dr Tanya Serisier and Dr Shaun Walsh. We thank you all for your important insights. The authors also wish to acknowledge the intellectual input of Dr Michael Salter in the early stages of the research project from which this book is drawn.

Most importantly the authors wish to thank all the young people (and some not so young people) who participated in the focus groups and online survey. This research would not have been possible without your participation.

Part I

Understanding Sexting by Young People

1

An Introduction to Sexting and Young People

Introduction

Young people integrate online and digital technologies into their everyday lives in increasingly complex ways. As McGrath (2009, p. 2) notes, '[y]oung people...see technologies (especially the internet) as a vital part of their social life and the building of their identity'. As mechanisms for socialising, education, relaxation, gaming, romance or communication between friends and peer groups, new technologies provide a key framework within which young people live their lives. Yet, the ways in which they incorporate romantic and sexual relationships and practices into this technology-dominated, virtual world has been relatively underexplored by researchers and, subsequently, it has become problematic for policymakers. Media and social commentators play an important role in drawing our attention to the intersections of digital technologies, sexuality and sexual practices of young people. However, such commentary has also seen these complex interconnections misunderstood and oversimplified. At the very core of contemporary debates around young people's online sexual practices, new technologies, social media, and childhood sexuality has been the phenomenon dubbed 'sexting'. While sexting has many meanings, which we critically explore in more detail below, it generally refers to the digital taking and distribution of images of a nude/semi-nude person through mobile phone or social networking sites.

There has been growing political, media and public concern about sexting in recent years, particularly sexting among children and young people. There have also been, in a range of jurisdictions, either reports of minors being prosecuted under child pornography or child abuse or child exploitation[1] laws for sexting-type behaviours. These two elements

3

of sexting – practices and perceptions, and regulation and legislation – form the core themes of this book. However, before we pursue these themes in depth, we need to set the scene. This introductory chapter considers how sexting is defined, discusses a number of scenarios said to constitute sexting, and introduces some of the conceptual frameworks used in this book to analyse practices of sexting by young people,[2] and laws and regulations which seek to govern such practices. The chapter also outlines the nature and structure of our research project, some of the key arguments we will be making in this book, and introduces the structure and content of the chapters that follow.

Defining sexting: complexities, discourses and terminology

The term sexting is a portmanteau first created by the media that derives from a conflation of the phrase 'sexy texts'. It was first used to describe the sending or receiving of sexually explicit text messages (Rosenberg 2011). However, the term has now expanded to include the digital recording of naked, semi-naked, sexually suggestive or explicit images and their distribution via mobile phone messaging, email, or through the internet on social network sites, such as Facebook, Instagram and YouTube (see, e.g., Joint Select Committee on Cyber-Safety 2011, [4.47]). As the Law Reform Committee of Victoria notes, the term sexting is evolving and 'encompasses a wide range of practices, motivations and behaviours' (2013, p. 15).

Thus, as Ostrager (2010, p. 713) notes, while sexting could be loosely described as a 'more technological approach to sending a flirtatious note' (see also Lenhart 2009), this scenario is only part of much bigger picture. The term sexting is now commonly attributed to the making and distributing of nude or sexual 'pics' within a wide range of quite different scenarios: from taking a picture of oneself and consensually sharing that image with a friend or intimate partner, to the non-consensual resending of an originally consensually made image to a third party or the non-consensual taking and distributing of the image, to simply uploading an explicit image of oneself onto a hard drive. Other scenarios include the recording of a sexual assault, or adults sending an explicit text to 'groom' a child (Law Reform Committee of Victoria 2013, p. 19). 'Sexts' may also be used as tools to harass, bully, threaten or even coerce a person to behave in a certain way. Depending on jurisdiction and the age of participants, these behaviours may or may not constitute criminal offences. Thus, the complexities of sexting require a thorough investigation of the practices it encompasses as well as the motivations, relationships, and perceptions of the actors involved.

Sexting as a term has been particularly salient in popular media and political discourse. It has, in a sense, discursively captured the public imagination. Indeed, sexting among young people has become a significant cultural phenomenon, a topic of major media discussion and the target of concern by law and policymakers. Over the past few years, news media in Australia, North America, Europe and other Western countries have reported numerous cases of sexting where minors have used digital technology to manufacture and distribute sexual images of themselves and/or other minors, in some cases falling foul of child pornography laws. Populist responses to this behaviour have ranged from liberal commentators calling for the decriminalisation of sexting, to conservatives insisting that sexting should be considered a form of child pornography (see Weins and Hiest 2009, p. 2). Media reports and public discourse about sexting tend to gravitate between moralising statements about the inappropriateness of such behaviour by young people, and the emotional and physical harms engaging in sexting potentially cause for young people, to concern that the current legal frameworks in some jurisdictions wrongly allow for the prosecution of young people under child pornography laws. There are reported cases across jurisdictions internationally that have seen young people added to sex offender registries or facing other extreme punishments; outcomes that well may have a significant negative impact later in their lives (see Chapter 4). To an extent, the broad range of activities that fall under the definition of the term sexting means that there is a lack of clarity over the need for a legal response to it (Moran-Ellis 2012, p. 116).

Before we outline the research and data covered in this book, we need to discuss the use of terminology. The term sexting is not commonly used by young people, even people who engage in the practice, as discussed in Chapter 9 in this book. Rather, young people refer to forms of technologically mediated sexual communication as 'nudes', 'dirty pics', 'nude selfies' amongst other terms. Sexting, to them, is a term used by 'out of touch' adults (Weins 2014, pp. 3–8). Largely, we agree that the term is problematic because, as we will argue in this book, sexting fails to distinguish the full range of behaviours, scenarios, motivations and emotions that characterise technologically mediated sexual communications. Despite this, we have decided to use the term sexting throughout this book as it is the term commonly used in academic and public discourse.

About this book

This book investigates the phenomenon of sexting by young people. We examined this under-researched but emergent contemporary legal and social issue using an inter-disciplinary and multi-methods framework asking the question: Are current legal and policy responses to sexting appropriate and are they reflective of young peoples' perceptions and practices of sexting? As such, the research that informs this book had three specific aims: to document young people's perceptions and practices of sexting; to analyse public and media discourse around sexting; and to examine existing legal frameworks and sanctions around sexting and develop recommendations for appropriate and effective legislative policy responses to the practice. The research consisted of a three-stage research project: quantitative surveys and qualitative focus groups with young people, recording their views and experiences of sexting; a media discourse analysis aimed at capturing the tenure of public discussion about sexting; and an analysis of existing laws and sanctions that apply to sexting. Importantly, this research sought to give voice to young people on this topic – a voice that has long been absent from such discussion (Karaian 2012). In doing so we are not suggesting that laws must slavishly respond to the voices of young people. However, their voices can help us to understand their various motivations for, and practices and experiences of, sexting. This in turn can assist in evaluating the effectiveness and appropriateness of existing laws and how laws and policies might best develop to address sexting.

Structure of this book

This book has four parts. The first part, which includes this introduction, explores how we might understand sexting. To begin we provide an overview of key conceptual frameworks we use in the book to explain and theorise sexting practices, as well as to frame existing research and literature on the topic.

Part II discusses what we currently know about sexting. It examines media, law and policy, and educational responses to sexting as well as assessing the already available research into sexting by young people. Chapter 3 begins with an exploration of media representations of sexting. Our analysis focuses on Australian and New Zealand media reports since 2002, and explains the emergence of sexting in the media discourse. We ask how sexting rose to be such a newsworthy topic and outline some of the key themes that have emerged from the media coverage on sexting.

Chapters 4 and 5 capture law and policy responses to sexting in Australia and internationally. We first look in Chapter 4 at significant sexting cases, primarily in the United States but also Australia, the United Kingdom and Canada. This is followed by an overview of child pornography laws to help understand how sexting has been conceptualised by the law and policy makers and why it can be prosecuted as child pornography.

In Chapter 5 we inquire whether and why young people have been charged, or not charged, for child pornography offences. We also explore why there has been a reluctance to legally remove young people from the possibility of being charged with child pornography. The chapter discusses topics such as the age of criminal responsibility, barriers to prosecution, defences to child pornography offences, constitutional protections, and the exercise of discretion.

Chapter 6 turns to the educational responses to sexting. It provides an overview of key international, Australian national and state-based awareness-raising campaigns. We identify the predominant voices and discourses in these campaigns and offer a brief evaluation of these existing approaches.

The final chapter of Part II offers an overview of the current empirical research. We critically assess methodologies and research findings relevant to sexting and young people. In exploring existing responses to, and knowledge of, sexting by young people, Part II of the book provides the contextual background for Parts III and IV.

Part III of this book contains the detail and analysis of the results of our quantitative and qualitative research into young people and sexting. Chapter 8 begins by outlining the findings from the survey component of our project. This includes, among other things, exploration of: the prevalence of sexting; the relationships between sexting participants; gender relations and sexting; the motivations for sexting; and young people's understandings of the legal consequences of sexting.

The qualitative element of our research is outlined in Chapters 9 and 10. In Chapter 9 we discuss perceptions and practices of sexting. This includes: how young people negotiate their online identity and privacy; how they define sexting; how they perceive motivations for sexting among their peers; and how they perceive the prevalence of sexting among peers; as well as their views on the social consequences and impact of sexting. In Chapter 10 we present young people's views on criminal justice interventions around sexting, based on their reflections on two case studies of legal responses to sexting. Part III concludes with an overall analysis and discussion of the findings of our quantitative and qualitative research in Chapter 11.

Part IV of this book draws together the themes of the book in order to critique existing responses to sexting by young people and to make suggestions for alternative law and policy approaches. We offer some concluding thoughts on sexting practices by young people in Chapter 13.

2
Conceptualising Sexting

Introduction

How should we understand both the nature and context of acts of sexting and socio-legal concern about such acts? In this chapter we discuss the conceptual frameworks through which this book views these different aspects of sexting. First we discuss the conceptual tools we use to understand the construction of sexting as a socio-legal problem, then we move on to how public perceptions and reactions to sexting might be understood. We then discuss our framework for understanding motivations for sexting, and finally comment on sexting and the nature of the image.

It would be useful to be able to conceptualise the practice of sexting, attempts to control the practice, the reactions of the social audiences, and the actors' motivations through a single framework. However, as our analysis will indicate, there is no one convenient conceptual framework through which to frame these various elements of sexting by young people. Rather, the multi-methods approach to the research that informs this book also requires multiple conceptual frames through which to view these issues. The conceptual frameworks we deploy are informed first and foremost by the collection and analysis of the research data – rather than being imposed upon it. Underpinning this, we also conceptualise the criminalisation of sexting by young people as a social process (Becker 1963); such a process requires an act and actor (an 'offender'), a social audience (media and/or public), a social reaction (policing, law, policy), and a (constructed or actual) victim. Our multi-methods approach sets out to capture this process and the interaction between each of these elements.

Sexting as a socio-legal problem

On the face of it, sexting appears to be a new practice and problem. Indeed, the problematisation of sexting seems to fit the schema of a moral panic – 'a condition, episode, person or group of persons emerges to become defined as a threat to societal values and interests' (Cohen 1973, p. 9). However, on closer inspection, there is justification not to treat the issue as a traditional moral panic. First, there is no clear 'folk devil' in the sexting practices of young people. Admittedly, there is a possibility of an online child sex offender sharing child pornography or 'grooming' young people, but he or she is not central to the practice – not a key actor on which to place anxiety as per Cohen's (1973) famous model. Second, while moral panic theory does not necessarily assume the cause of panic must be novel, it does assume something of a break from past ways of conceptualising a particular issue. Again, as we will discuss throughout the book, we do not believe sexting by young people fits this schema.

Rather, as a social 'problem' we can trace some of today's concern about sexting by young people back to much more long-held concerns about both new forms of media technology and expressions of childhood sexuality that come to be regarded as promiscuous. In analysing these issues, we draw on a range of social theories. First, we deploy critical theories of late modernity in order to understand both concerns about the dangers of new technologies and how the speed of new technologies is impacting upon and changing the nature of practice. Second, we draw on a far longer – seemingly continuous – history of social anxieties about childhood sexuality and attempts to regulate and govern its expression. Third, we make use of contemporary gender theories to understand the ways in which gendered 'double standards' play out in sexting behaviours that can create divergent experiences for boys and girls engaging in or affected by sexting.

Technology and sexual harms in late modernity

The social and cultural changes that commentators have variously termed 'late modernity', 'liquid modernity', 'second modernity' or 'post-modernity' have at their core notions of the collapse of time and space – or the increasing domination of time over space (Bauman 2000; Giddens 1991; Virilio 1986). Technological developments have allowed global communications and the transference of information to occur instantaneously. As Bauman (2000, pp. 10–11) notes:

> [T]he long effort to accelerate the speed of movement has presently reached its 'natural limit'. Power can move with the speed of the

electronic signal – and so the time required for the movement of its essential ingredients has been reduced to instantaneity. For all practical purposes, power has become truly exterritorial, no longer bound or even slowed down, by the resistance of space (the advent of cellular telephones may well serve as a symbolic 'last blow' delivered to the dependency on space: even the access to a telephone socket is unnecessary for a command to be given and seen through to its effect. It does not matter any more where the giver of the command is – the difference between 'close by' and 'far away', or for that matter between the wilderness and the civilized, orderly space, has been all but cancelled).

This mastery over space, a capacity to transfer information instantaneously, has accompanied and hastened significant social and cultural transformation. As Virilio (1986) would have it, this increase in speed can change the nature of events themselves. Indeed, one of Bauman's (2000) key observations about liquid modernity is that social forms now change so quickly, structural adjustment is all but impossible. Humans struggle to adjust to, and keep up with, the very changes their ingenuity facilitates, reflecting what scholars have termed 'reflexive modernisation' (Beck 1992; Beck et al. 1994). These changes thus appear disruptive and dangerous, and bring with them further risks that require further cultural and social adjustment.

In the 70 years that have passed since the mass adoption of the television in the developed world, our communications technologies have gone through unprecedented development and change. Key exemplars of communications technology illustrative of the changes Bauman suggests include the telephone, the photograph, the television and the internet. These four technologies converge in modern devices such as personal smart phones and tablets. These devices are liberated from the socket, instantaneous in nature and, now, found in the hands of the masses.

There is also little doubt that the speed and penetration of new technologies have presented significant challenges to the traditional notion of the sovereign state and its attempts to govern. Borderless (and ostensibly 'ungovernable') cyberspace undermines state-based regulation and security even as tougher laws attempt to reassert sovereignty (Aas 2007). Ever-blurring boundaries and borders 'that are no longer physical or territorial lines on a map' (Pickering 2008, p. 177) see states struggling to deal with the apparently unavoidable – a growing threat of cybercrimes of great variety. As such, the customary practices of criminal justice interventions, such as search, seize and arrest, are deemed inadequate for offences that take place in cyberspace (Fox 2001). In order to address cyberthreats, various state and non-state actors, politicians and the media have called for more rigorous state interventions, tougher legislation, practices of self-policing when online, the expansion of internet monitoring powers, censorship and parental controls, and unconditional cooperation with law enforcement in investigating offences (Howden 2011; Berg 2011; Jewkes & Yar 2010). The debate around crime in the age of digital technology incorporates a 'part of the problem' and a 'part of the solution' standpoint, in which searching for 'the solution' can potentially lead to 'new punitiveness' (Pratt 2000), pre-emptive justice policies and the violation of rights of internet users and others impacted by such policies.

Importantly, each new telecommunications device and its accompanying utilisation require new manners and etiquette (Marx 1995). Each advance in mediated communication brings an emergent cultural change with a 'set of interactional codes and symbolic manners appropriate to the technology' (Ferrell et al. 2008, p. 106). Like the technology itself, these codes and manners do not come fully formed. Just as the language of phone texting has developed with the technological advances of the mobile phone, the technical capacities of such phones to produce and disseminate images have opened up new capabilities and possibilities (McLuhan et al. 1967). But if we follow Bauman, the 'manners' – and ethics, procedures and practices – are always playing catch-up, as the liquid social form and modern technology shifts once again. And, like these manners, law and regulation also continually play catch-up. Also, if we agree with Virilio's (1986) notion that technology that is fast will win out over slower or outdated technologies, it is not surprising that sexting has gained popularity within a very short period of time. This new form of sexual communication has obvious significant advantages in terms of the rate at which sexual dialogues can occur.

Governing childhood sexuality: continuities

While much recent academic research and media reporting of sexting takes as its starting point the notion that sexting is a some what new activity – an activity essentially made possible by the development of new information and communication technologies – there are important caveats to this conceptualisation. As Garland (1997), drawing on the work of Foucault, tells us, we need to be wary in evaluations of the present that conceive of contemporary problems and anxieties as significantly different or largely discontinuous with those that came before them. Just as there is nothing novel in the production of pornography,[1] youthful sexual expression (or exploitation) is certainly not a new phenomenon (Fishman 1982). Of course new technologies have affected the delivery speed of such expression, just as they have affected the level of opportunity for some forms of exploitation. In this sense, genealogical and governmentality frameworks that often point to hidden continuities in discourse are also important analytical tools for understanding how sexting has become a pressing contemporary issue.

From a genealogical perspective, the history of present anxieties about childhood sexuality and telecommunications technologies is somewhat continuous. For example, the problematisation of childhood sexuality – how to suppress and/or regulate it – emerged in the late 17th/ early 18th century (Fishman 1982). While much of the early discourse around the management of childhood sexuality concerned masturbation, the 'experts' guiding this regulation have changed over time. By the 18th century, anti-masturbation pamphlets and pronouncements on the topic from figures as significant as Jean Jacques Rousseau proliferated (Fishman 1982). While the baton was passed to School Masters and the church in the 19th century, by the 20th century the discourse was dominated by clinicians, psychiatrists and social workers, who made sex education mainstream by introducing it into the public school system. The later 20th century became a period where childhood sexuality was no longer to be suppressed per se, but managed and regulated. Parents could give over the problem of regulating childhood sexuality to a state happy to outline a set of normalising principles. As Foucault notes:

> The sexualization of children was accomplished in the form of a campaign of health of the race – precocious sexuality was presented from the eighteenth century to the end of the nineteenth century as an epidemic menace that risked compromising not only the future health of adults but the future of the entire society and species. (1990, p. 146)

The key point here is that childhood sexuality has always been about something more than childhood sexuality – it has been both an instrument through which to manage, and an indicator of, the moral health of a nation. Any contemporary account of sexting needs to acknowledge this continuity, recognising an array of differing attempts at the governance of childhood sexuality.

A similar argument can be made in relation to telecommunications technologies. As Wartella and Jennings noted in 2000 (p. 31), '[c]omputer technology has ushered in a new era of mass media, bringing with it great promise and great concern about the effect on children's development and well-being'. Again though, there is continuity. Similar to historical debates around the emergence of new technologies (such as telephone, television, radio, movies), contemporary narratives are fuelled with concerns about the impact of new media on children's morality, ethical principles, and capacity to expose them to illicit sexual and criminal behaviour (Wartella & Jennings 2000).

Likewise, the governmentality perspective illustrates the ways in which the influence of neo-liberal politics has intersected with technology and childhood sexuality in the context of sexting by young people. This may explain why sexting by some groups – young people, and young girls in particular – may be problematised, while at the same time sexting among adults can be seen as a legitimate form of risk-taking, excitement or inter-relationship practice. As O'Malley tells us:

> The broad political rationality generates a cultural milieu in which risk taking may be regarded as a 'good thing' and be applied to all manner of domains other than those originally imagined. In the nineteenth century, prudence had been such a strong requirement imposed on the mass by Victorian liberal politics, that risk taking was generally frowned upon except among a privileged few who could afford the luxury... Neo-liberal governmental rationality has been 'innovated' into legally problematic practices by certain individuals or groups. Governmentality may be useful as a way of rendering intelligible the risky rationalities deployed by such individuals and groups, and the ambiguities of their relations with other rationalities such as neo-liberalism. (2010, pp. 14–15)

So while childhood sexuality may long have been a problem for government, the political contexts in which its regulation has occurred have shifted considerably. Nowadays, this means that the regulation and criminalisation of sexting by young people occurs in a context of a broader individualisation where online sexual expression is not only tolerated but in some cases will be expected; for example, some research suggests that there may be a greater use of social networking 'hook-up' apps in some gay cultures (see Gudelunas 2012, p. 348).

While continuing anxiety about childhood sexuality is a key component of the discourse around young people and sexting, there is also a more recent concern about child abuse. Concerns around child sexual abuse have grown significantly since its 'discovery' as a problem the early 1970s. With new, digital technologies, these concerns have been renewed and strengthened because of the very core of the online engagement: its perceived clandestine character and potential global reach. This, together with the very scale of the growth of online technologies, the threat of online predators and other unwelcome 'Others', and the vulnerability of potential victims, has resulted in 'a series of local and global moral panics' (Jewkes 2007, p. 5) that have purportedly warranted a quick and uncompromising response, mostly within a punitive framework.

Sexting as gendered practice

A range of existing studies into sexting have highlighted the often gendered nature of the practice. Gender has also provided a lens though which sexting by young people has been problematised, with educational campaigns often focusing on the way in which sexting can have negative effects on young women (see Chapter 6).

There are complex issues of consent and agency around the application of feminist theories to sexting that go to the heart of contemporary feminist debates. In particular, these revolve around the value and capacity of young women's sexual desire. Radical feminism, for example, might suggest that, given the girls involved are minors, and given the broader patriarchal power structures or post-feminist cultural pressures that produce sexualised forms of girlhood, young women's desires and self-construction are always bounded. This is seen to be the case even when the behaviour is consensual – in other words, young women's agency and, consequently, their consent is limited. On the other hand, post-structural feminist or post-feminist accounts may see such behaviours as legitimate expressions of young women's sexual desires, and understand attempts to regulate this as essentially the silencing of their voices or repressing displays of their sexuality. While these two positions are not mutually exclusive, they do provide analytical challenges we will expand on later in this book. Within the sexting scholarship, however, there are a number of issues relating to gender to be addressed.

Pressure and coercion

First, there is the argument that pressure and/or coercion is a key reason why young females (in particular) send images of themselves to others (usually young males). Englander (2012, p. 3) notes in relation to her own research that '[i]ndisputably, the most important motivation for sexting revealed in this study (and others) was pressure or coercion'.

However, one of the reasons why debates around pressure and coercion become circular is that the variety of forms and origins of pressure that might be experienced are not always well articulated. These presumed elements of pressure fall into three categories that overlap and intersect: individual pressure, peer group pressure and socio-cultural pressure.

Individual pressure operates within individual relationships between sexting participants (senders and receivers). Such pressure is likely to have some basis in the biographical particularities of individuals involved. This kind of pressure is also the type more likely to become coercive. At one end of the scale of individual pressures one partner in a relationship might ask for an image of the other which the other only sends because he or she feels obligated to for the good of the relationship – but which the sender might also enjoy sending. Pleasure and pressure are not necessarily mutually exclusive feelings – just as risk can be both exciting and dangerous. At the other end of the scale, an individual could be blackmailed into sending an image of himself or herself under the threat of some kind of shaming, humiliation or even violence (see eg. Keeley et al. 2014; Katz et al. 2014). The latter is probably more accurately a form of cyberbullying rather than sexting, but nonetheless an act of sexting might be the result (and also become the tool of further incidents of cyberbullying). The way such individual pressures are experienced (or not) are likely to be related to the status or position of power of the sender. That is, the biographical and socio-demographic characteristics of the individual being asked for a photo will place that individual differentially in relation to power.

Peer group pressure involves what criminologists refer to as midrange social dynamics of particular peer or social groups and might even extend to entire school cohorts, but they may be bounded geographically, be relative to a specific class or ethnicity, and be themselves specifically gendered. For example Peskin et al. (2013) noted that sexting is prevalent among ethnic minority youth. Indeed, it is clear from the currently available qualitative research (Ringrose et al. 2012, 2013; Albury et al. 2012) that particular peer and social groups are likely to influence normative behaviours where a member of such a group might feel his or her group membership is jeopardised by non-participation in sexting. At the other extreme, peers may actively coerce individuals to send images of themselves through abusive behaviours that have a continuum from the classroom and playground into cyber-space (Ringrose et al. 2013). We might conceive the dynamic of such peer groups through an interactional framework (Becker 1963; Lemert 1981) where labels (internalised and externalised) and group dynamics create incentives (or disincentives) to engage in sexting. Sexting behaviours may be positively reinforced within the group culture. *Socio-cultural pressure* is the general normative pressure in any social order. For example, the contemporary sexualisation of culture is said to have created normative expectations whereby women and girls may be expected to perform sexualised subject positions. There is a body of literature that sees young women as becoming increasingly sexualised and pornified in post-feminist cultural and social contexts where forms of sexualised selfhood are to be performed (Attwood 2009; Durham 2008; Gill 2012). Additionally, cultural (heterosexual) norms create a situation where particular displays of feminine (hetero-) sexuality might be rewarded or judged positively (or negatively). As Powell (2007, p. 11) argues:

> Subtle pressure relates to the gendered social norms or expectations as to what men and women are 'supposed' to do in a relationship ... this is further borne out in research which suggests that ideals surrounding love, romance and sex as well as gender-role expectations of sexual encounters, can influence the occurrence of unwanted or 'compliant' sexual experiences.

Gill (2012) has likewise questioned whether notions of young women's 'empowerment' through practices such as sexting may simply be reinforcing, reproducing and reflective of sexualised and sexist (hetero-) normative expectations. She notes that the term may have lost any analytical purchase given its co-option for consumerist and possibly exploitative purposes. As a result of pressure and coercion at these levels, it is legitimate to question whether young women in some instances are able to fully and freely *consent* to the activity, even where they produce and send the image.

Gendered double standards

As well as pressure to send, there are other key characteristics of sexting that reproduce gendered power relations. For example, there is likely to be a *gendered double standard* around how young women who send images of themselves are judged compared to young men who do the same thing. This double standard has been demonstrated in qualitative research (Ringrose et al. 2013; Albury et al. 2010, Albury 2013) but also in a number of high-profile incidences where young women have committed suicide as a result of the humiliation of having a digital image of themselves circulated. Here moral expectations of what 'good girls' should and should not do can be seen to collide with the expectation to behave in a sexualised way – as discussed above.

Connected to this double standard is the capacity for young women who send images, or whose images are forward distributed, to be 'slut shamed' (Ringrose et al. 2013). While young men who send images can be shamed there is no equivalent category of 'slut' that carries the same derogatory implications. Young women's behaviour might be constructed as inappropriate by young men, but also by their female peers. There is also the capacity for slut shaming to operate at the individual, peer and socio-cultural levels in much the same way as pressure – but almost as the opposite side of the same coin. So, potentially, young women may be under more pressure to produce and send images of themselves, but may suffer more severe public censure should their trust in the receiver be breached.

While slightly different to slut shaming, images of young women can be used by boys to bolster their own status. Ringrose et al. (2012, 2013) demonstrated though qualitative research how such photos can subsequently be used as trophies or, in some cases, be sent on to friends as a mark of male status between peers. In this sense, images form part of a digital online economy. They also note how boys take effective 'ownership' of young women's bodies, with some even writing across their breasts that they are the property of a particular young man, then photographing and sending this image (Ringrose et al. 2013). Albury et al. (2013) further advise that female peers can also label the young women sending erotic images as 'slutty'.

Young women can find their behaviours construed as much more problematic than young men by legislators and other moral guardians. Educational campaigns aimed at young women tend to operate via very different narratives to those aimed at young men (Salter et al. 2013; see also Chapter 6). Karaian (2014, p. 288) has noted how young women are also slut shamed in education campaigns where it is 'girls' responsibility to abstain from sexting'. The same is true of some of the well-publicised legal cases involving sexting, where young women's behaviours became the target of legal sanction in the form of forced education and training programs (Crofts & Lee 2013).

Gender theory has utility for both how we understand public reactions and broader perceptions of sexting, and how we understand motivations in regard to individuals who engage in the practice.

Motivations: Mauss and sexting as a gift

Marcel Mauss' work on the nature of gifting brings a novel framework to understanding motivations to engage in sexting and it is a key component of our analysis. Although Mauss' ethnographic and anthropological works are based in the study of non-Western 'traditional' societies, they have particular purchase for understanding motivations around sexting. Mauss himself notes, describing the universality of contract and exchange: 'It has been suggested that these (traditional) societies lack the economic market, but this is not true; for the market is a very human phenomenon which we believe to be familiar to every known society' (1969, p. 2).

Thus, Mauss' project does not simply outline the differences between traditional and modern societies; it also highlights the similarities between these gift economies and modern market economies. In concluding, he notes: 'Much of our everyday morality is concerned with the question of obligation and the spontaneity of the gift. It is our good fortune that all is not yet couched in terms of purchase and sale' (Mauss 1969, p. 63).

Further, Mauss was studying traditional societies – and the gift economies he saw as central to them – in their totality (Evans Pritchard in Mauss 1969, p. vii). This is important as it implores us not to simply study sexting as an isolated system of exchange but, to paraphrase Evans Pritchard in the introduction to Mauss' text, to see it as part of 'economic, juridical, moral aesthetic, religious, mythological, and socio-morphological phenomena' (1969, p. vii).

Scholars have made much of the utility of Mauss' work in later modern Western capitalist societies, and have applied it to the developing utopian dream of growth of the internet, and even to systems of online file sharing – of which the current topic could be seen as a sub-genre. The relevance for this project is how this particular gift economy of sexting fits with the idea of studying systems in their totality. What this means for the current study is that the gift giving around sexting cannot be divorced from the social institutions and norms in which the practice is embedded. As we will demonstrate, many young people conceptualise the sending of a sext as a gift to a boyfriend of girlfriend. This gifting occurs in a context where various normative values and beliefs influence the activity. Thus, we will place sexting as gifting within broader socio-cultural and normative contexts. We will also argue that this notion of gifting holds even in most cases where sexting is non-consensual.

Sexing the image

Finally, there are also conceptual and socio-legal debates around the nature of the image that must come into play in any analytical account of sexting. At the heart of such debates is whether a particular image is actually erotic or sexual at all. Images do not hold an innate truth; rather, they are subject to a variety of 'readings' that are in turn influenced by the socio-cultural context in which the reading takes place, the biographical background of the viewer, and the socio-legal context under which they are examined. As we will discuss, law has constructed nude and semi-nude photos of children in a broad range of ways.

Such diverse accounts of the image also touch on notions of agency, particularly in regards to images of minors. McDonald (2012) succinctly captures both sides of this debate. In drawing on Sontag (1977), he notes that, in modelling naked for an artist, the young subject's inability to 'consent' symbolises the sexualisation of the child and a resulting 'loss of the child's innocence' (McDonald 2012, p. 105). It is not the image itself that might be constructed as pornographic, but a context that labels it so. In the words of Sontag: '[I]t turns people into objects that can be symbolically possessed' (1977, p. 14).

Yet, that particular account, McDonald goes on to argue, does not accord with the experiences of child subjects of the particular artist in question. Rather, the experiences of these young people, even when grown, have been overwhelmingly positive. In this sense, critics of such photographs might actually be robbing the young subjects of 'the capacity to articulate an experience of performative engagement with the camera' (McDonald 2012, p. 106).

Conclusion

Sexting by young people involves a wide array of practices, but it also creates a significant social policy problem. This problem is exacerbated by difficulties defining and separating the range of practices. Consequently, conceptual and theoretical understandings and explanations of sexting are not – and should not be – straightforward. Such theorising is made more complex by the varying subjective accounts of the social actors themselves. With these factors in mind this book consists of a multi-conceptual approach that borrows from a number of theoretical traditions to help us conceptualise that various elements of sexting.

In Part II that follows we assess the current media, policy, legal and educational responses to sexting by young people. We also explore existing research into sexting and provides a background for contextualising our research into young people and sexting which forms the basis of Part III.

Part II

Young People and Sexting Discourses

3
Media Representations of Sexting

Introduction

In recent years, sexting as a concept has gained traction in popular and media discourse, becoming one of a suite of issues canvassed by the media that come under the umbrella of cyberporn, cyberbullying and other technologically facilitated 'harms'. While a growing body of work has begun to emerge about the experiences, understandings and perceptions of young people around the practice of sexting – which we explore in other chapters of this book – much less is known about the way in which the concept of sexting entered the public lexicon, the role of the media in this process, and the implications of media discourses on understandings of and attitudes towards sexting. Given that the media provide an important forum for the discussion and dissemination of a range of social issues, including crime and deviance (cf. Jewkes 2011a; Surette 2010), analysing media representations becomes important when trying to understand the responses of governments, agents of social control, the public and young people to the issue of sexting.

Drawing on analyses of media reports between 2002 and 2013 from Australian and New Zealand media outlets, this chapter outlines the emergence of the term sexting in the Australian and New Zealand media. Through the analysis of over 2000 media items, the chapter identifies some of the key themes to emerge from the data on media discourse and public statements about sexting, as well as the key groups, stakeholders or 'actors' involved in framing and informing debates around sexting and young people. Comparisons are also drawn with existing literature that explores media representations of sexting, young people and cyberbullying internationally.

Media in context

Young people and their exploits are a perpetual source of fascination for the media and the public alike. Concerns over the behaviours and activities of youth are as old as the media itself; history is littered with examples of media-driven moral panics over the way in which individuals and groups conduct themselves in society, with young people often at the centre of such panics, as either victims or offenders, or both (Cohen 1973; Taylor 1999). The proliferation of new and emerging technologies and the rise of social and digital media have only served to exaggerate these panics in modern times (Burke 2008). As Vanderbosch et al. (2013, p. 99) argue, 'the news media pay considerable attention to stories on internet-related risks and children, especially those involving sex and aggression'. A range of moral panics have been associated with the introduction and proliferation of digital technologies, particularly as they relate to young people. Potter and Potter (2001, p. 31), for example, argued that '[c]oncern with sexual predators [and] "cyberporn" became media-induced moral panics of the mid- and late-1990s', with much of the concern raised over the ability for children to access pornography on the internet.

Drotner (1992) and Draper (2012) go further, arguing that when it comes to the emergence of new technologies and new media forms, the moral panic model is lacking. They argue that the public reaction to these new forms of media, particularly in terms of young peoples' engagement with them, should instead be understood by what they term a 'media panic'. As Draper explains:

> like moral panics, media panics focus on young people as symbols of greater social unrest engaged in power struggles over ideological values. However, where in a moral panic the media is described as drawing attention to social issues, Drotner notes, 'in media panics, the mass media are both the source and the medium of public reaction' (1992, p. 44)...a reaction that may eventually result in regulation and censorship. (2012, p. 222)

Further, we might ask whether the 'folk devils' of the traditional moral panic model can be readily identified in the supposed moral panics of today; are they found in the young people themselves, or the technologies they are engaging with?

While there is no one theoretical or methodological approach that can capture the complex and diverse ways in which the media represent social issues (Greer 2010, p. 9), the media do play an important role in delimiting our social world. Thus, the way in which they approach these social issues, especially in the context of agenda setting, is open to analysis and critique. As Jewkes (2011a, p. 41) notes, the media set the news agenda by choosing to publish or broadcast certain stories and events over others. In turn, the ways in which these stories are framed have implications for the meanings that are attached to them. The tone taken, solutions offered, 'experts' cited, tropes replicated, and individuals or groups associated with an identified behaviour or activity all play an important role in shaping public discourse around a particular issue (Jewkes 2011a). Sexting is one issue that has gained increasing amounts of media attention over the last decade (Lee et al. 2013; Podlas 2014). Analyses of sexting stories reveal a number of themes in relation to the way in which sexting is framed in media and, subsequently, in public discourse.

Worth noting here too are the ways in which newsmaking processes impact on journalistic and editorial decisions to focus on particular stories and social issues. In the case of sexting, there is the potential for stories to fulfil a number of 'news values' – 'judgements that journalists and editors make about the public appeal of a story and also whether it is in public interest' (Jewkes 2011a, p. 42) – that journalists implicitly or explicitly seek out in the process of constructing news. Foremost in these news values are titillation (Chibnall 1977, p. 23) or sex (Jewkes 2011a, pp. 51–2); by its very name, sexting fulfils the criteria of being scandalous, appealing to the curiosity and voyeurism of readers. In addition, sexting evokes elements of personalisation, simplification, dramatisation, children and risk, as will be explored throughout this chapter (Chibnall 1977, p. 23; Jewkes 2011a, pp. 45–62).

Analysing media representations of sexting: methodology and data

The research presented in this chapter originates from an analysis of media reports that was particularly focused on understanding the role the media play in framing knowledge around the issue of sexting. Based on the collation and analysis of Australian and New Zealand media reports on sexting since 2002, the research sought to explore a number of themes on the way in which sexting has been articulated in the media, and what definitions and explanations were being used in news reporting. Of particular interest were the key stakeholders, 'actors' or spokespeople on sexting cited in the media, as well as recurrent themes to emerge from the data that appeared to define or position sexting as an issue of importance or newsworthiness.

The data collection phase of the study involved a number of stages. First, in order to contain the data to a manageable quantity and track the tenor of media and public sentiment in a discrete locale, the scope of the project was confined to Australian and New Zealand media publications. Second, using the ProQuest Australia & New Zealand Newsstand database, searches were conducted for the following terms:[1]

- 'sexting'
- 'sex text' or 'sex texts'
- 'nude selfie' or 'nude selfies'
- 'naked selfie' or 'naked selfies'
- 'banana pic' or 'banana pics'.

Search terms were developed following consultation with youth representatives on the NSW Commission for Children and Young People Advisory Group. As previously mentioned, while commonly used by and among adults to describe sexually suggestive, semi-nude, or nude personal pictures/videos, sexting is not the preferred term of young people (see Weins 2014, pp. 3–8; Moran-Ellis 2012, pp. 115–18 and chapter 9). For this reason, a wider range of terms were identified and used in the search in order to capture articles that may use alternative terminology that would otherwise be overlooked by the search engine.

Finally, the data was thematically analysed to identify information consistent with the interests of the broader research project. There were no set categories for this analysis; rather, the analysis was driven by a number of guiding questions, including:

- When did sexting emerge as a media discourse and how has it been defined?
- How do the media frame sexting? What are the common themes that emerge around sexting, particular as it relates to young people?
- How is 'harm' explored and/or defined?
- How are the causes of sexting explored and/or defined?
- Who are the key stakeholders, experts and/or primary definers of sexting in the media and in what context are they being cited?
- What are the responses (actual or recommended) to sexting and young people that are explored in the media? How are these responses framed by the media?
- What is being ignored or overlooked in media coverage of sexting?

Table 3.1 Number of sexting articles by year and media source

Media type and year	Newspapers	Wire feeds	Other sources	Total
2001	0	0	0	0
2002	2	0	0	2
2003	4	0	0	4
2004	13	0	0	13
2005	35	0	0	35
2006	12	0	1	13
2007	25	1	0	26
2008	10	1	0	11
2009	171	21	2	194
2010	198	22	1	221
2011	406	26	3	435
2012	433	27	1	461
2013	579	45	9	633
Total	**1888**	**143**	**17**	**2048**

Searches conducted on ProQuest determined that there were no relevant term matches before 2002, which resulted in a timeframe of 2002–13, inclusive, for data collection. Media formats examined within ProQuest included newspapers, wire feeds[2] and other sources (such as radio broadcasts, commentary, magazines and weblinks), culminating in the identification of over 2000 relevant articles across the 12-year period of study. As Table 3.1 and Figure 3.1 demonstrate, the prevalence of sexting-related articles in the Australian and New Zealand media grew significantly from 2009, and continued to trend upwards through to 2013.

The data also revealed that media interest in sexting was primarily confined to the print media, with newspapers far outweighing other media formats for the presentation of sexting-related articles. This may be explained by the capacity for newspapers to cover a wider range and degree of content than other media formats; it was evident in the analysis, for example, that newspapers included both local and international sexting stories, whereas wire feeds and other sources tended to cover only local examples.

The emergence of sexting: identifying and defining a concept

Before the term sexting entered the public realm, the term 'sex text' gained media coverage in Australia in 2003[3] via a high-profile cheating scandal involving Australian cricketer and celebrity Shane Warne. Warne, it was alleged, 'bombarded' South African woman Helen Cohen

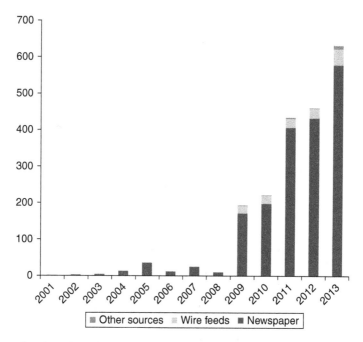

Figure 3.1   Number of sexting-related articles by year

Alon with 'sex texts' in which he claimed to be lying in bed naked with his wife Simone but thinking of Alon ('Your calls' 2003; Masters 2003). In a clear case of the convergence of the news values of titillation/sex and personalisation/celebrity (Chibnall 1977; Jewkes 2011a), following the Warne-Alon scandal 'sex texts' became a newsworthy topic for the Australian media. Between 2003 and 2006, for example, the largest number of sexting-related articles in the media reported on the alleged sexting behaviour of not only Shane Warne, but also high-profile English soccer player David Beckham (see English 2004).

However, Shane Warne was not the only one making headlines for allegedly engaging in adult sex texting in 2003. The article 'Man Fined for Sex Text' reported that a 39-year-old man from Adelaide, South Australia, was fined $250 for sending 'lewd text messages' to a woman he met through his job ('Man fined' 2003). It is noteworthy that at this time sexting was of concern in relation to adults, not young people.

When these instances of sexting hit the headlines, 'sex texts' referred to a practice somewhat different to today's conceptualisation of sexting.

While the first mobile phones with built-in cameras were released internationally in mid to late 2000, it was not until late 2003/early 2004 that camera phones enjoyed general circulation (Hill 2013). As such, 'sex texts' as they were known in 2003 primarily indicated the exchange of sexually explicit text messages, rather than images (Benns 2003).

By 2005, the term sexting began to feature in the Australian media. Cited in an article published in *The Daily Telegraph*, Sydney, on 2 July (James 2005), Shane Warne's mobile phone behaviours once again came under scrutiny and provided the first example of the use of the term sexting in the Australian media. Discussing Warne's actions, the article stated:

> A telling aspect of his sexual farragos is the use of his mobile for sexting (texting).
>
> Although 'kiss and sell' newspaper accounts must always be treated with caution, there is a suspiciously similar theme to the sexts.
>
> Three women, from different continents, have accused him of harassing them with unwanted calls or sexts. In one case, he was alleged to have performed a sex act during a call to her answerphone. Another claimed the sexts 'made my flesh creep'. (James 2005, p. 87)

The article appears to imply that 'sexts', 'sex texts' and 'sexting' in Warne's case went beyond the up-until-this-point text-based content, but were yet to include visual images. By 2007, however, a different picture emerges in the media about the practice of 'sex texts', or 'sexts', with reports developing about the sending and receiving of nude and sexual images via mobile phone. Such developments, not surprisingly, seem to mirror developments in mobile phone technology. Interestingly, the first mention in the media of visually based sex texts came via the case of a Northern Territory police officer, who was reportedly demoted after 'he was caught sending a nude picture of himself – via mobile phone – to a junior female colleague in December. The woman lodged an official complaint against the Darwin-based officer' ('Sex text' 2007, p. 2).

By 2008, such sexual images and their dissemination were being described by the media as sexting, resurrecting the term that was first used in 2005 to describe Shane Warne's alleged text-based 'sexts'. The start of media attempts to define the practice of sexting also emerged in 2008, with stories increasingly shifting their focus from the celebrity sexting scandals to cases of workplace harassment

(Cann 2008). Findings from a Western Australian survey were widely reported at this time, suggesting that sexting was part of a wider cyber-bullying problem facing children (Pritchard 2008). As sexting became a 'mainstream' issue, the media actively attempted to explain the practice for audiences:

> The new trend of 'sexting' – in which explicit photos of oneself are forwarded to friends or potential partners. (Porter 2008, p. 18)
>
> Sexting involves taking or sending an explicit photo of oneself and forwarding it to friends or potential suitors. (Battersby 2008, p. 3)

Gender and age feature prominently in many of these early definitions. Here, sexting practice is linked to the narrative of a young female victim and a male (ex-boyfriend, ex-partner) perpetrator who distributes the sexts:

> '[S]exting' ... [is a practice] in which a girl records her sexual activities on a mobile phone and sends it to her boyfriend, who then sends it to his friends. (Pritchard 2008)
>
> Last year, a year 10 girl from a private school in Mentone texted nude photos of herself to her boyfriend that quickly spread to his friends and beyond. The practice, which police say is becoming more prevalent among adolescent girls, has been dubbed 'sexting'. (Farrer 2008, p. 11)

The gendering of media reports on sexting reflects the findings of Draper's (2012, p. 226) study into television news coverage of sexting in the United States, which determined that in these reports girls were being depicted as the producers and distributors of such material in an effort to attract male attention, while boys were portrayed as merely recipients of images. Draper found that there was little evidence to support such gender roles, a theme we explore in Chapter 11.

As the literature shows, children as victims or offenders makes an issue inherently more newsworthy. As Mascheroni et al. (2010) argue, and in line with Draper's (2012) 'media panic' model, the evolution of media discourses on sexting demonstrates the media's tendency to frame issues negatively when they relate to young people and the internet.

Although the definition of the 'problem' of sexting changed signifi-cantly over the time period examined, going from an 'adult' activity to one that engaged young people, there was a consistently high number of articles that defined sexting as gendered practice with young girls explicitly portrayed as sexters, as noted above. In addition, while many of the early articles tended to describe images or 'sexts' as, for example, 'sexually explicit', there was greater tendency from 2011 onwards to use more euphemistic language, such as 'lewd' or 'inappropriate' messages. While it is difficult to attribute meaning to such changes, perhaps the shifting focus of the discourse, and a greater recognition of the complexities around the legalities of sexting, contributed towards a softening of the media rhetoric.

Sexting as newsworthy: the evolution of a discourse

By 2009, sexting had well and truly arrived on the news media agenda in Australia, with 194 sexting-related articles published during that year, up from 11 in 2008. The number of articles continued to rise in 2010, 2011, 2012 and 2013, with 221, 435, 461 and 633 sexting-related articles published in those years respectively (for analysis of similarly increased reporting in the United States, see Podlas 2014). While it is difficult to pinpoint the exact cause of the dramatic increase in reporting on sexting in the media over time, one possible explanation – aside from the moral or media panic models – may be the inter-media agenda setting effect, an effect similarly uncovered by Vanderbosch et al. (2013, p. 102) in their study of cyberbullying reporting. According to Golan (2006, p. 326), '[i]nter-media agenda setting refers to the influence of mass media agendas on each other'; that is, the coverage of particular stories in news media outlets is associated with subsequent coverage of these same stories in other news outlets. The increase in media coverage on the issue of sexting in the Australian media may be partly explained by this multiplication effect (Vanderbosch et al. 2013, p. 102).

More interesting than the sheer number of articles published, however, was the evolving discourse around sexting over this period, which maps out several phases in media discourse on sexting. Leaving aside the celebrity-focused period between 2003 and 2006, articles in 2007 and 2008 primarily focused on identifying sexting as a 'problem'. This focus specifically related to young people, whose sexual activities in the digital realm began to come to media and public attention, corresponding with Draper's (2012, p. 225) findings of a media discourse that promoted the 'notion that "good kids" are seduced by the accessibility of digital technologies into deviant activities'. As one Australian media report stated:

A peek into the lives of Australian teenagers has confirmed parents' worst fears about pornography, flirting with strangers in cyberspace and pressures to have sex...Sex Lives of Australian Teenagers, by Sydney author Joan Sauers, paints a graphic picture of what teenagers are doing. ('Sex life of teens' 2007, p. 3)

By 2009 and 2010, the 'problem' essentially became a moral panic, contextualising sexting in the intersection of young people and cyber-bullying, and the pornification of society and its effects on young girls. An article from 2009 titled 'Little girls the new sex objects', for example, claimed that '[b]y late primary school and early high school girls are "sexting" boys compromising photographs of themselves' (Jones and Cuneo 2009, p. 2). This was just one of many pieces published in 2009 that decried the pornification of young girls in modern society. Interestingly, Draper's US study, undertaken during the same period, likewise concluded that there was a noticeable trend within the media to 'conflate concerns regarding a perceived increase in teen sexuality brought on by the seductive powers of digital media with a yearning for an idealized past' (Draper 2012, p. 226).

The legal implications of sexting also came into focus during this period, with reports throughout 2009 and 2010 citing a number of legal cases in the United States and Australia related to sexting, typically involving male perpetrators or defendants. Such stories appear to fuel concerns about the involvement of young people in sexting, evident in the groundswell of articles subsequently published urging parents to protect their children, and 'their innocence' (Sinnerton 2009, p. 90). The risks of sexting and other technologically facilitated harms are artic-ulated in a number of ways. For instance, young people are portrayed as being at risk of falling victim to sexual predators, while authority voices highlighted young people's naivety and gullibility when online:

> [C]hildren as young as seven are putting themselves at risk from pred-ators and bullies online because they are flouting Facebook website age restrictions, police have said...Maitland police-school liaison officer Michael Steele said: Children...do not really understand there are paedophiles out there trawling cyberspace and that they've got no idea who they're chatting to. (Branley 2010, p. 1)

Young people are also shown as possibly contributing to their own victimisation due to this naivety. The process of responsibilisation – shifting the burden for protection from victimisation to young people, especially young girls (Salter et al. 2013; Draper 2012) – was also prom-inent in media reports in 2009–10:

'The problem is that kids don't really look at the what-ifs,' said one Brisbane mother who wanted to remain nameless. 'They don't realise that they are responsible for protecting their own privacy. 'I have two teenage daughters and they are good girls, but I can see they are very naive when it comes to the internet. Most kids don't realise that once you hit the send button, anything can come back to bite you. Kids all make mistakes, and they should be allowed to make mistakes without such drastic circumstances'. (Sinnerton 2009, p. 90)

News headlines also broadcasted sensational and exaggerated claims about the risk of criminal sanctions faced by young people, a theme that was also identified in studies of international media reports during the same period (see Draper 2012; Hasinoff 2013; Podlas 2014, pp. 137, 141):

Tougher laws on sexting – Teens may be caught in porn crime swoop. (Viellaris 2010, p. 7)

Kids can be charged under 'sexting' laws. (Anonymous, *The Daily Telegraph*, 19 March 2010, p. 3)

Court case displays worry of teens sexting each other. (Anonymous, *Fraser Coast Chronicle*, 22 October 2010, p. 16)

Along the same vein as educational campaigns launched around this time (see Chapter 6), the message in the media has been straightforward: parents must take action to stop their children's sexting practices, and rescue them from potential long-lasting consequences of sexting indiscretions. As one article explained, the prime responsibility falls to parents to educate their teens about these risks:

A NSW government campaign starting this week will urge parents to try to halt an alarming rise in the number of teenagers sending sexual images of themselves via mobile phone ... Schools will receive no-holds-barred fact-sheets warning parents that 'sexting' can haunt their kids for life, damaging careers and relationships. ('Parents urged' 2009)

These messages sat alongside reports that linked the rise in sexting and other technologically facilitated activities to the shortcomings of parental knowledge of technology. Parents were commonly described as being ignorant of new technologies, and unable to detect, let alone prevent, their children's misconduct in this space. Similar to educational campaigns described in Chapter 6, which argue that parental surveillance of young people's behaviour can reduce the incidents of sexting, monitoring of children's phones was seen as both required and desired, as supported by claims in the media that:

> Parents aren't good at monitoring their children's phone and Internet usage, partly because many of them are digital neanderthals so they don't understand what their 12-year-old can do on the computer or on the phone. ... Sexting is becoming more popular, which is horrifying parents across the nation, but how many of them actually check their kids' phones each day? (Carr-Gregg as cited in Squires 2009, p. 32)

Such rhetoric replicates the findings from Lynn's (2010) study on the reporting of sexting in major US newspapers between November 2008 and April 2009. Lynn found that during this period the press:

> uncritically disseminated stereotypical representations of parents as ignorant, technologically inept, and incapable of controlling their children's behaviors. Moreover, these articles aggressively propounded parenting strategies for addressing sexting in the family, preferring authoritarian solutions to less restrictive or confrontational solutions and invoking draconian legal consequences as justification for implementing harsh parental restrictions. (2010, p. 1)

Increases in reportage in 2011 and 2012 were shadowed by yet another shift in coverage. Dominant voices in the media around this time called for action in order to address the perceived risks of sexting and young people's engagement in it. Emergent discussion around 'responses' to sexting from schools and the government, as well as police blitzes on sexting/cyberbullying, characterised much of the media discourse during this period. Central to many debates were messages of abstinence; the key message that stakeholders were being asked to communicate to young people was that they simply should not sext. A commonly repeated phrase in media advice on sexting was: 'There is no such thing as safe sexting' ('Handy hints' 2012, p. 9).

Some of the 'facts' in these media reports, however, were difficult to verify; thus, it can be argued that the media exaggerated the risks those engaging in sexting face. For example, a number of articles cited unconfirmed figures to demonstrate that large numbers of children and teens were being charged for sexting:

> *Hundreds of teenagers* have been charged over producing or distributing child pornography amid growing concern that 'sexting' has reached *epidemic* levels.

In the past three years, more than 450 child pornography charges have been laid against youths between the ages of 10 and 17, including 113 charges of 'making child exploitation material'. More than 160 charges were laid in 2010 alone – 26 more than in 2008. (Tin 2011, p. 7, emphasis added)

The conflation of numbers such as these is not atypical, however. In his study of US newspaper reports of sexting, Lynn (2010, p. 9) found that almost 55 per cent of the articles he examined used the results from a single online survey, conducted by a private research agency with an unrepresentative participant base, to 'make the case that sexting among teens is widespread'. Such reporting, he argued, contributed to the media trope of a sexting 'epidemic', something that again mirrors the findings from this Australian study.

The sorts of figures touted by the Australian media contrast with reports of police taking measures to ensure young people are not being unfairly drawn into the criminal justice system (see Chapter 5). As this media report demonstrates, police have been cognisant of the dangers of over-criminalisation of young people in relation to sexting:

Tasmanian police have produced new protocols for dealing with sexually explicit text message and photographs exchanged by young people. Under existing child exploitation and pornography laws 'sexting' is considered child pornography and both the sender and recipient can be charged.

Detective Senior Sergeant Luke Manhood says the new protocols are designed to guarantee the law is being used in the way it was intended.

This particular legislation is about targeting adults that prey on children. It's not about criminalising the normal parts of growing up that children might be engaged in. ('New protocols for explicit texts' 2011)

In 2012, there were a greater proportion of articles themed around law reform and sexting, as well as articles critical of law enforcement responses to sexting (see Podlas 2014, p. 139 for a similar shift in focus in the United States). While only a few articles in 2011 questioned whether sexting among youth was inherently harmful, by 2012 there was a marked increase in such articles, with several canvassing both sides of the harm equation. Across the sample, however, a number of articles that depicted the 'harm' of sexting did so solely in terms of the risk of prosecution. This theme continued into 2013, with the Victorian

Parliamentary Inquiry into Sexting (Law Reform Committee of Victoria 2013) and the proliferation of mobile phone 'sexting apps' adding to debates over appropriate responses to sexting and the implications of criminal sanctions.

What the data demonstrated was that the discourse around sexting has primarily focused on its implications for young people. The tenor of the discourse has been one of fear; fear initially that young people might actually be sexting, then fear that young people may be at risk of exploitation or that they are being sexualised too early. The concerns then lead to fears over the consequences – legal or otherwise – of sexting for young people. Such fears are typically expressed by adults, rather than by young people themselves, leading to a range of reactions from parents, teachers, government officials, and criminal justice agents, who scramble for appropriate answers to the articulated problem. The end result remains unresolved; sexting by young people is still considered to be a problem, but the best approach for dealing with it is yet to be determined.

Moving beyond the moral panic model, which on the surface seems readily apparent in the media discourses about young people's sexting practices, Hier's rethinking of moral panic conceives moralisation 'in terms of rational, dialectic constructions of self and other that are transmitted through everyday discourses of risk management and harm avoidance' (2008, p. 174). He contends that we have seen a shift in the regulation of morality in recent times and, as a result, we see a growing number of everyday activities becoming moralised 'through what could be characterized as dialectical judgments pertaining to what is right and wrong, good and bad, healthy and unhealthy' (2008, p. 174; see also Hunt 1999, 2003). Such a proposition can readily be applied to sexting: judgments are made, advice is given, and behaviours are scrutinised when it comes to young peoples' sexting activities. In this way, young people 'are called upon to engage in ethical forms of individual risk management, and these forms of self-conduct exist in tension with collective subject positions of "harmful others"' (Hier 2008, p. 174).

What does the media teach us about sexting?

In discussing the overall arc the media has taken in discourses of sexting, it is important to analyse key themes that emerge from the data. Our research identified four key themes: how the media defines the causes of sexting; how harm is articulated; the primary definers of sexting in the news; and the responses to sexting that the media advance.

Causes of sexting behaviours

The vast majority of articles that depicted the harms of sexting as being the risk of prosecution tended to cite ignorance of the law as a reason why young people may engage in the behaviour. Such articles suggested that if adolescents knew the law, they would cease to sext. A small, but increasing number of the sample cited legal ambiguities or inconsistencies around legal responses to sexting, particularly with regards to the age of consent.

Of the articles that portrayed sexting as more generally harmful, the most common explanations given were technology; the pornification of society and raunch culture; and the psychological immaturity of young people. The introduction of mobile phone apps such as Snapchat, for example, were overwhelmingly discussed in negative terms, with media reports citing concerns that such applications may lead young people to think they can sext without consequences: 'Police say social media apps and websites such as Facebook, Instagram and Snapchat are of particular concern, with many young people wrongly believing they could permanently delete their racy pictures' (Pearson 2013, p. 1).

Some of the overarching explanations for the willingness of young people to engage in sexting were linked to the pornification of society; that is, 'little girls being too sexy too soon, children being pressured to look and act much older than they actually were' (Tankard-Reist as cited in Hills 2012, p. 12). Integral to such arguments were claims that young people are not mature enough to understand the long-term impacts of sexting. As child psychologist Michael Carr-Greg, a key commentator on children and technology in the media, wrote: '[T]echnology also brings challenges in the form of cyberbullying, sexting, malware and scams. We have created the perfect digital storm. We have brought together an immature teenage brain and a technology that is in the moment and of the moment' (Carr-Gregg 2012, p. 11).

Harms defined

Consistently, the most common harm identified in the sample was the risk of prosecution or criminal charges, accompanied frequently by reference to the risk of being placed on a sex offender's register. Other common harms cited across the sample were reputation, future career prospects and future relationship prospects, as well as the amorphous warnings that an image is permanent and out of the individual's control once it goes online. Interestingly, only in 2011 was the risk of the image ending up in the hands of paedophiles cited as harm, but this continued in 2012 and 2013.

Experts

The analysis of media reports indicated that there was a clear process of issue-claiming around sexting. While in the early media reports of sexting there was little in-depth analysis, primarily due to the subject being focused on celebrity sexters, once young people entered the debate experts were sought out by the media to provide comment about the issue. The most commonly cited experts in the sample were the police, who were often referenced as also being brought into schools as part of education campaigns around sexting (see Chapter 6). After the police, the developers of government programs and curricula designed for schools were the next most referenced issues claimers. While these two groups were often held up as experts, teachers and parents themselves were often depicted as lost and unable to respond to the 'problem'. As such, police and education experts were often positioned as advisers in media pieces, providing information and guidance to parents about how they should approach and deal with the issue of sexting specifically, and cyberbullying more generally. This was evident in a number of articles that provided handy 'tips' for parents in dealing with their teens, such as:

- Discuss any changes in mood or behaviour with your child as it may relate to cyber bullying – are they quieter than normal or more aggressive?
- Notify police immediately if you have serious concerns for your child's safety.
- Work with your child to save evidence of cyber bullying behaviour.
- Follow up with the child's school, internet service provider (ISP), mobile phone carrier or the police.
- Speak to your child's school. (Nelligan and Etheridge 2011, p. 5)

The sample also indicated a class of expert entrepreneurs – Maggie Hamilton (author on pornification), Susan McLean (ex-police officer; runs cybersafety training), Michael Carr-Greg (psychologist), Kath Albury (academic) and Nina Funnell (victim advocate, freelance opinion writer and researcher) – who commented regularly in the media as experts on sexting-related matters, providing definitions of the problem as well as their own authoritative solutions.

Teenagers were almost never quoted in media articles on young people and sexting, and when they were, their comments were almost always framed by expert opinion; an expert would quote a teenager in order to evidence his or her point on the harm or lack of harm of sexting. This replicated the findings of Lynn's (2010, p. 9) US research, which found that 82 per cent of the articles analysed cited 'adult experts' rather than young people in reports on sexting. Teens and young people have, for the most part, been excluded from the debates on sexting, and their voices and opinions overlooked in the discourse that has developed around sexting. As Albury (2013, p. S34) notes, young people are often locked out of the sexuality debate altogether when their needs are over-looked by educators and others.

Responses taken and recommendations

The measures advanced towards resolving the sexting 'problem' depended on the focus of the articles sampled. A number of articles discussed the use of charges or referred to police discretion options. Aside from these options, government programs, curriculum and teacher training were also mentioned as possible measures. Such measures were by far the most commonly referred to in the sample; however, from 2011 onwards, a small number of articles began to discuss efforts to reform legislation, culminating in the 2013 Law Reform Committee of Victoria Inquiry into Sexting, which focused on exactly this matter. Other measures raised during the same period reported the banning of mobile phones in schools. There were also reports of teenagers (or their families) suing the police in 2009, 2011 and 2012.

In 2009, several commercial apps were introduced that enabled parents to monitor their children's phones, and these continued to be discussed in the years following. Most experts, however, were fairly disapproving of this measure from 2010 onwards. Of the articles that presented views on what should be done about sexting, law reform formed an increas-ingly large proportion from 2011 onwards, and by 2012 there were over 30 articles addressing this, far more than for any other issue.

Other recommendations tended to remain reasonably constant across the sample and timeframe. The most common were for education of children about the dangers of sexting. The majority exhorted parents directly to educate their children, while a smaller number called for increasing education in schools or for forums run by police.

The next largest category of recommendations related to education, more generally, of youth about sexual ethics, healthy relationships and sexual citizenship – again these were most frequently an exhortation to parents and secondarily a call for school programs. The next largest set of recommendations called for the banning of mobiles and portable devices in schools or for their increased regulation.

Conclusion

The media has played an important role in generating, locating and guiding the debate around the issues of sexting, particularly in relation to young people. As has been demonstrated in the literature, discourses around sexting mirror many other concerns around cyberbullying and pornography on the internet, and tap into a range of fears in the community about the sexualisation of children (Salter et al. 2013; Lee et al. 2013). While parents, teachers, academics, police and government officials discussed the issues around sexting and the possible solutions, young people rarely featured in the discussions. Our research indicates that media discourses contextualised legal and social consequences in a familiar milieu of risk, while identifying young people as naive, vulnerable, prone to risky behaviour and in a need of protection. More education about sexting (by parents, schools and in the social context more broadly), legal reforms, and other measures aimed at minimising harm were predominant recommendations suggested by experts in the media reports.

The following chapter will explore how sexting has been framed legally primarily as child pornography.

4
Sexting as Child Pornography

Introduction

Prosecution of young people under child pornography offences has increasingly been the subject of public, media and academic debate. This is interesting, given that there are many other possible civil and criminal law responses, as well as non-legal responses, to sexting by young people. In civil law it is possible to bring an action for breach of privacy, breach of confidence, breach of copyright, defamation, nuisance, sexual harassment and so on. Such civil law actions are available where there is non-consensual distribution or reception of an image, and require that the individual concerned brings a complaint. As such, they will not be relevant where young people consensually take and share images. Also given that these actions are 'private law' they do not have the public censuring function of criminal law and may not excite the public imagination in the way that criminal prosecutions do. There are also a range of existing criminal law offences that may apply to sexting by young people, such as sexual offences, offences against indecency, stalking and harassment.

Despite such alternatives the primary focus of legal attention has been on child pornography offences. This may in part be due to the fact that such severe legal consequences for young people captures public interest and as a result media and other commentators tend to report only on child pornography cases. More than just due to skewed media reporting, however, such a focus may also be based on police practices under current laws. Presently the options for responding to sexting are regarded, at least in some Australian jurisdictions, as either prosecution under child pornography offences or diversion from formal proceedings or taking no police action.[1] Such practices and what legal and non-legal factors explain whether young people may or may not be prosecuted under child pornography offences are examined in more detail in Chapter 5. This chapter describes *how* young people can be charged and convicted of child pornography offences for sexting behaviours. It begins by giving examples of some of the cases in which young people have been prosecuted under child pornography laws before discussing legal definitions of child pornography and how reforms in recent years mean that sexting can fall under these laws. Chapter 12 returns to the theme of legal and non-legal responses to sexting and draws on the findings of existing research (Chapter 7) and research that we conducted with young people (Chapters 8, 9 and 10) to consider what might be appropriate ways of addressing sexting.

Sexting cases

There are vastly different circumstances in which naked, semi-naked or sexual images of young people are being taken and distributed by young people. These range from what Wolak and Finkelhor (2011) have identified as 'experimental' sexting incidents, in which young people consensually take nude images of themselves and/or one another and share these images with one another, to 'aggravated' sexting incidents. Aggravated cases may involve the production of such images in the commission of a criminal offence (e.g., an indecent or sexual assault) or where images are non-consensually distributed to third parties or where an adult is involved. Despite such widely varying scenarios, in all these situations and across many jurisdictions it is possible for young people who take, possess and distribute nude images of themselves or another young person to be prosecuted under child pornography laws. The following cases illustrate the varied situations in which young people have been convicted of child pornography offences. They show how it is possible that, despite the complexity of issues, sexting has come to be legally problematised within the framework of child pornography.

The most well-known cases of young people being prosecuted under child pornography offences come from the United States. In *AH v State of Florida*, 949 So 2d 234, Fla App LEXIS 484 (Fla App Ct 2007) a 17-year-old boy took digital images of himself having consensual sexual intercourse with his 16-year-old girlfriend. They then emailed the images to another computer. Neither party showed the images to anyone else, but when word got out about the photographs police obtained a search warrant for the computer and located the images. As a result, both young people were charged and found guilty of producing, directing or promoting a photograph or representation that they knew to include the sexual conduct of a child (§ 827.071(2), Florida Statutes (2005)). The young man was additionally charged with possession of child pornography (§ 827.071(5), Florida Statutes (2005)). The young woman appealed her conviction, but the majority of the appellate court dismissed the appeal and affirmed the finding of the trial court that there was 'a compelling state interest in protecting children from sexual exploitation' (see also *New York v Ferber*, 458 US 747 (1982)). It was found that this compelling interest exists whether the exploiter is an adult or minor and is 'certainly triggered by the production of 117 photographs of minors engaging in graphic sexual acts' (Fla App LEXIS 484, [236]). The court further affirmed the finding of the trial court that 'criminal prosecution was the least intrusive means of furthering the State's compelling interest' ([236]).

In *Miller v Skumanick*, 605 F Supp 2d 634 (MD Pa 2009) two 13-year-old girls in Wyoming were threatened with prosecution for the possession and distribution of child pornography when they, among other things, took digital images of one another in opaque bras. The images did not show sexual activity or the genital region of the girls. Nonetheless, the District Attorney of Wyoming County threatened to prosecute the girls unless they completed an educational program that included writing an essay on why their behaviour was wrong. The parents of the girls sought, and were granted, an injunction against the girls being required to complete the educational program. In both these cases the creation and distribution of the images was consensual.

In one case, only the *creation* of the naked images was consensual. In *State v Vezzoni*, 127 Wash App 1012, 2005 Wash App LEXIS 1686 (Was Ct App 2005) a 16-year-old boy took pictures of his 16-year-old girlfriend's unclothed breasts and genitals with her permission. A week later, after breaking up with his girlfriend, he developed the photographs and showed them to classmates.[2] He was subsequently found guilty of 'dealing in depictions of a minor engaged in sexually explicit conduct' (Wash Rev Code § 9.68A.050) and 'possession of depictions of a minor engaged in sexually explicit conduct' (Wash Rev Code § 9.68A.070).

In Australia, there are few detailed reports of young people being prosecuted for sexting. In *DPP v Eades* [2009] NSWSC 1352, Australia's 'first sexting case', an 18-year-old (so no longer a 'young person') who incited a 13-year-old girl to send a picture of herself in the nude by mobile phone, was found not to be in possession of child pornography. The Magistrates Court held that: 'there was no sexual activity depicted in the photograph. Rather, it was a photograph of the Complainant standing naked in her bedroom and it was determined that there was "no posing, no objects, no additional aspects of the photograph which are sexual in nature or suggestion"' (at [33]).[3] In another case, it was reported in a submission to the Law Reform Committee of Victoria that a 17-year-old took a video of himself and his 17-year-old girlfriend having sexual intercourse in 2005. When they split up two years later, he forwarded still images of the video to three young people. He was charged with producing and transmitting child pornography and pleaded guilty to these charges. He was fined $1000 and no conviction was recorded; however, he was placed on the sex offender register (Submission No S3 2013).[4]

Despite the lack of legally reported cases, many media reports offer contradictory indications of the degree to which young people in Australia are being prosecuted for child pornography offences. In 2008, *The Age* (Vic) claimed that, in the previous year, 32 teenagers had been charged with child pornography offences as a result of sexting in Victoria (Battersby 2008). In 2011, *The Sunday Mail* (Qld) reported that, in the previous three years, 450 child pornography charges had been laid against young people aged between 10 and 17, and that more than 110 charges were laid in 2010 (Tin 2011). Seemingly contradicting this, it was reported in 2012 that, in the previous four years, only two teenage boys had been charged with pornography offences under the Commonwealth *Criminal Code*, and five others had been let off with a caution for sexting (Bita 2012). In the same year, in evidence before the Law Reform Committee of Victoria Inquiry into Sexting, the Acting Commander of Victoria Police noted that no one under 18 years of age had been prosecuted under child pornography laws in Victoria for sexting alone (Paterson 2012, p. 13). While recognising that charging young people with child pornography offences was 'not widespread', in its submission to the Law Reform Committee of Victoria's Inquiry, Victoria Legal Aid (2012, p. 3) stated that it had represented 'a number' of young people who had been charged with child pornography offences for sexting behaviour and expressed concern that the outcomes for the young people involved were disproportionate to their behaviours.

Again, in contrast to these reports of low numbers being charged with child pornography offences, an article in the *Brisbane Times* in 2013 reported that the first five months of 2013 had seen 240 young people charged with producing and distributing child pornography (Feeney 2013). Such enormous differences in the reporting of the rate at which young people are charged with child pornography offences in Australia may be due, as noted in Chapter 3, to the media's construction of newsworthy stories – the over-estimation of legal intervention into sexting is an attention-grabbing tactic. Such differences may also be due to a lack of clarity over whether young people who come to police attention are actually charged or are convicted of child pornography offences. A further explanation could be that prosecutorial practice may well differ between various jurisdictions, with each State and Territory and the Commonwealth having variously defined child pornography offences and their own prosecution services and practices.

In the United Kingdom and Canada it appears that, until recently, young people were not being prosecuted under child pornography offences for sexting behaviours. However, in January 2014, the media reported that a 17-year-old Canadian girl was convicted of possessing and distributing child pornography and threatening behaviour after the girl sent sexually explicit texts, including naked images, of her boyfriend's former girlfriend and threatened her through social media (Matyszczyk 2014). She was 16 at the time these events occurred. Similarly, in 2014, media in the United Kingdom reported that a schoolgirl under 18 years of age had been investigated for distributing an indecent image of a child after she sent a picture of herself topless to her boyfriend (Eleftheriou-Smith 2014). The following gives an overview of laws on child pornography to show how these cases have come about.

Child pornography legislation and regulation

In recent decades there has been growing concern about the effect that new technologies are having on the production and distribution of child pornography. International agreements about how to effectively combat child pornography has meant that many states have adopted broadly similar offences and definitions of child pornography. The following gives an overview of some relevant laws, revealing their similarity and helping us understand how young people engaging in sexting can be charged with child pornography.

International framework

The United Nations *Convention of the Rights of the Child*, art. 34, requires that:

> States Parties undertake to protect the child from all forms of sexual exploitation and sexual abuse. For these purposes, States Parties shall in particular take all appropriate national, bilateral and multilateral measures to prevent ... [t]he exploitative use of children in pornographic performances and materials.

In light of growing concerns over the opportunities that new technology has provided for the creation, possession and distribution of child pornography and developing understanding of the harms associated with child pornography, there has been broad international agreement in recent decades about the need to strengthen child pornography laws.[5] For instance, at the First World Congress Against the Sexual Exploitation of Children held in 1996 in Stockholm, a Declaration and Agenda for Action called on States to: 'Criminalize the commercial sexual exploitation of children, as well as other forms of sexual exploitation' and 'Review and revise, where appropriate, laws, policies, programmes and practices to eliminate the commercial sexual exploitation of children'.

The International Labour Organisation *Convention 182* on the Worst Forms of Child Labour, art. 3 also called on states to eliminate the use of children for child pornography and defined a 'child' as a person under the age of 18. In line with such international concern, the UN adopted an *Optional Protocol on the Sale of Children, Child Prostitution and Child Pornography* in 2000, which entered into force in 2002. The Optional Protocol was designed to increase international cooperation and improve law enforcement at the national level. It sought to strengthen the protections provided by child pornography laws by expanding the definition of what amounts to child pornography and criminalising not just the creation and distribution of child pornography, but also its possession. The Optional Protocol employs a definition of 'child pornography' that includes 'any representation... of a child engaged in real or simulated sexual activities or any representation of the sexual parts of a child for primarily sexual purposes' (art. 2(c)). This broad definition is in line with the development of typologies of material that might be sexualised by an adult with a sexual interest in children. For instance, the Combating Paedophile Information Networks in Europe (COPINE) Project developed a ten-point scale, which ranges from sadistic/bestiality images at one extreme to indicative non-erotic or sexualised images at the other (see Taylor et al. 2001, p. 101). This index recognises that paedophilic interest in images of children may go beyond images of children directly involved in sexual activity and include images that in other contexts might be relatively innocent but are sexualised by the viewer. As Taylor and Quayle (2003, p. 193) note: 'The central quality of pictures that are attractive to adults with a sexual interest in children, therefore, is that they enable the generation and sustenance of sexual fantasy about children.'

The Optional Protocol also requires States to criminalise the mere possession of child pornography, whether or not there is an intention to distribute (art. 3(1)(c)). While there is no definition of the age at which a person should be considered a child for the purposes of child pornography in the Protocol, the Council of Europe Convention on Cybercrime (2001) set the age at 18, although it allows a State to have a lower age level, but not lower than 16 (art. 9(3)). Many jurisdictions have amended child pornography laws in line with these international obligations.

The broad international agreement to increase the age level for the purposes of child pornography often takes this age level out of line with the age of consent, which in many jurisdictions is lower than 18 (for instance in Canada, some States of the United States, some Australian jurisdictions and England and Wales).[6] So, in those jurisdictions where there is a disparity between the age of consent and the age at which a young person is considered a child for the purposes of child pornography laws, a child can lawfully consent to sexual activity, but not to the recording of the same activity. This higher age level for child pornography is justified, for example, by the Australian Commonwealth Attorney-General's Department on the basis that it is appropriate that the age threshold 'be higher than the age of consent because child pornography involves the exploitation (often for commercial purposes) of children' (2009, p. 6). A further justification often used is the more permanent and lasting consequences of recording such activities, which is considered more serious than the possible consequences of sexual intercourse. Some commentators, however, have criticised defining a 'child' for the purposes of these laws as a person under the age of 18. Gillespie (2010b), for instance, finds some weight in the argument that a person under 18 may still lack the maturity to decide whether to allow themselves to be photographed or filmed but notes that a test of maturity has not traditionally been applied to this area. Furthermore, given that the law allows a young person to make significant decisions about sexual conduct from the age of consent Gillespie questions 'why should a decision as to whether to be photographed be any different?' (2010b, p. 22).

Australia

Australia has a system of federal (Commonwealth) and state/territory criminal law. In line with its international obligations relating to combatting child pornography the Commonwealth Government has taken 'an important leadership role in this area' by creating new Commonwealth offences and definitions designed to 'provide a springboard to a national approach to this issue' (Slipper 2004, pp. 32035–6). Child pornography is defined in s 473.1 of the Commonwealth *Criminal Code Act 1995* as:

a. material that depicts a person, or a representation of a person, who is, or appears to be, under 18 years of age and who:
   i. is engaged in, or appears to be engaged in, a sexual pose or sexual activity (whether or not in the presence of other persons); or
   ii. is in the presence of a person who is engaged in, or appears to be engaged in, a sexual pose or sexual activity;
     and does this in a way that reasonable persons would regard as being, in all the circumstances, offensive; or

b. material the dominant characteristic of which is the depiction, for a sexual purpose, of:
   i. a sexual organ or the anal region of a person who is, or appears to be, under 18 years of age; or
   ii. a representation of such a sexual organ or anal region; or
   iii. the breasts, or a representation of the breasts, of a female person who is, or appears to be, under 18 years of age;
     in a way that reasonable persons would regard as being, in all the circumstances, offensive; or

c. material that describes a person who is, or is implied to be, under 18 years of age and who:
   i. is engaged in, or is implied to be engaged in, a sexual pose or sexual activity (whether or not in the presence of other persons); or
   ii. is in the presence of a person who is engaged in, or is implied to be engaged in, a sexual pose or sexual activity;
     and does this in a way that reasonable persons would regard as being, in all the circumstances, offensive; or

d. material that describes:
   i. a sexual organ or the anal region of a person who is, or is implied to be, under 18 years of age; or
   ii. the breasts of a female person who is, or is implied to be, under 18 years of age;
     and does this in a way that reasonable persons would regard as being, in all the circumstances, offensive.

It is noteworthy that the *Criminal Code Act 1995* (Cth) provides such an extensive definition of 'child pornography'. It covers depictions or descriptions and extends to cases where the depiction or description is not actually of a child but of an apparent or implied child and need not show sexual activity or a pose, provided this is apparent or implied. Furthermore, and particularly relevant to cases of sexting, the definition includes the depiction, description or representation for a sexual purpose, of the sexual organ, anal region or, in the case of a female person, the breasts. In all these instances, the depiction or description must meet a threshold test of whether 'reasonable persons' would regard it as being, in all the circumstances, offensive. This is designed to prevent overreach of the law and ensure that community standards are incorporated into the determination of whether the material should amount to child pornography (Krone 2005, p. 2). The age level under which a person is deemed a child for the purposes of child pornography is set at 18.

As the Commonwealth only has jurisdiction in certain criminal matters, the offences in the Commonwealth *Criminal Code* are linked to the mode by which the child pornography or child abuse material is accessed, transmitted or made available. Thus, it is a criminal offence to use a carriage service (service for transmitting communications, for example, telephone, mobile telephone, internet and so on (*Telecommunications Act 1997* (Cth), s 7)) to access, transmit or make child pornography available (*Criminal Code Act 1995* (Cth), s 474.19). It is also an offence to possess or produce child pornography with the intent to place it on the internet (*Criminal Code Act 1995* (Cth), ss 474.20, 474.23).

United States

In the United States, child pornography offences can be found in federal and state criminal law. Under US federal criminal law, child pornography is defined as the visual depiction (by photograph, film, picture or computer generated image) of a child engaged in or apparently engaged in sexually explicit conduct (18 USC § 2256(8) (2006)). 'Sexually explicit conduct' is defined in § 2256(2)(A) as:

actual or simulated—

i. sexual intercourse, including genital-genital, oral-genital, anal-genital, or oral-anal, whether between persons of the same or opposite sex;
ii. bestiality;
iii. masturbation;
iv. sadistic or masochistic abuse; or
v. lascivious exhibition of the genitals or pubic area of any person.

In instances where there is depiction of the genitals or pubic area of a person (interestingly this definition does not mention female breasts), something more than nudity is required for it to be considered child pornography. To fit the federal statutory definition of 'child pornography', the exhibition of the genitals must be lascivious. Various courts have attempted to articulate a test for determining lasciviousness. Many have relied upon a six-factor test that originated in *United States v Dost*, 636 F Supp 828, 832 (SD Cal 1986):

1. whether the focal point of the visual depiction is on the child's genitalia or pubic area;
2. whether the setting of the visual depiction is sexually suggestive, i.e., in a place or pose generally associated with sexual activity;
3. whether the child is depicted in an unnatural pose, or in inappropriate attire, considering the age of the child;
4. whether the child is fully or partially clothed, or nude;
5. whether the visual depiction suggests sexual coyness or a willingness to engage in sexual activity;
6. whether the visual depiction is intended or designed to elicit a sexual response in the viewer.[7]

Until the 1970s, in the United States, some types of child pornography were protected by the First Amendment (Shafron-Perez 2009). This changed in *New York v Ferber*, 458 US 747, 774 (1982), where the question arose whether child pornography was subject to protection as free speech under the First Amendment. In this case, a bookstore owner was convicted for selling films of young boys masturbating in violation of a New York statute that prohibited 'persons from knowingly promoting sexual performances by children under the age of 16 by distributing material which depicts such performances' (at 749). The Supreme Court granted the State's petition for review on the sole question of whether the State could regulate child pornography, regardless of whether it was obscene. The Court answered the question in the affirmative, holding that the State had more leeway in regulating 'works which portray sexual acts or lewd exhibitions of genitalia by children' (at 774). The Court traced the legal development of obscenity, which is 'not within the area of constitutionally protected speech or press' (at 754),[8] and determined five reasons it was not necessary for child pornography to meet the three-part test for obscenity to not be protected speech.[9] The Supreme Court therefore decided that child pornography did not deserve constitutional protection under the First Amendment.

Canada

Unlike the United States and Australia, Canada is a single criminal law jurisdiction with responsibility lying with the Federal Parliament. The

Canadian *Criminal Code* defines 'child pornography' in a condensed way that is broadly similar to the Australian Commonwealth *Criminal Code*:

> 163.1(1) In this section, *'child pornography'* means
>
> a. a photographic, film, video or other visual representation, whether or not it was made by electronic or mechanical means,
>   i. that shows a person who is or is depicted as being under the age of eighteen years and is engaged in or is depicted as engaged in explicit sexual activity, or
>   ii. the dominant characteristic of which is the depiction, for a sexual purpose, of a sexual organ or the anal region of a person under the age of eighteen years.

This definition extends child pornography beyond depictions of a child engaged in sexual activity or apparently engaged in sexual activity and includes reference to depictions of a sexual organ or anal region of a person under 18 where this is the dominant aspect of the image and it is done for a sexual purpose (*Criminal Code* (Can), s 163.1(1)). While this definition does not expressly mention the naked breasts of a female, Canadian courts have held that a sexual organ includes female breasts (*R v VPS* [2001] BCJ No 930). In *R v Sharpe* [2001] 1 SCR 45, 2001 SCC 2 the Supreme Court held that two questions are necessary to determine whether depictions of the sexual organ or anal region amount to child pornography. First, an objective assessment:

> The question is whether a reasonable viewer, looking at the depiction objectively and in context, would see its 'dominant characteristic' as the depiction of the child's sexual organ or anal region. The same applies to the phrase 'for a sexual purpose', which I would interpret in the sense of reasonably perceived as intended to cause sexual stimulation to some viewers. (at [50])

And second, the context and purpose of the depictions:

> Family photos of naked children, viewed objectively, generally do not have as their 'dominant characteristic' the depiction of a sexual organ or anal region 'for a sexual purpose'. Placing a photo in an album of sexual photos and adding a sexual caption could change its meaning such that its dominant characteristic or purpose becomes unmistakably sexual in the view of a reasonable objective observer: see *R. v.*

Hurtubise, [1997] B.C.J. No. 40 (QL) (S.C.), at paras. 16–17. Absent evidence indicating a dominant prurient purpose, a photo of a child in the bath will not be caught. To secure a conviction the Crown must prove beyond a reasonable doubt that the 'dominant characteristic' of the picture is a depiction of the sexual organ or anal region 'for a sexual purpose'. If there is a reasonable doubt, the accused must be acquitted. (at [51])

In *Sharpe*, the Supreme Court of Canada found that two exceptions had to be read into the Canadian legislation, which would otherwise capture the possession of certain material that would not normally be considered child pornography. Those exceptions were for 'written materials or visual representations created and held by the accused alone, exclusively for personal use' and 'visual recordings created by or depicting the accused that do not depict unlawful sexual activity and are held by the accused exclusively for private use' (at [99]). The Supreme Court ruled that such material would not harm, or had little risk of harming, children.

In the retrial of *R v Sharpe* in 2002 (*R v Sharpe* (2002) BCD Crim J 2149) it was found that the exception would be made out where the person possessing the recording personally recorded or participated in the sexual activity in question; the activity was not unlawful; all parties consented to the creation of the record; and the record was kept in strict privacy and intended exclusively for private use. Therefore, a teenage couple would not be affected by the law if they created and kept sexually explicit pictures capturing each other engaged in lawful sexual activity, provided that these were not shared beyond the couple (for further discussion see Akdeniz 2008, p. 149).

England and Wales

In England and Wales, according to the *Protection of Children Act 1978* (UK), s 1, taking an indecent photograph of a child is prohibited. The *Sexual Offences Act 2003* (UK) revised s 7(6) of the *Protection of Children Act 1978* (UK), redefining a 'child' as a person under the age of 18, in order to comply with international initiatives to harmonise child pornography laws (see Ost 2009, p. 62). Unlike the other jurisdictions discussed, there is no statutory definition of 'indecent' and the courts determine its meaning by reference to ordinary standards of decency (*R v Stanford* [1972] QB 391). The court must therefore apply community standards of propriety and must do so looking solely at the image without considering the context or intention of the maker of the image

(*R v Graham-Kerr* [1988] 1 WLR 1098).[10] This means the definition of indecency is potentially very wide in England and Wales (Gillespie 2010b, p. 211).

In 2001, the Sentencing Advisory Panel (SAP) provided advice to the Court of Appeal of England and Wales as to offences involving indecent photographs of children. The SAP analysed the seriousness of offences by reference to five points on a scale derived from the COPINE Project. However, in applying this advice in *R v Oliver* [2002] EWCA Crim 2766; [2003] 1 Cr App R 28, the Court of Appeal found that the lowest scale for pornographic images was 'images depicting erotic posing with no sexual activity', as 'it seems to us, neither nakedness in a legitimate setting, nor the surreptitious procuring of an image, gives rise, of itself, to a pornographic image' (at [10]).

Conclusion

This brief review of child pornography laws reveals that the concern to combat child pornography and the development of typologies of material that may be of interest to adults with a sexual interest in young people has led to a global expansion of child pornography laws. The following chapter will explore what may be leading to, or preventing, young people from being prosecuted under these laws and why there appears to be a reluctance to completely remove the young from the reaches of child pornography laws.

5

Factors Determining Whether Young People Are Prosecuted

Introduction

The review of the laws relating to child pornography in the previous chapter shows that while there are differences across jurisdictions in how child pornography is defined and criminalised, in recent years most jurisdictions have extended the definition of 'child pornography' beyond depictions of children engaged in a sexual act or pose or witnessing sexual acts. While, as the cases discussed in Chapter 4 show, young people may be prosecuted for child pornography offences for sexting in many jurisdictions, it does not appear to be the case that young people are being routinely prosecuted and convicted (see e.g., Wolak et al., 2012, p. 4; Paterson 2012, pp. 12–13). This chapter therefore explores the factors that may determine whether or not a young person will be prosecuted under child pornography laws. This involves looking at legal provisions that may prevent prosecution, such as general defences, child pornography specific defences and constitutional protections such as the right to free speech and privacy, as well as non-legal barriers to prosecution, such as the exercise of discretion to only prosecute certain cases of sexting. The chapter then considers why it is deemed necessary to retain the possibility of prosecuting young people under these laws.

Age of criminal responsibility

A primary determinant of whether a young person can be prosecuted under child pornography laws is the age of criminal responsibility (i.e., the age at which he or she can be held accountable for criminal behaviour as opposed to the age at which he or she can be prosecuted as an adult). The age level(s), and systems for determining criminal responsibility, vary across jurisdictions. It is notable that many common law countries have a relatively low minimum age level of criminal responsibility. This stems from the traditional position at common law that under the age of seven a child is never criminally responsible, and from this age until the age of 14 there is a presumption of *doli incapax*, which means a child's liability to prosecution depends on an assessment of whether he or she understood the wrongfulness of the act (for a history of the age of criminal responsibility, see Crofts 2002, pp. 5–35). This contrasts sharply with the majority of European states, where the minimum age is generally set between 12 and 16 (see Hammarberg 2006; for an international overview, see Cipriani 2009).

Some jurisdictions maintain this common law position of two age levels of criminal responsibility but in a statutory form; for instance, Washington State (§ 9A.04.050 of the *Revised Code*):

> Children under the age of eight years are incapable of committing crime. Children of eight and under twelve years of age are presumed to be incapable of committing crime, but this presumption may be removed by proof that they have sufficient capacity to understand the act or neglect, and to know that it was wrong.

That position is similar throughout Australia with all jurisdictions providing that no child under 10 can be criminally responsible for an offence while a child aged 10 years but not more than 14 years old can only be criminally responsible for an offence if it is proven by the prosecution that the child knew that his or her conduct or omission was wrong (see e.g., ss 7.1, 7.2 *Criminal Code Act 1995* (Cth)).

Other jurisdictions have moved away from this traditional common law position and have abolished the higher flexible age level of criminal responsibility, although this is generally done where the common law age level of criminal responsibility has been raised, for example, to 10 in England and Wales (*Children and Young Persons Act 1963*, s 16)[1] or 12 in Canada (*Criminal Code*, s 13).

Current research suggests that while some young people may begin to explore with sexting from the age of 9 to 14 prevalence increases from the age of 15 (see Law Reform Committee of Victoria 2013, p. 69; see also our findings on age and prevalence of sexting in Chapter 8). This suggests that depending on the jurisdiction the age level(s) of criminal responsibility in the common law world may provide some level of protection for younger sexters but not for those at age levels at which sexting is more prevalent.

Defences to child pornography offences

Some jurisdictions have defences that may apply to young people in relation to child pornography offences. For example, according to s 130E(2) of the Tasmanian *Criminal Code*, it is a defence to charges of producing, involving a minor in producing, possessing or accessing (but not distributing) child exploitation material to prove that 'the material which is the subject of the charge depicts sexual activity between the accused person and a person under the age of 18 years that is not an unlawful sexual act'. However, as Tallon et al. observe, 'given that the Tasmanian defence is silent about young people depicted in a sexual context, as opposed to a sexual activity, it does not guarantee that child pornography laws will never be applied against young people who engage in sexting' (2012, [5.7]).

Victoria also provides a defence which has a limited role by only applying to possession of child pornography where at the time of taking, making or receiving the material the possessor was not more two years older than the minor or where the possessor was the young person who was the subject of the material (*Crimes Act 1958* (Vic), s70(2)(d), (e)). This defence was perceived by the Law Reform Committee of Victoria to be problematic in being both too limited and too expansive. The first part of the defence was limited in not covering images received by third parties, such as where an intimate image was passed on by the receiver to another young person (Law Reform Committee of Victoria 2013, p. 132). The second part of the defence was considered to possibly exempt exploitative conduct in not requiring that there was a close age relationship between the subject of the image and the possessor (Law Reform Committee of Victoria 2013, p. 133). Other problems were that the defence only applied to one of the child pornography offences and was out of line with defences to sexual offences more generally (2013, p. 133). Based on its review the Committee recommended the development of new defences to child pornography offences (2013, p. 145). The Parliament of Victoria followed the recommendation and introduced new defences (discussed in Chapter 12) through the *Crimes Amendment (Sexual Offences and Other Matters) Act 2014* (Vic).

In England and Wales, when the age level for child pornography was raised to 18 (under s 7(6) the *Protection of Children Act 1978* (UK), revised by the *Sexual Offences Act 2003* (UK)), a defence was introduced where a child is aged over 16 and either married to or living together in an 'enduring relationship' with the other young person who is the subject of the photograph. Earlier drafts, but not the final version, of the legislation also provided that no offence would be committed if the child depicted in the photograph was 16 or over and the photograph was made with his or her consent. The European Council Framework Decision of 22 December 2003 on combating the sexual exploitation of children and child pornography, art. 3.2(b) also provides that Member States may exclude criminal liability for the production and possession of images of children where the image is taken with the child's consent, is for private use only, and the child is above the age of consent (see Ost 2009, p. 64). The desirability and appropriateness of such defences is considered in more detail in Chapter 12.

Constitutional protections

In the United States, prosecutions under child pornography offences have been challenged on the basis that sexting behaviour is constitutionally protected (see McLaughlin 2014). Depictions of naked children that do not involve a lascivious exhibition of the genitals do not fit the federal statutory definition of 'child pornography' and are protected by the First Amendment (see *United States v Horn*, 187 F3d 781, 789 (8th Cir 1999)). Furthermore, other constitutional rights may create barriers to prosecution. In *Miller v Skumanick*, 605 F Supp 2d 634 (MD Pa 2009), *Miller v Mitchell*, 589 F3d 139 (3d Cir 2010),[2] a school teacher found photos on a confiscated phone, including photos of girls in their underwear, and one girl who was topless with a towel around her waist. Three of the girls involved in these photos refused to attend probation or complete a program of 're-education', and the District Attorney threatened charges for the possession and distribution of child pornography. The girls argued that this was not child pornography and challenged the requirement to attend the re-education program on the basis that this infringed their First Amendment rights to free expression and to be free from compelled expression (in the form of being forced to write a paper about the wrongfulness of their actions). Their parents also argued that the re-education program infringed their Fourteenth Amendment rights to direct their children's upbringing. These arguments were successful and the girls obtained preliminary injunctive relief, and future prosecution was prevented.

However, while constitutional rights prevented the threatened prosecutions in *Miller v Skumanick*, they have not prevented other prosecutions of teenagers for sexting-type behaviours. This is demonstrated by the case *AH v State of Florida*, 949 So 2d 234, Fla App Ct 2007, detailed in Chapter 4. In this case, a 17-year-old boy took digital images of himself having consensual sexual intercourse with his 16-year-old girlfriend and emailed the images to another computer. Both were found guilty of producing, directing or promoting a photograph or representation that they knew to include the sexual conduct of a child (§ 827.071(2),

Florida Statutes (2005)). The young woman appealed her conviction, but the majority of the Appeal Court dismissed the appeal. The Court affirmed the finding of the trial court that 'criminal prosecution was the least intrusive means of furthering the State's compelling interest' (at [236]). The majority rejected the argument that the minor's right to privacy, which may protect acts of sexual intercourse, extends also to situations where the minor memorialises the sexual act through pictures or video (at [236]). It was held that there was no reasonable expectation of privacy in this situation for two reasons: first, because 'the decision to take photographs and to keep a record that may be shown to people in the future weighs against a reasonable expectation of privacy' (at [237]) and, second, because the Court found that, unlike adults in a committed relationship, these were minors in a sexual relationship who could not have a reasonable expectation that the relationship would last and therefore could not have a reasonable expectation that the other would not show the photographs to others, intentionally or not. A range of scenarios were imagined in which the photographs might be shown to others. For example, the majority of the Court noted that child pornography is lucrative and therefore a reason to show the photographs might be for profit. It was also noted that teenagers like to brag about their prowess and a 'reasonably prudent person would believe that if you put this type of material in a teenagers hands that at some point, either for profit or bragging rights, the material will be disseminated to other members of the public' (at [237]).

In *State v Vezzoni*, 127 Wash App 1012, 2005 Wash App LEXIS 1686 (Was Ct App 2005), a 16-year-old boy was found guilty of 'dealing in depictions of a minor engaged in sexually explicit conduct' (Wash Rev Code § 9.68A.050) and 'possession of depictions of a minor engaged in sexually explicit conduct' (§ 9.68A.070) after distributing pictures of his 16-year-old girlfriend's unclothed breasts and genitals. He argued that his convictions should be overturned because they violated his right to privacy, which covered engaging in sexual activity as a minor and also extended to the taking of photographs of that activity. As in *AH v State of Florida*, it was found that the right to privacy was not unlimited and was subject to the state's compelling interest in preventing the sexual exploitation of children. It was also argued that the legislature did not intend child pornography offences to apply to situations in which teenagers, who could consent to sexual intercourse, took nude pictures of each other. The Court rejected this argument, finding that:

The child pornography statutes are unambiguous and do not make age-based distinctions when defining specific criminal conduct. As the court stated in *D.H.*, '[t]he Legislature is well aware of how to create different degrees of criminal liability on the basis of a specific age disparity between the offender and the victim.' ... When the legislature declines to make distinctions based on age in the statute, '[t]here is no room for judicial interpretation ... beyond the plain language of the statute.' ... The legislature did not intend to exclude juvenile offenders from the child pornography statutes. (2005 Wash App LEXIS 864 [6])

Finally, Vezzoni argued that his convictions should be quashed because they violated his constitutionally protected right to free speech, which was not overridden because, in not showing his girlfriend engaging in sexual conduct or performing sexual activity, the photographs did not amount to child pornography. However, the Court of Appeal found that, given the photographs showed unclothed genitals and breasts, it was reasonable to assume that the photographs were taken in order to sexually stimulate the viewer and, as such, amounted to child pornography.

In Canada the Charter of Rights and Freedoms has arguably played a more significant role in restricting the applicability of Canadian child pornography laws in cases of sexting. In *R v Sharpe* [2001] 1 SCR 45, 2001 SCC 2 the Supreme Court read exceptions into the Canadian legislation for 'self created expressive material' made for personal use, and private recordings of lawful sexual activity for personal use. In doing so, it found that such material would not harm, or had little risk of harming, children, and the impact of the laws was not proportionate when analysed in terms of the Canadian Charter of Rights and Freedoms. The Court stated: 'The cost of prohibiting such materials to the right of free expression outweighs any tenuous benefit it might confer in preventing harm to children' (*R v Sharpe*). Gillespie (2013, p. 640), commenting on this case, states that:

> Sharpe shows that the central question is the extent to which the potential negative elements can justify the criminalisation of the material. At the heart of this decision is the fact that it has been said that the purpose of the child pornography law was the protection of children from exploitation, and this is true of the law in England and Wales too. The Canadian Supreme Court decided that there was little evidence that children were exploited in the production of self-generated material and in the context of consensual sexting that is at the heart of this discussion, this would seem to be correct.

The exceptions read into the Canadian legislation do not, however, prevent prosecutions where images go beyond private use and there is a breach of privacy. Therefore, in *R v Walsh* (2006), 206 CCC (3d) 543 (Ont CA), a 22-year-old male was prosecuted after he distributed sexts sent by his 15-year-old girlfriend after their relationship ended. Similarly, in *R v Schultz* (2008) 450 AR 37 (QB), a 20-year-old was prosecuted when he exposed intimate photographs of his 16-year-old ex-girlfriend on the internet and, in *R v Dabrowksi* (2007), 86 OR (3d) 721 (CA), it was held that threats to circulate intimate photos could mean that they were no longer being held for a mutual intimate purpose, thus preventing them from falling under the exceptions outlined in *Sharpe*. This contrasts with the operation of US constitutional protections. As Slane states, 'an image either attracts First Amendment protection (and hence is not child pornography) or it does not' (2010, p. 581). In Canada, on the other hand, an image may fall within protections afforded by the Charter, but can lose this protection if it is published or shared in a different context.

Requiring authority to prosecute

Requiring the permission of a higher office before prosecutions can be commenced against young people is a method of reviewing and controlling discretion at lower ranks in the prosecution and police service. In response to concerns about children and young people being prosecuted, the Australian Government amended the *Criminal Code Act 1995* (Cth) in 2010 to require the permission of the Attorney General to bring criminal proceedings in relation to child pornography against a person aged under 18 under Commonwealth law. A blanket ban on prosecuting young people was not thought to be appropriate to ensure that child pornography charges could be laid where the incident involved malicious or exploitative behaviour (Explanatory Memorandum 2010). It was also felt that the path to prosecution of young people should not be closed because there is a community interest in preventing the circulation of explicit images of minors (Explanatory Memorandum 2010). However, according to the Australia Federal Police, between 2008 and 2012, no person under the age of 18 had been charged under the Commonwealth *Criminal Code* for offences relating to sexting. The Australian Federal Police have also described the section as a 'safeguard' that operates in addition to the discretion accorded to law enforcement and prosecution agencies 'to take the circumstances of the particular case into account before proceeding to investigate or prosecute' (2012, p. 7).

Although not limited to young persons, in England and Wales the *Protection of Children Act 1978* (UK), which creates offences involving indecent photographs of children, similarly provides in s 1(3) that proceedings for an offence under the Act will not be instituted except by or with the consent of the Director of Public Prosecutions.

Discretion

Given that sexting can cover a wide range of behaviours, from the consensual sharing of images to non-consensual creation and distribution of images, child pornography laws clearly are not appropriate in all sexting situations. There is therefore a widespread reliance on discretion in deciding whether to report, investigate and prosecute young people for sexting. It is highly likely that only a small proportion of sexting cases will come to official attention (Paterson 2012, pp. 12–13). Incidents of sexting may be under-reported because the young people involved are consensually taking, distributing and possessing the images and therefore do not consider that a crime has been committed. Even where an image is distributed without consent, the young person may not want to report this to an adult because, as with under-reporting of crimes generally, he or she may feel 'not altogether blameless or wishes certain activities to remain secret' (Williams 2012, p. 83). A young person who feels shame about being the subject or recipient of such an image may wish to avoid facing the further embarrassment of official attention. Also, a young person may feel that sexting is wrong, but not realise that it could amount to an offence and therefore may not report it in the belief that it is too trivial or nothing can be done. Equally, knowledge that the behaviour could amount to such a serious offence as child pornography may actually deter a young person from reporting incidents because he or she does not wish to see anyone punished so severely or he or she may fear his or her own criminalisation or reprisals if he or she reports the behaviour (see Law Reform Committee of Victoria 2013, p. 136).

Where sexting does come to the attention of adults, they may be reluctant to report it to the police if they view it as normal childish (if inappropriate) behaviour and there are no circumstances suggesting coercion, exploitation or abuse. Adults who are aware of the potentially serious child pornography charges may also be reluctant to report because they do not think the behaviour fits the criminal law or deserves such a severe reaction. However, mandatory reporting requirements may mean that teachers and those with special responsibilities towards children do not feel that they have a choice in whether or not to report sexting behaviour.

Once sexting has come to official attention, discretion may be exercised to not pursue prosecution. Recent research in the United States into how police are dealing with cases of sexting suggests that police are using discretion not to prosecute young people for child pornography offences unless there are other factors that are less readily assigned to childish misbehaviour or normal childhood experimentation with sexuality (Wolak et al. 2012, p. 4). Such factors may include whether the image was distributed without the consent of the subject, for instance as an act of revenge, or where the image was taken of a criminal offence, such as a sexual assault. Police are also more likely to pursue prosecution if an adult is the recipient or the sender of the image (Wolak et al. 2012, p. 6).

Discretion is also widely used in Australia. For instance, the Acting Commander of Victoria Police gave evidence before the Law Reform Committee of Victoria Inquiry into Sexting in which he confirmed that police (at least in that state) were exercising discretion:

> We have gone back over the data in particular to look at the number of juveniles who have ever been investigated for the offences that I outlined earlier on, and through a manual search of the data we can certainly identify that there are six juveniles who have been investigated in the context of a 57A offence – that is, the transmission of child pornography – which best fits the sexting scenario. Only one matter proceeded to the Children's Court, but that matter was also complicated by the young person downloading child pornography from the internet, completely separate to the sexting-type offence. Of the remaining five juveniles, one was cautioned and four were subject to no further police action, which means that the matter was dealt with by police but no charges were laid and no caution was given for the young person. So from what we are seeing, whilst we understand the concept of sexting out there, there are not too many matters that are coming to police attention, and certainly of any of the juvenile matters that are coming to our attention, they are not being charged. We are exercising our discretion of the office of constable and dealing with the matters outside of the court process (Paterson 2012, pp. 12–13).

Similarly, in Queensland, Acting Detective Inspector Steve Loth commented that:

> There's a level of criminality considered here; the more serious the criminal behaviour – coercion, threats or exploitation of people – that behaviour is more likely to warrant criminal sanction as opposed

a young person who has exchanged an image with the consent of another young person ... We're not about prosecuting young people who are sharing images even though they may technically be criminal, bearing in mind prosecution needs to be in the public interest, but kids need to understand that once they send an image, they lose complete control of that image (cited in Feeney 2013).

New South Wales Police have also indicated that they typically refer sexting cases to a Youth Justice Conference, rather than pursuing charges. However, when they feel that behaviour has become 'malicious' rather than merely 'stupid' – for example, where the material has been disseminated to damage a person's reputation, or where the material was procured by coercion or otherwise with a lack of consent – they are more likely to prosecute (see Tallon et al. 2012, p. 19).

In their submission to the Law Reform Committee of Victoria Inquiry into Sexting, Western Australian Police noted that they have formulated a policy with the Office of the Director of Public Prosecutions, which provides that 'while technically an offence it is not in the public interest to charge and prosecute persons under the age of 18 years in respect to images of a child in an adolescent relationship, unless there is evidence to suggest that the child is being exploited' (Western Australian Police Force 2012, p. 2). This involves consideration of factors such as: the degree of malice involved in procuring the sexting; any imbalance of power between the parties; and whether bribery, coercion, threat or violence was involved. The Western Australian Police also note that when the images have been distributed, serious consideration is given to prosecuting the child responsible for the distribution.

In England and Wales, the Crown Prosecution Service's (CPS) Code for Crown Prosecutors specifies that the interests of a youth must be taken into account when deciding whether to prosecute, with regard to be had to the United Nations *Convention on the Rights of the Child* and the principle aim of the youth justice system: the prevention of offending by children and young people. Moreover, in relation to sexual offences committed by a young person (under *Sexual Offences Act 2003* (UK), s 13), the Crown Prosecution Service guidelines on Youth Offenders state that:

It should be noted that where both parties to sexual activity are under 16, then they may both have committed a criminal offence. However, the overriding purpose of the legislation is to protect children and it was not Parliaments [*sic*] intention to punish children unnecessarily or for the criminal law to intervene where it was wholly in appropriate. Consensual sexual activity between, for example, a 14- or 15-year-old and a teenage partner would not normally require criminal proceedings in the absence of aggravating features. The relevant considerations include:

- the respective ages of the parties;
- the existence and nature of any relationship;
- their level of maturity;
- whether any duty of care existed;
- whether there was a serious element of exploitation. (Crown Prosecution Service, undated)

The Association of Chief Police Officers (n.d.) has published a statement of its position on sexting-type behaviours. While acknowledging that it is a crime 'to take, make, permit to take, distribute, show, possess, possess with intent to distribute, or to advertise indecent photographs or pseudo-photographs of any person below the age of 18' (at [1.6]), it also states that:

First time offenders should not usually face prosecution for such activities, instead an investigation to ensure that the young person is not at any risk and the use of established education programmes should be utilised. CEOP accept that in some cases, e.g. persistent offenders, a more robust approach may be called for- for example the use of reprimands. It is recommended that prosecution options are avoided, in particular the use legislation that would attract sex offender registration. (at [1.8])

There are some suggestions that police in Canada are also exercising discretion not to prosecute (Slane 2010, p. 587). In the case of *Walsh*, discussed above, a few of the victim's classmates were involved in the distribution of the sexual images, including by email; however, one girl's case appeared to have been resolved 'by other means', rather than via the criminal justice system. Slane states that such discretion explains the lack of reported cases involving malicious distribution in Canada (2010, p. 588).

Aside from situations where there are aggravating factors, research in the United States has found that arrests were made in 18 per cent of cases where the sexting was deemed to be experimental and there were no aggravating factors involved (i.e., where there was no adult involved in the sexting and there was no indication of a malicious intent or reckless misuse) (Wolak et al. 2012). This demonstrates that such broad discretion can result in arbitrary consequences, with young people engaging in sexting behaviour either attracting or escaping the operation of the criminal law due to the decisions of peers or adults (parents, teachers etc) to report their activities, and law enforcement officials to prosecute. For example, in Farmington, Utah, 28 teenagers were investigated for sharing naked pictures of themselves via their mobile phones; however, the prosecutor charged most of them with misdemeanour crimes, rather than with distributing child pornography (see Kimpel 2010, p. 335). This can be contrasted with the decision to prosecute the minors in *AH v State of Florida*. Such discrepancies confirm Wolak et al.'s conclusion based on their research 'that some youth may be facing exposure to criminal treatment in cases that might be better handled informally' (2012, p. 9).

Why retain the possibility of prosecuting young people for sexting under child pornography laws?

The above discussion has shown that it appears that young people are, in the main, only prosecuted where there are aggravating factors (such as malicious intent, coercion,[3] or exploitation) involved in the sexting behaviour. Also, as the media analysis in Chapter 3 has shown, concern about the negative effects of such prosecutions has increased in recent years (particularly in Australia). This raises the question as to whether the legislators intend that young people who sext should be captured by such laws, and why it is thought necessary to retain the option of prosecution of young people for such offences.

As noted in the previous chapter, child pornography laws were strengthened in response to the concern that new technologies were seen to be escalating the dangers of exploitation of young people by adults (Commonwealth Attorney-General's Department 2009). Increasing attention to the negative impacts of young people being prosecuted for child pornography offences has made some question the appropriateness of allowing the prosecution of young people under child pornography laws. Nonetheless, there has generally not been an appetite to remove young people completely from the reaches of child pornography laws. This suggests that concerns over the harms that sexting poses form part of the argument for using such laws to deter this behaviour. The following examines the numerous linkages that have been made between sexting and direct or indirect forms of harm to young people and how these form part of an argument that such conduct should be dissuaded by the possibility of prosecution under child pornography laws.

Direct harm

A main concern regarding the criminalisation of the creation, possession and distribution of child pornography is the direct harm to the
child involved as the subject of that material. As the Attorney-General's
Department of the Australian Government notes:

> Offences directed at possession and distribution should recognise
> the sexual exploitation which such images represent. Dealing in
> child pornography or abuse material fuels market demand, thereby
> increasing the incidence of actual abuse of children. It reflects varying
> scales of harm involving the initial abuse of the child (from images
> taken of an unknowing child playing naked on the beach, to images
> of serious rape/torture) and varying scales of harm relating to the
> subsequent exploitation (from private access within the home to
> large-scale commercial exploitation). (2009, [238])

Similar rationales can be identified in other jurisdictions. In *New York
v Ferber*, 458 US 747 (1982) the Court justified the regulation of child
pornography that did not necessarily constitute obscenity because the
use of children in images was harmful to their 'physiological, emotional
and mental health' (at 756–8). Similarly, Slane has argued that the types
of images prohibited by Canadian law are those involving an exploitative element (2010, p. 56). As the Court of Appeal stated in *R v Hewlett*
(2002) 312 AR 165, [24]:

> [T]he protection afforded by the legislation extends to all children
> under 18, no matter their age, and rightly so. Society has recognized
> the legitimate need to safeguard all children in this category from
> exploitative conduct. Children are not adults and cannot be expected
> to exercise judgment as if they were.

Evident from this is the concern that minors cannot be expected to
appreciate the exploitative nature of sexual photography, and the legal
system has an obligation to protect these vulnerable persons (Slane 2010,
p. 564). This rationale calls for a clearer understanding of the forms of
behaviour that we understand as sexting. Direct harms are likely to differ
significantly depending on whether the image was created and distributed consensually, at the one extreme, or, at the other, was created and
distributed without consent or was the result of a sexual offence.

In the US case of *AH v State of Florida* the Court stated that there
could be direct harm to the participants even if the images were taken

consensually and were not distributed to anyone other than the two young people involved because it could cause psychological trauma. Such an argument in favour of prosecution overlooks the more likely and deeper psychological harm that may be caused by receiving a criminal conviction in such circumstances. It may reflect a general discomfort adults might feel about young people expressing their sexuality. It could also indicate inter-generational differences in engagement with new technologies. Arcabascio (2009–10, p. 5) notes, '[i]t is unlikely that today's teenagers recognize or recall a world without cellular phones and texting'. There is evidence that many young people may not view sending naked images as anything other than a bit of fun or modern day 'love letters' (see Chapters 8 and 9). The Joint Select Committee on Cyber-Safety noted that 'Australia now has a generation of people who have never been without online access and have integrated it fully into their lives' (2011, [1.33]). The Committee also commented that: 'Sexting has become "normalised behaviour" in adolescent culture' (2011, [4.54]).

Some may consider that a young person is harmed by the creation of the images even if he or she gives apparent consent because he or she may have felt coerced into making or distributing the image, either directly by a partner exerting pressure or through peer group pressure. Researchers have identified a gendered dimension to sexting, with images more likely to be of girls and distributed by boys (see discussion in Chapter 7). There is a degree of evidence suggesting that young girls feel particular peer pressure to send naked images. This can have negative impacts for the young person's privacy and reputation, which can lead to 'poor self-esteem and self-image, isolating behaviours, school avoidance, eating disorders, self-harm and suicidal ideation and behaviours' (Joint Select Committee on Cyber-Safety 2011, [4.60]). The gendered nature of sexting is further explored in our survey and focus groups, and is discussed in Chapters 8 and 9.

As Ryan (2010) notes, when images are initially taken consensually and free from coercion, direct exploitation has not occurred and, although a young person may later regret taking the image, especially if he or she is faced with consequences if the image is shared, that experience is 'drastically different from victims of traditional child pornography' (p. 371). She argues that using such laws to criminalise conduct willingly engaged in by minors is contrary to legislative intent (2010, p. 371). This is also evident in Judge Padovano's dissent in *AH v State of Florida* where he stated that the intent of the statute was to protect children from abuse by others, and not by themselves.

Haunting harm

If there is no direct harm, it could be argued that there will be no haunting harm. However, this depends on whether the image is distributed beyond the originally intended recipient(s) and whether a young person changes his or her view of whether the material is harmful. In *AH v State of Florida*, the view was expressed that, given the immaturity of young people's relationships, there can be no reasonable expectation that the relationships will last, and hence no reasonable expectation that the images will not be disseminated to others.

If the images are then distributed to others, they could be a source of haunting harm and could result in far-reaching consequences for the minors involved (Joint Select Committee on Cyber-Safety 2011, p. 143; Law Reform Committee of Victoria 2013, p. 55). This scenario is continually reinforced by media campaigns, as noted in Chapter 3. Education campaigns also focus on the idea of continuing damage to reputation caused by the sharing of these photos, particularly at the end of a relationship, and the lasting consequence this can have in areas such as employment. A 2009 US study found that colleges and universities use social networking websites as part of their evaluation of applications (Anderson 2009). Similarly, a 2014 survey on a US job website found that 51 per cent of employers had not hired a candidate due to content, including provocative or inappropriate photos, which they had found on social media websites (CareerBuilder 2014).

However, as Ryan notes, although young adults face the same psychological and reputational consequences as adults who engage in sexting, these laws only reflect a concern with protecting minors from these consequences 'because the law presumes that adults are able to make fully informed, responsible decisions and predict the consequences of such decisions once they reach the age of majority' (2010, p. 369).

Enticing harm and whetting the appetite of child abusers

As Moran-Ellis observes, sexts may also be accessed by sexual offenders if they are posted on social media websites (2012, p. 126). Therefore, sexting could involve the creation of sexual images of minors that eventually provide a means of whetting the appetite of child abusers, and enticing other children to participate in child pornography. These concerns were evident in the US decision of *Osborne v Ohio* 495 US 103 (1990), where the Court referenced evidence suggesting that child pornographic materials are used to entice young people into sexual behaviour (at 111). Similarly, in *R v Schultz* (2008) 450 AR 37, it was stated:

> The distribution of child pornography causes harm beyond that caused by the exploitation and abuse of children portrayed in existing pornographic material, including:
>
> (i) The promotion of 'cognitive distortions' causing the possessor to view child abuse as normal (at para. 87);
>
> (ii) The fueling of fantasies and consequence of making paedophiles more likely to offend (at para.89); and
>
> (iii) The facilitation of new production of child pornography by using existing materials to groom or seduce victims (at para. 91).
>
> Incidental to preventing harm to children, the law recognizes the need to prevent 'attitudinal harm to society at large' (Sharpe at para. 82).
>
> These concerns apply equally to the hypothetical distributor. She contributes to harmful attitudinal shifts, fuels fantasies, and provides material that may be used to exploit and traumatize future victims. (at [130]–[132])

However, most of these harms arise from the consensual material being passed on to others who were never intended to receive them. The mere possibility of such images being passed on does not justify the prosecution of the young person who creates such a consensual image as a child pornographer.

Encouraging problematic sexual behaviour

A more indirect concern that has not been clearly articulated in the legal literature is that sexting could encourage 'deviant' sexual behaviour among the young. This depends on what sort of behaviour is considered problematic and why. Some research has associated sexting with a gamut of negative risk factors, including 'risky' sexual behaviours (see, e.g., Dake et al. 2013). There are questions about the validity of such research and the hetero-normative stance concerning what is regarded to be risky sexual behaviour which are discussed in Chapter 7.

Negative associations between sexting and sexual practices constructed as 'risky' or 'deviant' are unsurprising, given the social discomfort that may be felt by adults about young people as emerging sexual subjects. In the United States, Kimpel comments that society is 'deeply uncomfortable with adolescent sexuality' (2010, p. 310). As Jackson states, '[c] hildren are still not generally treated as sexual beings and the possibility that they might be makes many of us feel uneasy' (1982, p. 3). Faulkner (2011b, p. 53, n 11 emphasis in original) similarly notes that:

> The 'child' is reduced, in the common imagination, *to one without worldly experience or desire*: a passive object of *others'* protection, abuse and control. It is thus difficult for some to conceptualise the transition to the activity and knowledge of adulthood. And this is especially so concerning *sexual* activity and knowledge.

Some adults believe that stigmatising young people who engage in sexual behaviour, such as sexting, will benefit the wider class of young people as a whole by deterring them from engaging in such behaviour (Kimpel 2010, p. 312). As Kimpel states, 'the subtext is that the photograph contains a dangerous power because it constitutes evidence that adolescent sexuality exists' (2010, p. 314). The images also tend to beautify and give the subject importance and value (2010, p. 313). Considering adults' uneasiness with young people's sexuality, we can see why law targets such signs of its existence (2010, 313).

Criminalising sexting precludes sexually active 16- and 17-year-olds (in some jurisdictions) from any visual representation of their sexual life, even to one another. This leads Albury et al. (2010) to question whether this excludes young people from the rights and forms of citizenship enjoyed by adults. Criminalisation also effectively silences the voices of young people as participants in sexual behaviour (Karaian 2012). Furthermore, as Kimpel notes, criminalising behaviour which if undertaken by consenting adults would not amount to an offence could actually be harmful to the development of young people's intimate citizenship: 'Branding sexually active minors who seek to memorialize their private intimate conduct as criminal delegitimizes the relationships and sexual autonomy of adolescents' (2010, p. 332).

In fact, sexting could amount to a positive experience, allowing young people to explore their sexuality in a relatively safe cyber environment (rather than in real life), and allowing them to take control of it (see eg Cupples and Thompson 2010). As Levick and Shah argued in their amicus brief to the Third Circuit Court of Appeals in the case of *Miller v Mitchell,* adolescents develop and discover their identities by 'thinking and experimenting with new areas of sexuality' (cited in Arcabascio

2009–10, p. 7). Given that gender and sexual identity is constructed and performed (Butler 1990) new technologies offer young people a new space to explore their identity, especially facets that might be stigmatised, such as sexuality (Buckingham 2008, p. 8). In doing so there is 'opportunity for identity play, for parody and subversion of the kind promoted by queer theory' (2008, p. 9). Simpson similarly argues that mobile technologies allow young people to free themselves from the traditional constraints imposed on their sexuality by adults and to construct their own paradigms of sexual life (2013, p. 692).

Sexting reflects young people's pervasive use of new technology and therefore it is naturally used as a means for their sexual exploration. Young people experimenting with their sexuality is nothing new; rather, it is the vehicle of that exploration that has changed. As Cummings questions: 'Are there differences between youth playing face-to-face versus online "Strip Poker," or between children investigating each other's body parts while playing "Doctor" and teens sharing cell phone images of their naked bodies?' (2009, p. 9). Bond also notes that 'the mobile phone has become embedded in children's social worlds in later modernity' (2011, p. 590). Hence, the virtual space provided by the mobile phone has replaced the bike shed as the place where fumbling adventures into sexual and romantic relationships take place (2011, p. 587). The major difference with sexting is that when such experimentation is undertaken it is digitally stored and possibly transmitted, and the sender loses control over its further dissemination.[4]

Conclusion

Despite the fact that child pornography offences can apply to young people who sext, and despite initial media concerns that there are high rates of young people being prosecuted, it seems that young people are not being prosecuted in large numbers for consensual sexting. There is a range of legal and non-legal factors that determine whether prosecutions will be forthcoming. The greatest factor appears to be discretion. A large amount of discretion is exercised by young people themselves, thus where sexting is consensual it is unlikely to come to official attention. Subsequently, the question of prosecution generally arises where the sext enters the hands of an adult (such as a teacher confiscating a phone) who feels compelled to do something (whether morally or due to mandatory reporting requirements) or where the young person reports the sexting because there are other aggravating factors involved (such as a malicious intention or an adult). Police and prosecutors also use discretion to divert young people from the criminal justice system where the sexting is consensual, in recognition of the fact that in such cases the behaviour does not fit the rationale for child pornography offences. The case is different where aggravating factors are involved and where there is a perception that prosecution is necessary to avert the harms that may flow from sexting. The question remains, which will be discussed further in Chapter 12, whether such harms are of the same magnitude as those underlying the creation and use of child pornography laws. The following chapter will explore the ways in which educational material has developed to respond to sexting by young people.

6
Sexting Education

Introduction

This chapter explores the current educational responses to sexting. While education 'remains a key component of how society should respond to sexting' (Australian Privacy Foundation 2012, p. 2), not all educational campaigns are equally valuable. Moreover, it could be argued that, despite a plethora of educational campaigns across the developed world, 'educators are struggling to keep up with the phenomenon of sexting' (Law Reform Committee of Victoria 2013, p. 4). In this chapter, we demonstrate that some educational campaigns perpetuate gender stereotyping and victim blaming, in much the same way that early sexual assault campaigns tended to blame the victims for their own behaviours that led to their victimisation (Matthews 1994, p. 11). Such campaigns often miss the mark with young people; they are not responsive to the concerns and voices of those they seek to protect. While there are potentially negative consequences to sexting that in some cases may be severe, there is a distinct tendency in the campaigns to date to overemphasise the risks related to sexting. In so doing, the negative consequences of sexting for young people are articulated in ways that may neglect some of the potentially positive experiences this practice might have, such as the empowerment young people may feel through engaging in sexting behaviour (see for instance, Simpson 2013).

This chapter will first look at the origins of educational responses, followed by an overview of key international, Australian Commonwealth and state-based awareness-raising sexting (internet-based and audio-visual) campaigns. In the second part of the chapter, we outline the predominant voices in educational campaigns and their messages, as well as common themes of grassroots initiatives in Australian schools.

Finally, the chapter concludes with a brief evaluation of existing Australian and international educational initiatives.

The origins of educational responses to sexting in Australia

Social commentators have recently argued that '[i]t is clear that the practice of sexting has taken the adult world by surprise. It was not foreseen that young people and children with mobile phones and computers with cameras would start sending intimate pictures of themselves to each other' (CASA Forum 2012). Yet sexting among adults has not generated the same concern or – as some critics call it – hysteria (Shafron-Perez 2009; James 2005) as teenage sexting practices. As we noted in Chapter 3, in Australia sexting featured in the media for the first time in relation to celebrities such as David Beckham and Shane Warne attract. Rather than creating a sense of moral concern as with young people sexting these adult exploits have been treated more as a source of entertainment, with the 'offenders' facing public ridicule and tabloid attention. At the same time, popular magazines such as *Cosmopolitan* run articles educating adults on how to better sext, and sometimes how to sext safely (Miller 2012; Nagi 2013). It is only since sexting has been linked to young people, and in particular young females, that this practice appears to have generated a moral conundrum that has seen a range of social actors joining a united front to 'protect our children' (Ventre and Doukas 2012). As will be demonstrated in this chapter, and as we argue throughout the book, such attention to the issue has its roots in ongoing anxieties about childhood sexuality.

In Australia, 'one of the first cases of illegal sexting' (Labi 2009) involved an incident in a Sydney Catholic school in which a 13-year-old girl sent a nude photo of herself to her teenage boyfriend. While the image was sent during the pair's relationship, after their break-up the photo was circulated widely, seen by 'dozens of students' and reported by the principal to the police (Labi 2009). This incident sparked a response from the education system, putting the issue on the broader social agenda for the first time. Responding to the situation, a Catholic Education Office Child Protection Officer indicated that the girl 'understands that she's made a very serious mistake', adding that they were 'working with her on developing her understanding of her own self-worth and dignity and respect for the human body, within our Catholic values context at the college' (cited in Labi 2009).

From the suggestion that to send sexts is a serious mistake, one that requires an intervention in which restitution of a young girl's self-worth and dignity in light of Catholic values is essential to repair the damage, we can infer that sexting in general is intrinsically harmful.[1] Further, by identifying young girls as most at risk, this initial response suggests that sexting is a gendered practice, in which young women are likely victims, and young men typically the perpetrators. It also positions young women as responsible for both their victimisation and for failing to implement risk-reduction strategies (Salter et al. 2013). Finally, such response situates young people as in need of rescue; by sexting they degrade themselves so much so that authorities such as governments, schools and teachers need to intervene as moral entrepreneurs, with the difficult task of 'straightening out' the strayed youth. Although this initial case is specific in many ways, as this chapter will demonstrate, key messages (both implicit and explicit) describing preliminary responses to sexting have set the tone for the majority of the contemporary educational campaigns concerning sexting in Australia and beyond.

International and Australian educational campaigns and their audience

It has been argued in the literature that responses to sexting, like other behaviours that involve use of technology, should be located within 'the holy trinity of reg[ulation], tech[nology] and ed[ucation]' (Svantesson 2011, p. 300). Yet some commentators maintain that '[t]he government's reaction to sexting compares with the fear of witches in the Middle Ages' (Nelson 2013a). While it is perhaps not surprising to see a Catholic college 'paint any and all critical responses to sexting as somehow "irrational" or "unreasonable"' (Albury et al. 2010, p. 4), this incident resonates with the conventional remedies the majority of educational campaigns both in Australia and elsewhere call for. Innately linked to narratives of gendered vulnerability and youth at risk of everlasting consequences that can ruin their reputation, job options, and future relationships, mainstream education campaigns aim for nothing less than deterring sexting practices: an abstinence-style model.[2] In this context, the concept of an ungoverned and unregulated cyberspace in which pictures can never be completely erased and/or discarded is used as an omnipresent threat that can wreck our youth's future. As Ryan (2010, p. 363) points out, 'now minors and young adults can instantly transmit the fruits of their exploration ... leaving the subject of such images "susceptible to humiliation" on a much larger scale'. This is the perceived danger from which young people need to be rescued, even if this means focusing on the negative risks associated with sexting, with parents and carers being the target audience of such interventions.

The UK's *Parents Protect!* (2014) campaign, as well as one of the first anti-sexting campaigns in Australia, the NSW Government's 2009 initiative *Safe Sexting: No Such Thing*, were aimed exclusively at adults, primarily at parents and teachers of young people who might be at risk of sexting. Drawing on entrenched fears of sexual predation online, the information sheet for parents on *Safe Sexting* suggests that 'images sent by mobile phones can easily fail into the wrong hands, and once they are in cyberspace it is impossible to remove them or control who sees them' (NSW Government 2009). Similarly, the Australian Government's 2010 campaign *Fact Sheet: TXTing/SEXTing* as a part of *The Line* initiative focuses on parents, arguing that, with sexts, '[t]he image is shared publicly, with the suggestion that your child is interested in sexual contact' (Australian Government 2010). This notion was further reinforced in the NSW Government's 2011 initiative *Sexting and Cyber-Safety: Protecting Your Child Online* (NSW Government 2011). Each of these campaigns implied young people's naivety in relation to online behaviour, arguing that they send sexts 'often without a real understanding of the consequences', which can be 'potentially devastating' (NSW Government 2009).

Such rhetoric is common across educational responses to sexting. As noted by the NSW Secondary Principals Council:

> One of the greatest risks to young people is the permanence of the postings made on the internet. This concept is not fully understood by Gen Y and Gen Z. Government needs to consider protections to reduce the permanence of postings for under 18s. (Joint Select Committee on Cyber-Safety 2011, p. 142)

While predominantly speaking to the parents, these campaigns have a clear message for young people: do not sext and do not distribute sexts sent to you (NSW Government 2009; NSW Government 2011).

A slightly different approach was taken by the United Kingdom and Australian Government's *ThinkUKnow* internet safety programs, launched in 2007 (UK) and 2010 (Australia).[3] The key aim of the *ThinkUKnow* campaigns in both countries was to deliver interactive information on online safety, including sexting, to both adults and young people. *ThinkUKnow UK* was developed by the Child Exploitation and Online Protection Centre (CEOP) – part of the National Crime Agency, and ChildLine. The campaign includes four websites for children of different ages, and two for adults (parents and teachers/trainers – ThinkUKnow UK 2014). Developed by Australian Federal Police and Microsoft Australia, the Australian program produced two separate websites accessible from the landing page: ThinkUKnow Youth (for 11- to 17-years-olds) for young people, and ThinkUKnow for parents, carers and teachers.

Through fact sheets, educational videos, and strategies for young people to 'stay in control' while online, these sites also provide advice on what to do when sexting happens. While we will outline key messages such campaigns promote later in the chapter, it is important to note here that they suggest that '[u]nfortunately, some people think that this is part of a normal relationship but the reality is that only a small proportion of young people sext' (ThinkUKnow 2014a). In addition, as part of the *ThinkUKnow* educational segment for adults, sexting is compared to 'up-skirting' and 'down-blousing' practices of taking covert photos of female anatomy and child pornography (ThinkUKnow 2014b). As such, these campaigns do little to challenge some of the negative discourses around sexting practice and may be out of touch with young people's practices and perceptions of sexting (as we explore in Chapters 8 and 9).

In June 2011, following criticism of current responses to sexting, the Australian Joint Select Committee on Cyber-Safety tabled its report on an inquiry into cybersafety called 'High-Wire Act: Cyber-Safety and the Young'. The inquiry established by the Committee resulted in a list of recommendations on a range of cybersafety issues, with several focusing on education measures targeting schools and teachers. The inquiry's report called for the inclusion of young people in educational campaigns, arguing that 'if we don't listen to what [young people] have to say...we are going to go down some dead ends' (Helen McGrath, Australian Psychological Society, cited in Joint Select Committee on Cyber-Safety 2011, p. 454). As a consequence of the inquiry, in 2011 the Commonwealth Government released the $120 million *CyberSmart* campaign, a national cybersafety and cybersecurity education program aimed at children, teenagers, parents and primary and high schools. The *CyberSmart* website included activities, games, blogs, multimedia, policies and lesson plans for school children, as well as an online training course, *Connect.ed*, for teachers (CyberSmart 2014a). While the campaign aimed to give more of a voice to young people, the 'So you got naked online' leaflet, located in the teens section of the website to provide advice to young people on how to deal with sexting, implicitly fed into many of the gender narratives that have developed around sexting. Similar to some earlier examples, this leaflet is a customised version of a UK-based 'Would you get naked online?' leaflet, part of a wider *Staying Safe Online* campaign by the South West Grid for Learning and UK Safer Internet Centre. While the pamphlet explaining sexting used gender-neutral language, images of tearful and scared young women dominated visually, contributing to suggestions that girls are more likely to be victimised in sexting (CyberSmart 2014a).

Notions of individualised risk and young people's gullibility were also reinforced in the campaigns. For example, *Parents Protect!* (2014) warned parents that, while 'this "finger on the pulse, share all" culture has some benefits, it can also create an environment in which teenagers and young people make impulsive decisions without thinking through the possible consequences'. Similarly, while key overarching messages of 'this is not the end of the world' and 'take control of your privacy' were embedded in the *CyberSmart* campaign, the notion of abstinence as best practice is clearly articulated (CyberSmart 2014a). Commentators have argued that such campaigns 'simply advocate abstaining from sexting' (Atkin 2011) and do little to advance understandings of the consequences of sexting.

Audio-visual anti-sexting campaigns

Audio-visual campaigns have also played an important role in educating teenagers about sexting. The practice of sexting presented in educational videos, however, is mostly a variation of one sexting scenario, with a naive female victim and a male perpetrator/distributor of sexts. In 'Exposed', an educational video part of the *ThinkUKnow* UK campaign, 15-year-old Dee sends naked pictures to her boyfriend Si. She is subsequently shattered by the consequences of his betrayal when he shares the photos with his friends. Dee responds by smashing her phone, but she cannot run away. In the video sequence she meets a 'smarter' version of herself who tells her that what she did was 'fun and stupid' because 'as soon as you hit that button, it's out of control. You can't undo and you can't go back'. Dee questions herself: 'What about when someone who wants to give me a job searches my name, what then?' Her alter ego answers, 'Well, we will just have to face that if it happens', noting that she needs to 'stop blaming anyone else! You send them first, you have to face up to it'. On urging Dee to go to the authorities, her alter-ego points out that 'just because you made one bad choice doesn't mean you have to make the wrong one next time'. The final message of the video is: 'You've got to always think before you send or share. Think about how it will affect others and yourself. Remember, pictures you send and share might become public and permanent, and the police might get involved' (ThinkUKnow UK 2014).

In 'Megan's Story', a two-minute educational video produced by the Australian Federal Police, Microsoft, NineMSN, CEOP and Virtual Global Task Force launched in 2010 as a part of a *ThinkUKnow* internet safety program, the female victim is positioned as a vulnerable, reckless female student who sends an image of herself to a boy in her class. During the class, the message goes viral while Megan's schoolmates and teacher keep giving her disapproving looks, making her increasingly anxious. After she leaves the class, the closing statement asks: 'Think you know what happens to your images? Who will see them? How they will affect you? Think again' (ThinkUKnow 2010). Similarly, in an educational DVD entitled 'Photograph', produced by the CentaCare Sandhurst Loddon Mallee Cyber Safety Project, 'Developing Ethical Digital Citizens' and funded by the Telstra Foundation, the main protagonist, 15-year-old Holly, sends a photo to her then-boyfriend who goes on to distribute the image after the breakup. The video 'focuses on the emotional impact on the girl, her parents and her friends and the legal and emotional impact on the boy and his parents' (Cyber Safe Kids 2010).

In the same vein, the 'Sexting' video from Australian-based KidsHelpline pictures a young girl who, under pressure, sends an image of herself to the most popular boy in her school. After he distributes the image, she points out that 'there is no way I can get the photos back and everyone has seen them. I am so embarrassed; I can't go back to school…There are some things that are too private to give away to anybody, no matter what they tell you' (KidsHelpline 2013). The notion of the irreversibility of sexting was also reinforced in a one-minute educational video from Canada launched in 2013. 'I shared a photo' is a visual ad from the Children of the Street Society that depicts a young woman who, in Bob Dylan style, presents boards to the screen with messages written on them. Sticking to the scenario of 'I sent a photo to someone I trusted and now, thousands of people I don't know, know me', the video's closing statement argues that '[t]here is no such thing as "just one photo"' (Khosravi 2013). Similarly, American-based interactive video 'Your Photo Fate' suggests that, once you send the message, 'the decision is out of your hands now', further intimating that paedophiles might receive such images eventually (National Center for Missing and Exploited Children 2014). Finally, 'Tagged: What you do online could tag you for life', a video developed by the Australian Communications and Media Authority's *CyberSmart* program, presents the story of a young woman Kate, whose ex-boyfriend, after she tags his current girlfriend in a photo with another boy, distributes naked pictures of her to other students in the school. After changing schools, Kate finds out that her past follows her everywhere she goes. Lou, a girl Kate meets in her new school, tells her: 'I know who you are. I have seen the pictures. Don't worry. It will be old news soon.' Kate replies: 'Yeah. That is what my counsellor says.' After the conversation, Lou helps Kate to find a classroom and the video ends (ACMA Cybersmart 2011, 15:50–15:55).

While each of these video scenarios was developed in order to educate young people about the dangers of sexting, youth commentators have dubbed them 'cringeworthy' (Birdee 2013), and suggested that they 'insidiously promote a humiliating shame-culture at the expense of the victim' (Nelson 2013a). Moreover, some argue these videos do not acknowledge that 'young women may send provocative images of their own accord without the pleas of a significant other or the like' (Khosravi 2013). Such campaigns further reinforce an unsophisticated victimisation/over-sexualisation dualism of young women that dominates the mainstream sexting discourse (Salter et al. 2013), and emphasise the damage sexting practice might have for (mostly female) victims' future. They also inadequately capture the many and varied scenarios in which sexts are sent and distributed, further demonstrating how such narratives are out of line with young people's perceptions and practices of sexting.

Voices in anti-sexting campaigns and their messages

As we have discussed elsewhere (Lee et al. 2013), childhood sexuality has historically been suppressed and managed by the state through a set of normalising principles of accepted sexual behaviour and with the silent agreement of all key parties involved in the process (psychologists, teachers, schools, parents). This attention has been reignited with the rise of a neo-liberal state that refocuses on young people as a problem (Furlong and Cartmel 1997). To date, the notions of suppressing and regulating sexting behaviour make up the predominant message communicated in educational campaigns. At the same time, the dominant voices heard in anti-sexting campaigns are of those in positions of authority (policymakers, teachers, sexting 'experts', law enforcement – as we noted in Chapter 3), while voices of young people are rarely heard.[4]

One of the key pillars upon which the mainstream discourse in educational campaigns has been built is anxiety about the risk that new technologies pose to the wellbeing of a child, and the vulnerability of young people in cyberspace more generally (for more on this, see Lee et al. 2013). The notion of the internet as 'a bottomless hole where your indiscretions will be exposed and magnified to the point of crime, haunting you forever' (Nelson 2013b) and the concept of 'losing control' over an image once it has entered cyberspace, as well as one's inability to 'ever get it back' (Karaian 2014), have been reinforced in every educational campaign. Young people's 'digital footprint' has become a precious object worthy of protection, while social humiliation has been identified as an inevitable consequence of sexting (see, e.g., Parents Protect! 2014; KidsHelpline 2013). Worst-case scenarios, where sexts find their way to child pornography collections (such as in 'Your Photo Fate'), have additionally fuelled an already sizzling debate about young people and the perils of modern technology (Karaian 2014; Salter et al. 2013). Supported by messages such as '[y]ou run the risk of parents seeing it, schools seeing it, your best friend seeing it and your future boyfriends, girlfriends and employers as well' (Atkin 2011), the campaigns' key motto is that '[t] here never should be a reason for engaging in this behaviour' (Patrick Kelly, Australian Federal Police Youth Advisor, cited in Atkin 2011). Indeed, the message that your parents, prospective college/university, or future employers and even your kids (!) can see sexts you sent as a teenager (ThinkUKnow 2014a; see also Parents Protect! 2014) aim to scare young people into ceasing sexting practices, rather than educating them about safe ways to sext. Put simply, young people are instructed to '[not] create any of these images/videos/texts' (ThinkUKnow 2014a). Focus on abstinence and 'containing the beast' (MTV 2014) that resides within is nothing new when it comes to young people's sexuality; what is new are the avenues of control used to achieve such a goal. Some commentators believe that the threat that sexts can 'haunt you at a later day' (Joint Select Committee on Cyber-Safety 2011, p. 143) and be used to bully and harass young people (Department of Education and Early Childhood Development 2013) is 'a cocktail of paranoia, fire and brimstone' that can have serious, negative impacts on adolescents (Nelson 2013a).

Deeply rooted in an ever-increasing anxiety about teenage sexuality and naivety of today's youth, as well as perceived lack of awareness about the possible legal consequences of sexting (Law Reform Committee of Victoria 2013, p. 55), the notion of young people at the edge of doom dominates educational responses to sexting. Young '[p]eople simply do not realise that the Internet never forgets' (Joint Select Committee on Cyber-Safety 2011, p. 143) and that '[s]exting is a phenomenon where this communication has significant negative consequences, often beyond the thoughts of the young people involved' (Hugh Stevens, member of the Victorian Privacy Commissioner's Youth Advisory Group, cited in Fisher et al. 2012, p. 3). Raising awareness about the legal consequences of sexting is, thus, a second key message of sexting education campaigns (Salter et al. 2013). As one of the leading Commonwealth campaigns put it: 'You don't want to ruin your future because of a silly mistake as a teenager' (ThinkUKnow 2014a). By implying that sexting is a result of the recklessness and gullibility of young people, this discourse subtly implies victim blaming for any potential negative consequences of sexting.

As indicated above, anti-sexting campaigns mostly feature one variation of sexting: a young, white, heterosexual, middle-class woman who sends a picture to someone she trusts, only to find the picture resent to her peers. By focusing on her recklessness and the consequences, such as the loss of reputation, and by asking her to 'think again' – as in 'Megan's Story' – education campaigns engage in victim blaming, similar to the way we have seen issues around sexual violence during the last century play out (Galfoway 2010; see also Karaian 2014). As Karaian (2014, p. 284) investigated in the context of Canadian Centre for Child Protection's campaign *Respect Yourself*, anti-sexting education campaigns 'harness slut shaming in order to responsibilise...teenage girls for preventing sexting's purported harms'. The act of sharing the picture is omitted from the video, contrary to public humiliation a female victim experiences (Salter et al. 2013). Similarly, in 'Tagged', the female victim (Kate) is portrayed as a wicked person who publicly shames her ex-boyfriend, refuses to apologise and then bears the consequences of both this incident and her previous wrongdoing – sexts that have gone viral and follow her to a new school. The important question to be asked here, as one commentator recently posed, is

> why would she need to feel so ashamed? We grow up being made to feel ashamed of sex. ... What kind of harm does the circulation of the picture do to her? Sure, some harm, but not much – unless you make her feel ashamed by adult inquiries and prosecution. (Nelson 2013b)

In this broader setting, paternalistic notions that young people need to be saved from both expressions of their own premature or misguided (yet often consensual and constitutional) sexual desire (Karaian 2014) and their unwanted consequences is another key element in the majority of anti-sexting campaigns. This is achieved by promoting the 'don't sext' message, but also through urging parents to take control and increase surveillance of their children's online behaviour (see, e.g., Ryan 2010). In *Fact Sheet: TXTing/SEXTing* it is suggested that '[r]esearch shows that when parents put a limit on phone usage or the number of texts their teen's phone can send the likelihood that their teen will be involved in "SEXTing" decreases' (Australian Government 2010). Similarly, in *Safe Sexting: No Such Thing* parents are advised to 'learn how to use and monitor their children's mobile phones' and 'check photo galleries on their children's Facebook and MySpace accounts' (NSW Government 2009). Such responses are reflective of education programs and campaigns launched to address youth sexuality in the context of teenage pregnancy and STD infections, which are largely based on the notion that young people are unruly and reckless, biologically prone to risk taking and poor decision making. In such a context, parents and educators are called in to intervene and prevent/regulate young people's sexuality (see more in Lee et al. 2013). By focusing on the lack of agency of young people and by speaking largely to their parents and educators, anti-sexting campaigns reinforce the need for interventions 'from above', interventions that will (hopefully) save children from the doom of their own mistakes. In doing so, such campaigns also neglect some potential 'risk-imposing' factors for sexting, such as poverty, alienation, and corporate promotion of certain products and lifestyles (Ratcliffe et al. 1984), but also the role sexting might have in the sexual development of young people and any potential empowering effects of the practice. Importantly, all educational campaigns call for a more grassroots approach to combat sexting, with special emphasis on school curricula.

Combating sexting at the grassroots: education in schools

Education at the school level, as a part of wider campaigns on internet safety or sexting as described above, or as independent initiatives, seems to be a priority for policymakers. Some commentators maintain that 'educational programs at schools [need] to teach young people about the dangers of sexting' (Tomazin 2013) and that '[a] key issue behind why young people still partake in sexting is due to a lack of relevant and engaging education in our school systems' (Fisher et al. 2012, p. 3; see also Ryan 2010). In 2013, at the conclusion of the Victorian Government's two-year long inquiry into sexting, three key recommendations out of 14 related to education, particularly on the need to educate young people about sexting, both through broader educational campaigns and within schools (Law Reform Committee of Victoria 2013). Recommendations suggested adopting 'holistic, integrated programs for internet and communication technologies awareness and safety into the school curriculum' (recommendation no 2), and encouraged 'current and pre-service teachers to take part in professional development programs focusing on cybersafety education' (recommendation no 3; Law Reform Committee of Victoria 2013, p. 23). Schools were identified as key messengers in communicating information about sexting risks to young people. It is not surprising, then, that the majority of Commonwealth and state-based educational campaigns in Australia include programs for sexting education in schools. The *CyberSmart* campaign, for example, comprises of lesson plans on sexting for primary and secondary school students (Fisher et al. 2102). As a part of this campaign, 63,000 'So you got naked online ...' sexting brochures were distributed in Australian schools in only one month (Herrick 2011). As of December 2012, over 5288 Victorian teachers had participated in *CyberSmart's* one-day training sessions, while 208,000 teachers, students and parents had attended a one-hour presentation on sexting (Law Reform Committee of Victoria 2013). As indicated on the *CyberSmart* website, due to high demand, '[o]ver 2015 the [Australian Media and Communication Authority] will be placing a high priority on visiting those schools who have already registered, but have not yet received, one of our presentations' (CyberSmart 2014d). The *ThinkUKnow* and *CyberSmart* campaigns were also developed for school use (ThinkUKnow 2014c; CyberSmart 2014c).

In addition to these nationwide campaigns, state-based and independent campaigns about sexting have also been developed. Over the last couple of years, the Australian state of Victoria has developed a number of programs to educate both young people and parents about sexting. While resisting the pathway many American schools have taken recently, in which schools implement a formal policy to ban sexting (Ryan 2010), educational campaigns in Australian schools follow the basic principles of intervention outlined earlier in the chapter. In 2012–13, Victoria's South Eastern Centre Against Sexual Assault launched a campaign called *Respect me, don't seXt me*. Set up as a comic book, the leaflet identifies a young woman as a victim who, upon succumbing to peer pressure, sends a picture that ends up on social networking websites and stays 'online forever' (SECASA 2012). In 2013, the Victorian Department of Education and Early Childhood Development launched a two-page sexting advice pamphlet as part of its broader *BullyStoppers* campaign, highlighting the social and legal consequences of sexting, and providing tips to parents on how to deal with the issue (Department of Education and Early Childhood Development 2013).

Furthermore, the Victorian Government has recently partnered with the Alannah and Madeline Foundation to deliver the *eSmart* program to all government and some independent and Catholic schools across Victoria. Key features of the program include embracing technology's benefits and reducing students' and teachers' exposure to risk by providing a range of resources, research, tracking tools and training to both students and teachers (Law Reform Committee of Victoria 2013). What is consistent across these school-run campaigns is that they mostly promote abstinence from sexting (see, e.g., *Say No to Sexting*, Women's Health Grampians and Ballarat High School: SayNo 2014), and often include law enforcement officers and NGO activists as educators on the issue (Henry 2010; Forde 2011).

Evaluation and future developments

Educational campaigns can help young people to be aware of risks associated with online communication and to develop strategies to reduce such risks (Crofts and Lee 2013). The diversity of sexting practices and scenarios makes sexting 'a classic example of a situation in which one size does *not* fit all' (Australian Privacy Foundation 2012, p. 2, original emphasis). It is also important to note that sexting represents a very small proportion of overall incidents of child victimisation (Berkman Center for Internet and Society 2008). However, the intervention in this area, including educational campaigns, has so far focused on reactively managing, rather than understanding, explaining and mapping out risk in relation to sexting (Lee et al. 2013). By focusing on legal and social consequences of sexting, the desired goal of education campaigns has been to 'strongly discourage all forms and context of sexting' (Law Reform Committee of Victoria 2013, p. 57). Educators claim that, by focusing on risks and repercussions of sexting, they have been able to 'make the greatest impression on youth' (Law Reform Committee of Victoria 2013, p. 54).

Society's anxiety about young people's sexuality is perhaps a much bigger problem than sexting images (Nelson 2013a). Importantly, anxieties about the sexuality of Gen Y, together with concerns about the pitfalls of technology and child pornography, have coalesced around the issue of sexting (Jewkes 2010). Promoting self-regulation and abstinence, while at the same time neglecting motivations and potential empowerment and pleasure young people might get out of sexting, has resulted in some educational campaigns being assessed as 'boring, uninteresting and unworkable', or as 'dull, slow and fail[ing] to engage many viewers' (Fisher et al. 2012, p. 3). As Nelson (2013a) accurately notes: 'At 14 are we expected to be lawyers already, where any indiscretion is unpardonable and will stunt our career?' Importantly, as Karaian (2014, p. 284) compellingly argues, such education campaigns 'reify and mobilize a culture of sexual shame in order to responsibilize certain girls for their own, and others', safety', constituting 'meaning-making projects that reproduce and reify gendered, racialized, classed and hetero-normative ideas of sexual value, propriety, privilege and blameworthiness'.

As demonstrated in this chapter, one of the major failings of educational campaigns is their lack of communication and consultation with young people. When key participants are silenced and identified as being in need of protection, such campaigns rely on contemporary moral entrepreneurs to identify risk, suggest remedies for repairing the harm, and develop future prevention strategies. They ignore the importance of risk-taking as a key developmental process through which we learn key social skills (Coleman and Hendry 1999) and promote risk-curbing behaviour in which young people are, via a variety of scaremongering tactics, urged to practice abstinence or face the consequences. As Professor Karen Vered recently stated:

> I increasingly find it very interesting that we continue as a society to deny young people's interest in sexual experience, for instance. We simply do not want to accept the fact that teenagers are sexually active, and by ignoring that and by pretending it is not so we make a lot of mistakes, and some of them have consequences for young people's health that they wear for the rest of their lives. It is that kind of thing. We really need to be realistic about what young people are doing with their time, whether we approve of it or not. You might not like it, but the fact is that if young people are engaged in certain behaviours and if we still feel responsible for them then we need to provide them with the tools, the means and the guidance to make those activities safe for them. (cited in Joint Select Committee on Cyber-Safety 2011, p. 137)

Young people acknowledge that 'telling students to abstain [from sexting] just won't work. (Duh!)' (Birdee 2013), and that 'reinforcing a patronizing view of young people ... alienates them from their sexuality' (Nelson 2013a). In that context, sending a message that '[w]hat you do online can affect your whole world' (CyberSmart 2014b) or that sexts are there to stay and might come back to haunt you may lead to self-harm and depression amongst youth (Dr Helen McGrath, cited in Joint Select Committee on Cyber-Safety 2011, p. 143).

As noted in the literature (Albury and Crawford 2012; Dobson et al. 2012; Salter et al. 2013), educational responses to sexting focus predominantly on individualised notions of 'risk' and 'shame', neatly located in the mainstream gendered assumptions about accepted and deviant sexual behaviour, and appropriate gender roles. Emphasis on responsibilisation and criminalisation 'overlook sexting as part of a broader pattern of gendered sexual negotiations' (Salter et al. 2013, p. 304). Locked in 'expert' discourses outlined above, educational campaigns on sexting largely reinforce hegemonic values of gender, class and sexuality and are arguably more concerned about the development of a (female) child as appropriately self-regulating and self-censoring citizen, rather than the actual harm some practices of sexting might pose to today's youth (for more, see Lee et al. 2013; Dobson et al. 2012). This can have significant consequences and 'often places the onus of responsibility on victim/survivors (mostly young women), rather than perpetrators' (Gregory 2012). Such approaches 'demonise the girl rather than looking at the general climate in which it exist which allow this kind of inappropriate sexting to take place' (Dr Tim Hawkes, the Headmaster of Kings private school in Sydney, cited in Atkin 2011). As a consequence, the recent Victorian inquiry into sexting recommended that educational campaigns in the future focus on the act of dissemination of sexting images and online etiquette, rather than the sexting practice itself (recommendation no. 4, Law Reform Committee of Victoria 2013).

Moreover, anti-sexting campaigns incorrectly locate all sexting behaviour as exploitation, especially when the active participant is a young woman. As we have argued elsewhere, responses to sexting need to move away from gendered narratives of sexting in which young men are always exploiters and young women victims, ultimately positioning young women as responsible for their own victimisation (Lee et al. 2013). They need to recognise the broader social context in which anxiety about youth sexuality and new technologies is not followed by similar anxiety about adults. Quite the opposite: sexting for adults is a normalised and encouraged behaviour (Lee et al. 2013; Shafron-Perez 2009). Popular culture 'provides a wealth of evidence that a sexual presentation of oneself to the world enhances a person's profile, rather than detracts from it' (Law Reform Committee of Victoria 2013, p. 63).

Another important part of the puzzle that is missing in education campaigns is the potentially different value young people give to (offline and online) privacy. As a recent study in the US demonstrates, young people today share more information than they have in previous years, minimising the scope of what is considered private (Farber 2014).

Education needs to be built on a broader understanding of how privacy has been conceptualised among young people, not on adults' (mainstream) understanding of what privacy entails (Law Reform Committee of Victoria 2013). Education campaigns also need to encourage 'a fundamental lifelong respect for their own and other people's privacy against unwanted intrusions from any source, including government and businesses as well as "criminals"' (Australian Privacy Foundation 2012, p. 5).

Contemporary education campaigns also fail to penetrate the part of cyberworld where young people spend most of their time. Young people are 'often the earliest to adopt newly developed technologies' and 'are at the forefront of online usage' (Australian Privacy Foundation 2012, p. 5). Yet campaigns are mostly located on websites and distributed in schools, while a large cyberworld of social networking sites (such as Facebook, Tumblr, Instagram and similar), where young people spend most of time online, remains out of reach.

Finally, there has not yet been evaluation of existing campaigns. While research shows that young people are aware of risks online and that they modify they behaviour as a consequence of that, it is not known whether this is a direct result of educational campaigns (Crofts and Lee 2013). As one social campaigner concluded, 'we have no way of assessing whether [any campaign] actually alters behaviour' (CASA Forum 2012). While it would perhaps be unwarranted to argue that 'existing sexting education programs are having no impact' (Birdee 2013) or that we should leave the issue alone (Nelson 2013a), an evaluation of existing educational programs is a necessity, given their rapid development, overarching influence and presumably hefty cost to the taxpayer. The following chapter looks at existing international and Australian research on sexting.

7
Review of Existing Research

Introduction

In line with the critical approach of this book, it is useful to precede our own contribution to the field of research with a discussion and evaluation of the methods and approaches to researching sexting that have been used in research to date. This chapter starts with a critical analysis of the existing surveys into sexting practices by young people and then looks more closely at current qualitative research. A review at the time of writing identified ten such quantitative surveys.[1] Most of these are aimed at identifying the prevalence of sexting among young people and only a small proportion drill further into the practices of, and the motives or reasons for, sexting (National Campaign to Prevent Teen and Unplanned Pregnancy 2008; Mitchell et al. 2012; Dake et al. 2013), or the emotional or practical consequences of sexting (Dake et al. 2013; Phippen 2009; National Campaign to Prevent Teen and Unplanned Pregnancy 2008; Strassberg et al. 2013; Mitchell et al. 2012; Tallon et al. 2012).

   Three methodological approaches can be identified in these group of surveys – internet-based (often self-selection) surveys, telephone-based random sample surveys, and more traditional targeted paper-based surveys – almost exclusively administered through specific schools. We will look at the benefits and limitations of each of these briefly in order to situate the arguments that follow and our own empirical research. Reviewing this research also helps us to discover whether there is any existing evidence which appears to justify current laws that criminalise sexting by young people as child pornography. Taken together with our research this will provide an important background for assessing in Chapter 12 whether the current approaches to sexting are appropriate or whether there are better ways of understanding and responding to sexting.

Internet-based surveys

Internet-based surveys collect a sample of respondents through links to a web-based survey via a pool of volunteers, or by emailing potential respondents, or by using popular web pages or social media to recruit respondents. The first major study into sexting was an internet-based 'Sex and Tech' survey in the United States conducted in 2008 (National Campaign to Prevent Teen and Unplanned Pregnancy 2008). This survey sampled some 1280 respondents (653 'teens') 'from among those that volunteered to participate in TRU's online surveys' (20, p. 5). Data was weighted and stratified according to US Census data. Cox (2009) also conducted an online survey with a sample comprising 655 US teenagers aged 13 to 18. Results were weighted for a range of demographic variables. Although it is not clear, it appears that, like the Sex and Tech survey, volunteers were recruited from a pool of registered volunteers – in this case through Harris Interactive.

The strength of both surveys is that their online nature may have given young people a sense of anonymity likely to elicit relatively 'honest' responses. Both also ask something about motivations or reasons for sexting. Mitchell et al. (2012), however, identify an initial flaw in both; that is, that the sample of 'teens' includes those aged 18 and 19 (in the case of Sex and Tech) for which many sexting practices will be legal given that they are, by most definitions, adults. Importantly, the broad definition of sexting – which includes texts (SMS messages, as opposed to MMS) – dilutes the data in relation to the production and sending of images. The latter is our key focus. And from a more empiricist perspective, neither study was peer reviewed, nor was either sample a probability sample.

Phippen (2009) also conducted an online survey. In this UK-based study, 535 respondents aged 11 to 18 were recruited from 18 schools. While the study suffered from many of the methodological flaws of the previously discussed internet surveys in terms of its sample and the definitions of sexting, it also did not ask individual sexters about their own practices, choosing instead to ask only for respondents' *perceptions about sexting*.[2] As we will argue below, this is an important distinction.

Telephone surveys

The second set of surveys into sexting was conducted by telephone. There are two key surveys of this genre (Lenhart 2009; Mitchell et al.

2012), both of which included significant representative population samples (Lenhart n=800; Mitchell et al. n=1560). Only Mitchell et al. (2012), however, was peer reviewed. Lenhart (2009) is limited by the fact that only 'cell phone' traffic is assessed – the sending of images via computer and other devices was thus excluded. Lounsbury et al. (2011) also pointed out that the definition of 'semi-nude' is unclear in the Lenhart survey. However, there will always be definitional problems when it comes to deciding what is a sexualised 'semi-nude' image.

Mitchell et al. (2012) constitutes the most solid survey from a purely empirical perspective and collected a significant amount of data on motivations and demographics. However, both of these surveys had a procedural limitation that does not affect internet surveys as significantly: in both cases interviewers asked to speak to an adult in the household first to seek informed consent to speak to a young person. Taking Mitchell (2012) as an example, the interviewer then told the adult/parent that the interview with the young person was confidential. Informed consent was then obtained from the youth. Yes/no questions were asked in order to ensure confidentiality and regular checking was conducted by asking the youth if the conversation was private. It strikes us, however, that this adult filter process would disincentivise young people from providing accurate accounts of their sexting activities, with both the formality of the process, and the awareness of the proximity of an adult, acting as disincentives. The methodology may have also excluded young people who had strained relationships with their parents and spent less time in the home, or those whose parents refused to consent to their participation. So while, from a purely statistical perspective, this is a strong model, it has significant shortcomings.

Hard-copy questionnaires

Finally, there is a group of surveys administered via 'hard-copy' questionnaires to school students – and computer-based variations on this that use school computers 'off line' to run the surveys. These surveys tend to draw their recruits from a school or schools in a particular area(s). Strassberg (2013) sampled 606 students from a single private high school in the Southwest of the United States. The sample constituted some 98 per cent of the total students at the school. Although it provided an excellent snapshot of prevalence at that particular school, the results are not generalisable given, among other things, the nature of the particular school. This survey was also very brief and asked little about motivations apart from whether it was wrong or right to send a sext, or whether participants felt positively or negatively about sexting. Similarly, Peskin et al. (2013) surveyed 1034 tenth grade 'ethnic minority' urban school students in a single school in southeast Texas, United States. The study did not ask about motivations or intent and again is not generalisable.

Tallon et al. (2012) conducted ten consultations at eight schools across New South Wales, Australia, following which 'around 800 students' took a survey, with 70 of these taking the survey online. While this survey was largely aimed at identifying what respondents knew and thought about the laws around sexting and cyberbullying, and did not ask about motivations, it did ask the students what behaviours they deemed the most harmful (and most harmless). The framework of harm here, while useful in the legal context of the survey, did not allow respondents to express positive feelings they may have about sexting. The students were also asked to take the survey after they had viewed a presentation that sought to inform them of the laws and penalties that apply to sexting and cyber-bullying in an 'honest and frank manner' (Tallon et al. 2012, p. 27). While the research was designed to ensure that it 'would contribute to young people's knowledge and understanding of the law' and to give young people a voice, it is highly likely that the presentation would have influenced young people's perceptions of sexting and the associated harms and thus their survey responses.

While Englander's (2012) research was computer based and online, it focused on a select 617 'college freshman' from Bridgewater State University in Massachusetts. Respondents anonymously completed surveys with those reporting that they had sexted being asked a series of follow-up questions, including about the outcomes of their activities.

Dake et al. (2013) administered surveys to of 1289 students in 35 schools in the Midwest of the United States. The study constituted a stratified random sample. Essentially it asked respondents about their sexting practices – defined broadly to include sexual texts – and, more problematically, about what the researchers presumably see as a range of negative risk factors in youth development. We will begin the next section using the Dake et al. (2013) survey as an example of how a focus on adult-constructed moralising risk evaluations of sexting practices can blinker researchers to other possible motivations for such behaviours.

Motivations and Perceptions

Clearly, understanding what motivates young people to send sexual images to one another is important for a broader understanding of the practice itself, but also in terms of the legal frameworks that attempt to regulate sexting. At its most banal we might ask if sexting between young people is actually motivated by an attempt to distribute child pornography? – as the legal framework in many jurisdictions would have it. More subtly, however, the existing research identifies sets of power relations, especially gendered power relations (which are also reflected in the education campaigns discussed in Chapter 6) as being important in understanding motivations for sexting.

The gendered dynamics of sexting between young people has rightly been a significant focus of much research in this field. Scholars have, for example, suggested that there can be a continuum of abusive behaviours from childhood to adulthood of which sexting and/or other forms of cybercrime can form a part (Powell 2010; Salter et al. 2013). Subsequently, power relationships between young women and young men have become of great interest, particularly the interrelated notions of pressure or coercion that were discussed in Chapter 2. But it is important to reflect on just how often pressure and coercion do play a role, and in what ways.

Dake et al. (2013, p. 3) situated their survey in the literature by suggesting: 'Peer pressure seems to be an important reason for sexting, with 23% of teens saying *they felt pressured* by a friend and 51% of teenage girls saying *they felt pressure* from a boy to send sexually explicit messages' (emphasis added).

This data is attributed to the first large-scale survey on the topic by the US-based National Campaign to Prevent Teen and Unplanned Pregnancy – the survey generally known as 'Sex and Tech'. However, Dake misinterpreted the Sex and Tech Survey. The Survey does not establish that 51 per cent of girls felt pressure from a boy. Rather, what Sex and Tech (National Campaign to Prevent Unplanned Teen and Unplanned Pregnancy 2010, p. 4) actually says is: '51% of teen girls say pressure from a guy is a reason girls send sexy messages or images; only 18% of teen boys cited pressure from female counterparts as a reason'.

There is an important distinction here that is more clearly illustrated when we look at exactly what the Sex and Tech survey asked these young people. The question was not, 'For what reason *did you* post/send sexy messages or pictures/videos of yourself?' Rather, it was, 'What do you *think* are the reasons that girls send/post sexy messages or pictures/video of themselves?' (National Campaign to Prevent Teen and Unplanned Pregnancy 2010, p. 9, emphasis added). That is, the question asked the *entire sample cohort* of female respondents – most of whom had never sent a sext according to the survey results – why they *think or perceive* that girls send the images, as opposed to asking the motivations of those who actually did it.

However, the Sex and Tech survey did ask about the motivations of those who had actually sent messages/videos. These results indicated that only 10 per cent of *all* teenagers reported that they felt 'pressure to send it' in response to the question: 'What are the reasons that *you've* sent/posted suggestive messages or nude/semi-nude pictures/videos (of yourself)?' (National Campaign to Prevent Teen and Unplanned Pregnancy 2010, p. 9). Contrary to Dake et al.'s (2013) assertion, the most common reason for sending sexy content was to be 'fun or flirtatious', with 66 per cent of girls and 60 per cent of teen boys responding thus. Of the teen girls, 52 per cent said the sext was a 'sexy present' for their boyfriend; 44 per cent of both teen girls and teen boys said they sent sexually suggestive messages or images in response to receiving such content; 40 per cent of teen girls said they sent sexually suggestive messages or images as 'a joke'; 34 per cent of teen girls said they sent/posted sexually suggestive content to 'feel sexy'; and finally only 12 per cent of *teen girls* said they felt 'pressured' to send sexually suggestive messages or images (National Campaign to Prevent Teen and Unplanned Pregnancy 2008, p. 4). Importantly, respondents could choose all the responses that applied, so the fact that 'pressure' had such a low response rate is significant.

This eliding of perceptions and expressed personal experiential motivations pervades much of the research and literature on sexting and young people, including two of the current author's previous scholarship (Salter et al. 2013). Thinking back to the typologies of pressure discussed earlier, we might be problematically confusing various levels of pressure and even over-determining pressure all together. However, before moving into these more conceptual discussions, let us explore what other surveys have found in relation to pressure as a motivation for girls to send sexts to boys.

Englander (2012, p. 3) asked her cohort about their motivations for sexting. She states that:

> Indisputably, the most important motivation for sexting revealed in this study (and others) was pressure or coercion. Girls were more likely than boys to report that they had sexted, but the gender difference was entirely due to the girls being more likely to report that they had been pressured, coerced, blackmailed, or threatened into sexting.

This sounds straightforward, but there is little detail on the types of questions asked in this survey. From the snippets in the report, there appears to be limited scope for respondents to report any pleasures or other positive experiences of sexting.

Mitchell et al. (2012) is the other key survey-based study that touches on motivations. Respondents were asked why they thought the sexting incident(s) *they* were involved in occurred. The vast majority of those producing and sending (51%) and receiving (54%) said it was part of a romance or existing relationship. Another 23 per cent (sending and producing) and 11 per cent (receiving) suggested it was a joke or prank; and trying to start a relationship (5% and 11% respectively), or getting someone's notice (3% and 7%) were also factors. Only 3 per cent and 2 per cent respectively reported being blackmailed or coerced or threatened into the activity, and zero per cent and 1 per cent respectively reported it to be related to conflict or revenge. Similarly, zero percent and 1 per cent respectively reported it was the result of bullying or harassment.

While Mitchell et al. (2012) provide no specific gendered breakdown of the small numbers of respondents reporting negative motivations and negative responses to their actions, the figures do not suggest that large numbers of girls involved in the behaviours report being pressured to do so. Of those engaged in creating and sending, or receiving, images, a quarter or less reported *any negative emotions* about this involvement: 'Twenty-one percent of respondents appearing in or creating images reported feeling very or extremely upset, embarrassed, or afraid as a result, as did 25% of youth receiving images' (Mitchell et al. 2012, p. 16).

While there is again no gendered breakdown, there is little evidence to conclude that a majority of girls felt negatively or expressed negative feelings about their involvement in the practice.

Phippen (2009) notes that those personally impacted (presumably negatively, but this is not clearly articulated) by 'sexts' were very much in the minority. However, he highlights that a larger number were aware of friends who have been 'affected': 30 per cent of respondents said they knew a friend affected by the problems introduced by sexting. While we do not wish to downplay this finding, it is important to note that only secondary knowledge is used here. There is no sense whether these 'effects' might be positive or negative from the way the question is framed. Moreover, we can infer from the aforementioned surveys that non-sexters are likely to judge the behaviour of those that engage in the activity quite negatively.

Our argument that those who engage in the activity are less likely to judge it negatively is supported by the research of Strassberg et al. (2013). These researchers found that students who sent explicit pictures of themselves were more likely than others to positively evaluate the behaviour. Indeed, only one in seven who actually sexted reported generally negative feelings (2013, p. 19).

Returning to the Sex and Tech survey (National Campaign to Prevent Teen and Unplanned Pregnancy 2010), there is even stronger affirmation that the majority of those engaged in sexting activities had positive feelings about their involvement. Respondents were asked: 'Thinking about suggestive messages or nude/semi-nude pictures/videos that you ever received, how did getting them make you feel?' The responses were 'surprised' (55%), 'amused' (54%), 'turned on' (53%), 'excited' (44%), 'happy' (40%), 'more interested in hooking up with the sender' (27%), and 'more interested in dating the sender' (22%). Far fewer respondents had negative feelings with some being 'creeped out' (22%), 'grossed out' (18%), and 'turned off' (15%). The clear conclusion is that the vast majority of those receiving sexts did not view this negatively.

In summary, the majority of the current survey results taken together, as imperfect as this data is, indicates that when respondents (including young women) are expressly asked about their sexting motivations, they rarely express pressure or coercion as *the* key driver. It is certainly an issue for some girls and one motivation among others – a serious one – but, according to the available data, it is a significantly lower-order issue than what might best be described as motivations of 'pleasure' or 'romance'. But, drawing on our typology of pressures, what type of pressure are we talking about? The survey model is most likely to tap into whether individual pressure was applied 'by a boyfriend of girlfriend', for example. Indeed, many of the surveys asked a version of this question. Respondents are in a sense asked to phenomenologically bracket their experience to the one-on-one exchange. More difficult from the survey model is the job of measuring peer group or socio-cultural pressure. There may be an argument that questions asking the entire cohorts about their perceptions of others that sext might be tapping into evaluations of these peer group and socio-cultural pressures? However, this is again speculation and is not clearly conceived. It is more likely that the higher levels of pressure identified as a result of the perceptions questions are reflective of the gendered double standard that sees both males and females evaluating the sexting activities of others more harshly than they would their own. That is, they are reflective of (hetero-) normative moral judgments of females who sext.

The self-image of acting with agency does not mean there is no underlying gendered social pressure or coercion. Equally, however, given our aim is to explore how young women perceive their engagement in sexting, such pressures should not be unquestioningly apportioned. However, it is worth noting that Cox (2009) found that 90 per cent of those who had sent a sext reported no negative fallout from the activity.

We now turn to the existing qualitative evidence to assess whether these other levels of pressure might be better identified through such methodologies.

Qualifying motivations

In assessing the current state of qualitative data concerning motivations of young people to produce and send sexual images, it is useful to start with the more recent publications, for example, Phippen's (2012) report *Sexting: An Exploration of Practices, Attitudes, and Influences*. This report for the NSPCC in the United Kingdom attempts to expand on earlier research by Ringrose et al. (2012). Phippen's (2012, p. 40) first paragraph of the introduction helps situate the study:

> In May 2012 a report by Ringrose et al. 'A qualitative study of children, young people and "sexting"', commissioned by the NSPCC, produced ground breaking research understanding the nature of sexting for young people and identified a number of concerning issues around power and coercion, 'casual' sexual abuse in school environments and how technology is used in the production and distribution of self generated indecent images. However the research, while highly detailed, has issues of generalizability due to the small number of students (35) and the fact that all in the sample we [sic] drawn from two inner-city schools.

Phippen rightly points out the issues with generalisability, but as this introductory paragraph makes clear, the author also takes at face value these issues of pressure and coercion. Indeed, his research methodology indicates that he introduced sexting to his respondents through the lens of the parable of Amanda Todd – a Canadian teenager who, after exposing herself on webcam in Year 7, and subsequently experiencing serious bullying and ridicule, committed suicide in 2012. Rarely in his research agenda is there capacity to tease out the pleasures or positive feelings that might be associated with sexting behaviours.

Moreover, Phippen (2012, p. 8) notes that 'it was also made clear that we wanted to explore issues that affect young people of their age, *rather than their own personal experiences*' (emphases added). That is, members of this cohort were not reporting on their own experiences, but on their perceptions. This is not to say some would not have had first-hand experience, but the participants 'were asked specifically not to talk about what they had done', possibly for ethical reasons.

Despite the methodological issues, Phippen does not find the coercion and pressure he expects to. He concludes that:

> There is a clear gender imbalance here – boys would request pictures of girls and girls *may* send pictures as a result of the invitations. It was considered highly unusual for a girl to request a picture of a boy... some [respondents] were aware of instances where girls had responded to [sic] request but in many other cases they simply refused. (2012, p. 10, emphasis in original)

He goes on to suggest that 'just because a boy asked for a picture it did not mean they had to respond' (2012, p. 11). Some girls even suggested that among their peers were individuals who viewed 'a request for a picture, or other forms of online attention, as flattering – being asked to send a picture made you feel like you were attractive' (2012, p. 11). Among boys, they saw no problem in 'giving it a try'. So, while the practices identified were gendered, it is an overgeneralisation to call this coercion or pressure at either an individual or peer group level, and certainly that is not how the majority of girls conceptualised the exchange.

This begs the question: why did Phippen prioritise coercion and pressure over other motivations? As Phippen noted, he took his lead from the work of Ringrose et al. (2012). It is therefore worth examining that research more closely. Ringrose et al. (2012) developed a detailed methodology for their qualitative research. Indeed, their research instrument is reproduced in full as Appendix 3 of their report, and clearly indicates that none of their questions were leading.[3]

There is little doubt Ringrose et al.'s (2012) research identified a troubling range of gendered practices among the cohort of 35 Year 8 and Year 10 students interviewed across two inner-city schools in London. Such practices where technology was concerned included girls regularly receiving unsolicited explicit photos and boys asking for, and often receiving, semi-nude photos of their girlfriends for their default messaging image. However, such behaviours were largely extensions of the kinds of gendered sexualised behaviours already conducted in these school grounds. That is, for this cohort of students, gendered power relations played a large part in their day-to-day school lives. These gendered power relations manifested through sexualised activities in the school grounds, including: verbal harassment; being touched up; being rushed; being pushed down; and 'daggering', a range of harassments that often result in a boy thrusting his penis against a girl from behind or masturbating against a girl from behind.

There were then, at least in the two schools where Ringrose et al.'s (2012) research took place, serious ongoing problems or harassment of some girls by some boys – the kind of sub-legal 'everyday violence' identified by Stanko (1990) – although in this instance some of these activities were clearly criminal offences. Thus, the use of technology for these young people was an extension of existing behaviours. Ringrose et al. (2012, p. 8) suggest though that technology is not simply neutral; rather, 'it amplifies the problem': '[T]he specific features or affordances of mobile phones, social networking sites and other communication technologies facilitate the objectification of girls via the creation, exchange, collection, ranking and display of images' (2012, p. 8).

We do not disagree. However, there was also a specific context to this. As the authors point out in positioning their research:

> The study set out as an exploratory inquiry into differently positioned young people's experiences of 'sexting' in the UK. ... Over 50% of the students at both schools are from minority ethnic backgrounds. Both schools serve mixed socioeconomic status (SES) populations, though School One has a higher proportion of students eligible for free school meals. Both schools are located in geographical areas associated with gang activity and crime. (2012, p. 19–20)

While these practices were highly gendered in these schools, and while coercion and harassment clearly took place, the high level of such behaviours among 35 students in two ethnically mixed and somewhat disadvantaged schools does not provide evidence that such behaviours are dominant across all schools or among young people more generally. As the authors comment:

> Although the extent of sexting cannot be determined from a small-scale qualitative study ... *some* had experienced or *knew of others* who had experienced sexting, also important was the finding that most felt in some ways oppressed by perceived sexual pressure – to perform, judge and be judged – from peers. Such pressures may vary by context, but the specificity of sexualisation pressures – for example, expectations on appearance (being very thin, having large breasts or big muscles) or actions (viewing porn, tripping and touching up, performing blow jobs, sending images of own body parts) – should be discussed in order to undermine the culture of silence that further harms youth, especially girls. (2012, p. 8, emphasis added)

There are a number of points here. First, the authors acknowledge the limitations in terms of generalisability of their study; second, only *some* of the 35 participants had engaged in sexting – most accounts were secondhand; third, the placing of sexting practices in the context of broader forms of harassment is both a strength and a weakness of the study – while it provides context to online practices, it also creates an inclination to slip between the two unproblematically and see much sexting as an extension of such behaviours; fourth, the various levels or pressures and the role of sexualisation could be further explored.

For a broader analysis, it is worth then also placing Ringrose et al.'s (2012) work in the context of some of the surveys outlined above. A clear finding from those surveys was that sexting practices were more widespread among ethnic minority groups (Peskin et al. 2013; Tallon et al. 2012). Given this, it seems likely that the kinds of behaviours identified by Ringrose et al. (2012) may be more prevalent in particular schools, with particular social demographic characteristics, in particular geographic areas. So the pressure and coercion that Ringrose et al. (2012) identify may be a mix of the individual and peer group-type pressures identified in our typology, overwhelmingly experienced by students already marginalised and disempowered by a range of intersectional socio-demographic factors, including race, status, ethnicity, sexuality, and class. As such, the influence of broader socio-cultural sexualisation pressures will be heavily mediated by the presence (or not) of these other levels of pressure.

Finally, Albury et al. (2013) conducted a small number of focus groups with 16- to 18-year-olds in New South Wales, Australia (n=16). Despite the small sample, the researchers selected students from a range of differing backgrounds. While the gendered nature of sexting practices was a key element of the discussions in these focus groups, the question of coercion or pressure appears not to have been central to them. Rather, participants noted the different gendered interpretations of sexting practice and the likelihood of girls who sext being judged differently to boys who do so; that is, the gendered double standard in play when sexting occurred. However, girls in the focus groups did distinguish between boys who asked for photos – who they deemed more likely to share them without consent – and those who were sent photos as part of a relationship.

Conclusion

There is a small but growing body of research and scholarship that deals with sexting by young people. Assessed critically, this research suggests that there is a disconnect between perceptions and motivations of sexting by young people. While surveys may fail to pick up the subtle ways in which pressure and power relations may play a part in sexting practices, it remains unclear just how much and at what level pressure or coercion play a part, even through the more nuanced qualitative methods deployed by some researchers.

In the following section we explore our own empirical data, both qualitative and quantitative, in order to explore these perceptions and motivations further. While sexting between young people is no doubt constitutive of sets of power relations, there is little in the existing body of literature to suggest that it is motivated by a will to produce and distribute child pornography.

Part III
Sexting: Young People's Voices

8
Online Survey Data

Introduction

While sexting between young people has become a significant cultural phenomenon, a topic of popular media discussion, and the target of concern from law and policymakers, when it comes to young people themselves our knowledge of their practices and perspectives in relation to sexting is still relatively limited. The little we do know of young peoples' engagement with sexting comes from the handful of medium-scale quantitative surveys, and an even smaller number of qualitative studies discussed in the previous chapter.

In order to explore how young people in Australia perceive and practise sexting, we conducted an internet-based survey. This chapter presents a number of key themes that emerged from an analysis of survey responses. These themes relate to: the prevalence of sexting; between whom sexting takes place; gender and sexting; motivations and intent; feelings and fallout; legal consequences; and the sending of images to third parties. The purpose of the chapter is simply to present the data. Further analysis and discussion of the data will take place in Chapter 11.

The survey

The online survey aimed to capture data on young people's perceptions of sexting, their practices of and motivations for sexting, and their understanding of the law in relation to sexting. The survey questions were developed over a 12-month period and were aided by consultation sessions with the NSW Commission for Children and Young People's youth advisory group. This group provided valuable feedback on the constitution of the questions and usage of terminology. Following these consultations, questions were adjusted accordingly, resulting in the final survey, which consisted of 34 items.

In addition to collecting data on young people's perceptions and practices of sexting, the survey also aimed to collect demographic information, including the age, religion, gender, city/country, sexuality, and ethnicity of respondents. While the respondents to the survey were not a representative population sample, the large number who participated made the results compelling. Moreover, given the pros and cons of existing survey methods for this type of research, the online survey methodology constituted a very useful approach for this particular sample cohort.

The survey was of a self-selection style, administered through the University of Sydney Law School Survey Monkey platform. It was made available online between July 2013 and October 2013 and promoted through a range of sources, including the Triple J Hack program,[1] Facebook, Twitter, the Universities of Sydney, Western Sydney and New South Wales, as well as a large range of youth service providers. While the survey was aimed at 13- to 18-year-olds, older participants were also able to complete the survey, enabling us to capture useful comparative data. The data was statistically analysed using the SPSS program.

Respondents

There were 2243 respondents who attempted the survey, with 1416 completing every question (63.1 per cent completion rate). The sample cohort consisted of 48 per cent males and 52 per cent females, with <1 per cent of respondents (0.5 per cent) identifying as 'other'. In terms of age breakdown: 28 per cent of respondents were aged 13–15; 42 per cent were aged 16–18; 9 per cent were aged 19–21; 7 per cent were aged 22–5; and 13 per cent were aged 24 and above. This spread of age groups allowed us to make some comparisons between different groups of young people, and between young people and adults.

The survey also captured data on sexuality, with 9 per cent of respondents indicating they were bisexual, 3 per cent indicating they were gay, 1 per cent indicating they were lesbian, and 6 per cent indicating they were 'questioning'. While 36 per cent of respondents were from the state of NSW, there was a good spread of respondents from across the Australian states and territories. In addition, data captured on the location of respondents showed that 15 per cent of respondents resided in rural areas. While the majority of respondents were born in Australia and of Anglo-Saxon origin, respondents identified as belonging to one of 15 different ethnic groups. Reponses on religious background also revealed the majority of respondents did not identify with any religion (57 per cent), with a significant number identifying with Christianity (28 per cent). There was low representation from other religious groups.

Turning to the use of new technology, the vast majority of respondents reported having 'sent and received text messages' (96 per cent) and having a 'social networking profile' (98 per cent). A sizeable minority 'viewed pictures on dating or singles sites' (10 per cent), and a smaller number 'had a profile on a dating or singles site' (8 per cent). A majority of the sample 'read or viewed blogs' (61 per cent), 'shared photos on social media sites' (94 per cent), 'shared pictures or videos via MMS on a mobile phone' (87 per cent), 'sent or received pictures or videos on a computer' (83 per cent), and 'posted or shared videos through social media' (74 per cent). A smaller but significant minority had 'written a personal blog' (33 per cent), 96 per cent had 'used a computer or tablet without adult supervision', and 97 per cent had 'used a mobile phone without adult supervision'. These numbers demonstrate that the majority of respondents were relatively technologically engaged.

Our survey defined sexting relatively narrowly as 'the sending and receiving of sexual images or videos', with specific questions dealing with whether the images were of oneself or others. While the definition could possibly include sexual images that would not contravene the current legal definitions of 'child pornography material', it was agreed – with the input of the young people with whom we consulted – that this was the most accurate way in which to capture sexting by young people that, in Australian jurisdictions at least, is criminalised.

Prevalence of sending and receiving

The survey sought to establish just how prevalent sexting was within our cohort and across a range of demographic characteristics. In the following section we break this down with regard to the sending and receiving of sexual digital self-made images.

Of the entire sample (broken down by age below), 49 per cent of respondents reported having *sent* a sexual picture or video of themselves and 67 per cent of respondents reported *receiving* a sexual image. While all methodologies have great limitations with regards to the question of prevalence, we are likely to have oversampled those who had sent and received pictures, partly due to the modes of promotion of the survey, discussed above. Despite this, these figures reflect the fact that the practice of sexting is more widespread in Australia than much of the existing Australian and international research indicates.

Age: sending and receiving

The data presented in Table 8.1 reports the prevalence of sexting broken down by age category. As indicated, younger respondents were much less likely to have sent an image or video of themselves than any other age cohort. Nonetheless, with 38 per cent of 13- to 15-year-olds having sent an image, a significant minority of the younger cohort had engaged in the practice. Moreover, 50 per cent of the 16- to 18-year-old cohort had sent a sexual image or video.

A similar distribution is revealed on the question of receiving images or videos (see Table 8.2). These results indicate that high numbers of respondents received images or videos in every age category. The 13- to 15-year-old group had received fewer images or videos than other cohorts, at 62 per cent. Tables 8.1 and 8.2 indicate that all age groups are far more likely to receive than to send an image or video. This data indicates that sexting is not a marginal activity in any of the age groups surveyed. While young people are sending images less than their adult counterparts, they are receiving them more frequently.

Gender

Much of the academic and popular commentary about sexting has focused on the differing dynamics of gender. As the results in Table 8.3 indicate, at the overall cohort level there no statistically significant difference in prevalence rates between males and females.

Table 8.1   Have you ever sent a sexual picture/video (by age)?[a]

	Yes	No	Total
13–15	172 (38%)	276 (62%)	448
16–18	340 (50%)	346 (50%)	686
Adult (19+)	256 (59%)	179 (41%)	435
Total	768	801	1569

Note: [a] Pearson $\chi^2(2) = 34.15$, $p < 0.001$.

Table 8.2   Have you ever received a sexual picture/video (by age)?[a]

	Yes	No	Total
13–15	276 (62%)	169 (38%)	445
16–18	479 (70%)	204 (30%)	683
Adult (19+)	296 (68%)	138 (32%)	434
Total	1051	512	1562

Note: [a] Pearson $\chi^2(2) = 37.15$, $p < 0.001$.

Table 8.3   Have you ever sent a sexual picture/video of yourself (by gender)?[a]

	Yes	No	Total
Male	326 (48%)	349 (52%)	675
Female	438 (50%)	447 (50%)	885
Total	764 (49%)	796 (51%)	1560

Note: [a] Pearson $\chi^2(1) = 0.22$, $p = 0.64$.

Table 8.4   Have you ever received a sexual picture/video (by gender)?[a]

	Yes	No	Total
Male	480 (72%)	191 (28%)	671
Female	564 (64%)	319 (36%)	883
Total	1044 (67%)	510 (33%)	1554

Note: [a] Pearson $\chi^2(1) = 10.44$, $p = 0.001$.

The issue of gender is a factor in the receiving of images however. As the results presented in Table 8.4 indicate, of the overall cohort, women and girls were reportedly less likely to have received a sexual image or video than men and boys.

Number of sexting partners

Respondents were also asked about the number of people they had sent images or videos to, and how many people they had received images from in the past 12 months. This question aimed to explore just how many sexting partners respondents conversed with, something not yet addressed in the available research. As Table 8.5 indicates, the majority of respondents of every age and gender cohort had either not sent anyone an image or video in the past 12 months, or had only done so to one person. Nonetheless, in the younger age and gender cohorts those who *had* sent images were more likely to have sent to more than one person, compared with the adult cohort.

Across the gender groups, males who were active 'senders'[2] were more likely to have sent to two or more people (41 per cent) than females (29 per cent), indicating a significant overall difference in behaviours between males and females. That is, males overall were likely to send images or videos to more sexting partners than females. However, post hoc tests indicate that only adult females were significantly less likely than other groups to have sent to more than five people.

Table 8.6 shows the number of people that respondents had received sexual images from. Of those who had ever received a sext, the largest percentage of young people from all the gendered categories (except 16- to 18-year-old

Table 8.5 How many people have you sent a sexual picture/video of yourself to?[a]

	Male 13–15	Male 16–18	Male adult	Female 13–15	Female 16–18	Female adult	Total
No one in past 12 months	11 (16%)	18 (12%)	22 (22%)	10 (10%)	32 (18%)	36 (23%)	129 (17%)
One person	30 (42%)	67 (44%)	42 (42%)	47 (48%)	94 (52%)	91 (59%)	371 (49%)
2–5 people	19 (27%)	46 (30%)	24 (24%)	34 (34%)	38 (21%)	26 (17%)	187 (25%)
More than 5	11 (16%)	21 (14%)	11 (11%)	8 (8%)	18 (10%)	2 (1%)	71 (9%)
Total	71	152	99	99	182	155	758

Note: [a] Pearson $\chi^2(15) = 44.16$, $p < 0.001$.

Table 8.6 How many people have you received a sexual picture/video from?[a]

	Male 13–15	Male 16–18	Male adult	Female 13–15	Female 16–18	Female adult	Total
No one in past 12 months	6 (5%)	22 (9%)	24 (21%)	8 (5%)	27 (12%)	46 (26%)	133 (13%)
One person	40 (33%)	74 (31%)	44 (38%)	52 (35%)	104 (44%)	88 (50%)	402 (39%)
2–5 people	51 (42%)	103 (43%)	29 (25%)	54 (36%)	73 (31%)	34 (19%)	344 (33%)
More than 5	26 (21%)	39 (16%)	19 (16%)	36 (24%)	30 (13%)	9 (5%)	159 (15%)
Total	123	238	116	150	234	177	1038

Note: [a] Pearson $\chi^2(15) = 104.50$, $p < 0.001$.

girls) had received a sexual image from two or more people in the past 12 months. Post hoc tests confirmed that the younger cohorts of females were more likely than adult females to have received images or videos from more than five people in the past 12 months (24 per cent). They also confirmed that males aged 13–15 and 16–18 were similar to girls aged 13–15 in that they were more likely to have received from multiple persons. For both adult groups and the females 16–18 post hoc tests indicate that the majority received from one or no partners in the past 12 months.

Sexuality: sending and receiving

The survey also sought to understand the correlation between sexuality and sexting. As we argue below, while sexuality is often discussed as a key factor in the prevalence of sexting, little research has been undertaken into this variable. As the data in Table 8.7 indicates, respondents identifying as gay were significantly more likely to have sent or received an image or video (81 per cent). Both lesbian and bisexual identifying respondents were also more likely to have engaged in the practice than their heterosexual counterparts.[3]

As Table 8.8 further indicates, a similarly significant distribution was also found in relation to the receiving of images or videos, with 92 per cent of gay respondents having received such material. Lesbian and bisexual

Table 8.7   Have you ever sent a sexual picture/video of yourself (by sexual preference)?[a]

	Yes	No	Total
Hetero	526 (45%)	636 (55%)	1162
Lesbian	13 (65%)	7 (35%)	20
Gay	30 (81%)	7 (19%)	37
Bisexual	89 (67%)	44 (33%)	133
Total	658 (49%)	694 (51%)	1352

Note: [a] Pearson $\chi^2(3)$ = 40.81, $p < 0.001$.

Table 8.8   Have you ever received a sexual picture/video of yourself (by sexual preference)?[a]

	Yes	No	Total
Hetero	755 (65%)	407 (35%)	1162
Lesbian	13 (65%)	7 (35%)	20
Gay	34 (92%)	3 (8%)	37
Bisexual	103 (77%)	30 (23%)	133
Total	905 (67%)	447 (33%)	1352

Note: [a] Pearson $\chi^2(3)$ = 19.10, $p < 0.001$.

respondents were also more likely than heterosexual respondents to have received an image, although less likely than their gay counterparts. While the sample sizes of these groups were relatively low and the results thus not statistically significant, Table 8.9 demonstrates that respondents identifying as gay, followed by those identifying as bisexual were the most prevalent sexters. Moreover, gay respondents were more likely to send to multiple partners, followed by bisexual respondents. The same dynamic played out with regards to the receiving of images and sexuality. As Table 8.10 shows, gay identifying respondents appear to be the most likely recipients of images or videos although the sample is too small to draw firm statistical conclusions.

Relationships: sending and receiving

The survey sought to establish the types of relationships between those who send pictures or videos to one another. Implicit in much of the current discourse on sexting has been that it is a practice that is engaged in by singles or those in the early stages of a relationship; that is, it is part of getting to know someone, or attracting the attention of the receiver so that a relationship of some kind might ensue. Assumptions are also made about sexting being a behaviour that is 'out of control' (News.com.au 2009; Higgins 2014).

Table 8.9 How many people have you sent a sexual picture/video to (by sexual preference)?[a]

	Hetero	Lesbian	Gay	Bisexual
No one past 12 months	90 (17%)	3 (23%)	6 (20%)	11 (13%)
One person	271 (52%)	8 (62%)	5 (17%)	46 (52%)
2–5 people	123 (24%)	1 (7.5%)	11 (37%)	23 (26%)
More than 5	42 (7%)	1 (7.5%)	8 (27%)	9 (10%)
Total	526 (45% of total hetero n)	13 (65% of total lesbian n)	30 (81% of total gay n)	89 (70% of total bi n)

Note: [a] Pearson $\chi^2(9) = 23.50$, $p = 0.005$.

Table 8.10 How many people have you received a sexual picture/video from (by sexual preference)?[a]

	Hetero	Lesbian	Gay	Bisexual
No one past 12 months	101 (13%)	2 (15%)	2 (6%)	7 (7%)
One person	310 (41%)	8 (62%)	7 (21%)	39 (38%)
2–5 people	244 (32%)	2 (15%)	11 (32%)	37 (36%)
More than 5	100 (13%)	1 (8%)	14 (41%)	20 (19%)
Total	755	13	34	103

Note: [a] Pearson $\chi^2(9) = 30.00$, $p < 0.001$.

Table 8.11 Have you ever sent a sexual picture/video of yourself (by relationship status)?[a]

	Not in a relationship	Just started seeing someone	Casual/dating relationship	Long-term relationship	Married	Other	Total
Yes	288 (40%)	63 (53%)	86 (62%)	218 (62%)	18 (41%)	27 (53%)	700 (49%)
No	435 (60%)	56 (47%)	52 (38%)	132 (38%)	26 (59%)	24 (47%)	725 (51%)
Total	723	119	138	350	44	51	1425

Note: [a] Pearson $\chi^2(5) = 61.02$, $p < 0.001$.

Conversely, as the data reported in Table 8.11 indicates, those in some kind of relationship, particularly those in a long-term relationship (with the exception of married respondents), were more likely to have sent a sexual image or video of themselves than those who were not in a relationship, or than those who had 'just started seeing someone'. This suggests that those who send pictures of themselves do, in the vast majority of instances, send them to someone with whom they have an established relationship. We cannot conclusively say that those in a relationship are actually sending the pictures to their partner *in that relationship*, nor can we establish with certainty that the respondent was in a relationship when he or she sent or received an image or video.

As Table 8.12 indicates, those dating or in long-term relationships were more likely to have received an image or video. Those not in a relationship were least likely to have received and image or video, followed by those that were married.

As Table 8.13 illustrates, those who reported being in a long-term relationship were also most likely to have sent images or videos to only one person. The same was true of respondents who were married.

Similarly, as represented in Table 8.14, those who had received images or videos were more likely to be in a relationship, with the exception of married respondents.

Perceptions of sexting

As discussed in Chapter 6, previous studies have often confused perceptions with practices or motivations. Our survey therefore sought to differentiate perceptions from practice by asking respondents a range of questions about what they knew of and perceived about sexting more generally, rather than just their own behaviour.

Where did they hear about sexting?

Respondents were initially asked how they came to know about sexting in the first place. As the data in Table 8.15 indicates, the highest

Table 8.12 Have you ever received a sexual picture/video (by relationship status)? [a]

	Not in a relationship	Just started seeing someone	Casual/dating relationship	Long-term relationship	Married	Other	Total
Yes	435 (60%)	91 (77%)	115 (83%)	256 (73%)	24 (55%)	35 (69%)	956 (67%)
No	288 (40%)	28 (23%)	23 (17%)	94 (27%)	20 (45%)	16 (31%)	469 (33%)
Total	723	119	138	350	44	51	1425

Note: [a] Pearson $\chi^2(5) = 45.93$, $p < 0.001$.

Table 8.13 How many people have you received a sexual picture/video from in the past 12 months (by relationship status)? [a]

	Not in a relationship	Just started seeing someone	Casual/dating relationship	Long-term relationship	Married	Other	Total
No one past 12 months	51 (18%)	13 (21%)	11 (13%)	38 (17%)	5 (28%)	2 (7%)	120 (17%)
One person	112 (39%)	26 (41%)	33 (38%)	144 (66%)	11 (62%)	13 (48%)	339 (48%)
2–5 people	87 (30%)	18 (29%)	36 (42%)	25 (12%)	1 (6%)	7 (26%)	174 (25%)
More than 5	38 (13%)	6 (10%)	6 (7%)	11 (5%)	1 (6%)	5 (19%)	67 (10%)
Total	288	63	86	218	18	27	700

Note: [a] Pearson $\chi^2(15) = 70.49$, $p < 0.001$.

Table 8.14 How many people have you received a sexual picture/video from in the past 12 months (by relationship status)?[a]

	Not in a relationship	Just started seeing someone	Casual/dating relationship	Long-term relationship	Married	Other	Total
No one past 12 months	45 (10%)	8 (9%)	12 (10%)	46 (18%)	10 (42%)	1 (3%)	122 (13%)
One person	146 (34%)	25 (28%)	38 (33%)	139 (54%)	10 (42%)	13 (37%)	371 (39%)
2–5 people	168 (39%)	39 (43%)	44 (38%)	54 (21%)	3 (13%)	12 (34%)	320 (34%)
More than 5	9 (26%)	19 (21%)	21 (18%)	17 (7%)	1 (4%)	9 (26%)	143 (15%)
Total	435	91	115	256	24	35	956

Note: [a] Pearson χ^2(15) = 93.16, $p < 0.001$.

Table 8.15 Where did you first hear about sexting?[a]

Age	School teacher	Friend	Police	Internet	Parent/ Guardian	Sibling	Social networking	Media	This survey	Other	Total
13–15	74 (14%)	187 (36%)	43 (8%)	2 (<1%)	20 (4%)	5 (1%)	58 (11%)	117 (22%)	7 (1%)	14 (2.7%)	527
16–18	96 (12%)	304 (39%)	71 (9%)	3 (0.4%)	18 (2.3%)	6 (0.8%)	70 (9.0%)	175 (22.6%)	1 (0.1%)	31 (4%)	775
Adult (19+)	17 (3%)	156 (31%)	5 (1%)	2 (<1%)	5 (1%)	2 (<1%)	31 (6%)	255 (51%)	5 (1%)	19 (4%)	497
Total	187 (10%)	647 (36%)	119 (7%)	7 (<1%)	43 (2%)	13 (<1%)	159 (9%)	547 (30%)	13 (<1%)	64 (4%)	1799

Note: [a] Pearson χ^2(18) = 194.83, $p < 0.001$.

percentage younger cohorts heard about sexting from friends, whereas the higher percentage older respondents reported hearing about sexting from the media.

Perceptions of sexting by gender

Respondents were asked about their perceptions of sexting; specifically, why they *think* people engage in sexting, as opposed to why a person does actually engage in it. Table 8.16 presents respondents top three responses to the question: 'Why do you think girls send sexual pictures/videos?' The data shows which answers were the most popular choices and what percentage of respondents selected each response as one of their three choices (thus percentages do not add up to 100 per cent).

As the results indicate, the most popular options for males and females were: (1) to get attention, with 54 per cent of males and 65 per cent of females choosing this response; (2) because of pressure from the receiver, with 42 per cent of males and 46 per cent of females choosing this response; or (3) according to the perceptions of males, as a 'sexy present' (38 per cent) or, according to females, to get a girl or guy to like

Table 8.16 Why do you think girls send sexual pictures/videos?

	Frequency	Frequency Male (% of males)	Frequency Female (% of females)	χ^2	p value
Get or keep a guy/girl's attention	1078	445 (54%)	633 (65%)	21.02	0.00**
Bf/gf pressured them to send it	794	343 (42%)	451 (46%)	3.46	0.06
As a sexy present for bf/gf	610	314 (38%)	296 (30%)	12.03	0.00**
To feel sexy or confident	424	191 (23%)	233 (24%)	0.11	0.74
To get a guy/girl to like them	504	186 (23%)	318 (33%)	22.00	0.00**
Pressure from friends	98	41 (5.0%)	57 (6%)	0.49	0.49
To get compliments	365	157 (19%)	208 (21%)	1.49	0.22
To be included/fit in	151	58 (7%)	93 (10%)	3.53	0.06
To be fun/flirty	334	202 (25%)	132 (14%)	36.15	0.00**
To get noticed or show off	436	191 (23%)	245 (25%)	0.85	0.36
Because she received one	156	78 (9%)	78 (8.0%)	1.27	0.26
I don't know	44	25 (3%)	17 (2%)	3.31	0.07
Other (please specify)	59	30 (4%)	29 (3%)	0.65	0.42

Note: **Indicates significance at the $p < 0.001$ level.

them (33 per cent). In short, there was a general perception that girls might be pressured or feel compelled to send an image to get a potential partner interested in them. There were also some difference across gender categories with females more likely to select 'getting a guy/girl's attention' and 'to get a girl/guy to like them' than males. However, males were significantly more likely than females to perceive sexting as a 'sexy present for a boyfriend/girlfriend' or a way 'to be fun and flirty'.

Those respondents who selected 'other' did so for a number of reasons, including because they 'Liked them and trusted them', for 'Self validation', 'To feel empowered', or several variants of 'To help keep a relationship alive while her partner is working away'.

In comparison, per Table 8.17, when respondents were asked to select their top three reasons why males send sexual images/pictures, responses were quite different. This perhaps reflects the stereotypical notion that boys predominantly pressure girls to send images – but also reflects a gendered double standard that constructs girls as 'sluts' and boys as active agents 'doing what boys do'. Both male and female respondents believed that males were likely to send images to: (1) 'get noticed or show off', with 54 per cent of females and 34 per cent of males choosing this response; or (2) 'get or keep a guy/girl's attention', with 37 per cent of females and 34 per cent of males choosing this response.

Table 8.17 Why do you think guys send sexual pictures/videos?

	Frequency	Frequency Male (% of males)	Frequency Female (% of males)	χ^2	*p* value
Get or keep a guy's/girl's attention	637	278 (34%)	359 (37%)	1.83	0.18
Bf/gf pressured them to send it	156	84 (10%)	72 (7%)	4.55	0.03*
As a sexy present for bf/gf	495	227 (28%)	268 (27%)	0.02	0.90
To feel sexy or confident	443	182 (22%)	261 (27%)	5.11	0.02*
To get a guy/girl to like them	355	170 (21%)	185 (19%)	0.96	0.33
Pressure from friends	192	51 (6%)	141 (14%)	31.09	0.00**
To get compliments	341	130 (16%)	211 (22%)	9.42	0.00**
To be included/fit in	155	49 (6%)	106 (11%)	13.08	0.00**
To be fun/flirty	435	234 (29%)	201 (21%)	15.17	0.00**
To get noticed or show off	878	350 (43%)	528 (54%)	23.31	0.00**
Because he received one	476	252 (31%)	224 (23%)	13.71	0.00**
I don't know	128	68 (8%)	60 (6%)	3.05	0.08
Other (please specify)	87	37 (4%)	50 (5%)	0.26	0.61

Note: * Indicates significance at the $p < 0.05$ level.
       ** Indicates significance at the $p < 0.001$ level.

Significant differences in male and female responses were apparent, however, with the third most popular choice for male respondents, 'because he received one' (31 per cent) and for female respondents 'as a sexy present' (27 per cent). There were also some statistically significant variations in responses to particular items between males and females. More males than females endorsed the items 'boyfriend or girlfriend pressured them to send it', 'to be fun and flirty' and 'because he received one'. More females than males endorsed the items 'to feel sexy and confident', 'to get compliments', 'to be included and fit in', and 'to get noticed or show off'.

Specific questions were also asked with regard to the posting of sexual pictures on social networking platforms, and the pressure to do so. When asked whether they agreed or disagreed with the statement 'There is pressure among people my age to post sexual pictures/videos in their (social networking) profiles', overall there was no significant difference between those that believed there was pressure and those that did not (see Table 8.18).

However, when broken down according to gender (see Table 8.19), post hoc tests confirmed that significantly more females than males agreed or strongly agreed with the statement that 'there is pressure to post sexual pictures/videos on their (social networking) profiles'. Significantly more females neither agreed nor disagreed and significantly more males strongly disagreed with the statement. Again, these responses demonstrate a gender disparity in perceptions about sexting.

We also broke this down further in relation to age. As Table 8.19 indicates a high percentage of 13- to 15-year-old females either agreed or strongly agreed that there was pressure to post sexual pictures on networking sites (65 per cent), while 54 per cent of 16- to 18-year-old females also endorsed this statement.

Table 8.18 There is pressure among people my age to post sexual pictures/videos in their (social networking) profiles[a]

	Strongly agree	Agree	Neither agree nor disagree	Disagree	Strongly disagree	Don't know	Total
Male	75 (12%)	168 (27%)	119 (19%)	173 (27%)	87 (14%)	12 (2%)	634
Female	147 (17%)	268 (31%)	120 (14%)	213 (25%)	82 (10%)	23 (3%)	853
Total	222 (15%)	436 (29%)	239 (16%)	386 (26%)	169 (11%)	35 (2%)	1487

Note: [a] Pearson $\chi^2(5) = 22.27$, $p < 0.001$.

Table 8.19 There is pressure among people my age to post sexual pictures/videos in their (social networking) profiles[a]

	Strongly agree	Agree	Neither agree nor disagree	Disagree	Strongly disagree	Don't know	Total
Male 13–15	34 (19%)	31 (23%)	43 (24%)	39 (22%)	14 (8%)	7 (4%)	178
Male 16–18	37 (13%)	101 (34%)	49 (17%)	69 (23%)	37 (13%)	4 (1%)	297
Male adult (19+)	4 (3%)	26 (16%)	27 (17%)	65 (41%)	36 (23%)	1 (1%)	159
Female 13–15	63 (27%)	88 (38%)	34 (15%)	33 (14%)	9 (4%)	7 (3%)	234
Female 16–18	68 (19%)	123 (35%)	53 (15%)	81 (23%)	21 (6%)	10 (3%)	356
Female adult (19+)	16 (6%)	57 (22%)	33 (13%)	99 (38%)	52 (20%)	6 (2%)	263
Total	222 (15%)	436 (29%)	239 (16%)	386 (26%)	169 (11%)	35 (2%)	1487

Note: [a] Pearson $\chi^2(25)$ = 204.81, $p < 0.001$.

Motivations

The survey also sought to unpack individual motivations expressed for sexting. As the data presented in Table 8.20 shows, respondents were asked to select three reasons why they were motivated to send a sexual image or video. While the perceptions data above suggests that people engage in sexting due to pressure, 'motivations' responses suggested that pleasure or desire were the driving motivations for those who actually engaged in the sending of images or videos. We have disaggregated the responses the responses by age and gender.

This data suggests that teenage girls send images: (1) 'to be fun and flirty'; (2) 'as a sexy present'; and (3) to 'feel sexy and confident'. This was very closely followed by 'because I received one'.

Teenage boys' responses differed. Responses suggested that they were motivated to send an image or video: (1) 'to be fun and flirty'; (2) 'because I received one'; and (3) 'as a sexy present'.

Again there were also some statistically significant variations between groups on particular items that warrant some discussion. Male and female adult groups endorsed the item 'as a sexy present for a boyfriend of girlfriend' significantly more than their teen counterparts although all groups endorsed this in relative high numbers, Similarly, adults in both groups were more likely to have chosen the popular overall response of being motivated 'to be fun and flirty' than their teen coun-terparts. Female adults (28 per cent) were more likely to suggest that it made them 'feel sexy and confident' than other groups. Males overall were more likely to report be motivated to send 'because they received one', although this was a popular category for all groups. Adult males

Table 8.20 Why did you send a sexual picture/video of yourself?

	Frequency total	Male teen	Male adult	Female teen	Female adult	χ^2	p value
Get or keep a guy's/girl's attention	194	51a (10%)	26b (16%)	85b (14%)	32a, b (12%)	5.87	0.12
Bf/gf pressured me to send it	136	19a (4%)	4a (3%)	77b (13%)	36b (13%)	42.49	0.00**
As a sexy present for bf/gf	361	83a (16%)	57b (35%)	112a (18%)	109b (40%)	80.26	0.00**
To feel sexy or confident	239	45a (9%)	29b (18%)	90b (15%)	75c (28%)	50.17	0.00**
To get a guy/girl to like me	118	25a (5%)	12a, b (7%)	56b (9%)	25b (9%)	8.44	0.04*
Pressure from friends	30	7a (1%)	1a (1%)	19a (3%)	3a (1%)	7.67	0.05
To get compliments	130	25a (5%)	18b (11%)	53b (9%)	34b (13%)	16.03	0.00**
To be included/fit in	43	6a (1%)	4a, b (3%)	31b (5%)	2a (1%)	20.86	0.00**
To be fun/flirty	397	119a (23.2%)	60b (36.8%)	132a (21.4%)	86b (31.9%)	23.50	0.00**
To get noticed or show off	132	39a (8%)	24b (15%)	50a (8%)	19a (7%)	9.53	0.02*
Because I received one	288	116a (23%)	46a (28%)	86b (14%)	40b (15%)	26.99	0.00**
I don't know	60	18a, b, c (4%)	2c (1%)	36b (6%)	4a, c (2%)	13.92	0.00**
Other (please specify)	108	39a	11a	35a	23a	2.32	0.51

Note: *Indicates significance at the $p < 0.05$ level.

**$p < 0.01$ level.

(15 per cent) were more likely than the other groups to nominate 'to get noticed or show off' as a motivation. While there were only 13 per cent of both female teens and adult females who endorsed the response that a boyfriend of girlfriend pressured them, they did so significantly more than males of either category. Male teens were less likely to suggest they were motivated to 'get a girl or guy to like them' (5 per cent) or 'to get compliments' (5 per cent) than the other groups. Female teens, though in small numbers (5 per cent), were more likely than the other groups to be motivated 'to be included or fit in'. Female teens were more likely to nominate 'I don't know' as a response than other groups – but in very small numbers.

Overall then, respondents reported positive motivations for their sexting behaviours. Only small numbers reported being motivated by pressure or coercion in any group. Nonetheless, this picture is more mixed for younger females than their male and older counterparts with, for example, around 13 per cent endorsing a range of responses that could be interpreted as pressure.

Feelings and fallout from sexting

Respondents were asked to nominate from a number of selections which three reasons might discourage them from sending sexts (see Table 8.21). Young males reported that the risk of getting in trouble with the law was the primary factor that would discourage them from sexting, and while young females endorsed damage to their reputation as their most popular choice, they also endorsed getting in trouble with the law in high numbers. This suggests that young people are generally aware of the laws around sexting and their capacity to fall foul of them. This response contrasted significantly with the adult cohort, who were much less likely to be criminalised under existing laws and perhaps less concerned with this as a risk.

For each age and gender cohort the notion that 'I might regret it' was also a very popular reason not to engage in sexting. For adult females 'potential embarrassment' of their behaviour being revealed to others was a strong motivation not to sext, with 46 per cent choosing it as one of their three options.

Sending pictures to third parties

When asked how strongly they agreed with the statement 'personal pictures/videos usually end up being seen by more than the people

Table 8.21 What might discourage you from sending a sexual picture/video of yourself?

	Frequency total	Male teen	Male adult	Female teen	Female adult	χ^2	p value
Past bad experience	180 (10%)	48 (8%)	11 (6%)	93 (14%)	28 (9%)	18.79	<0.001***
Disappoint family	391 (22%)	149 (24%)	18 (9%)	197 (29%)	27 (9%)	70.42	<0.001***
Disappoint friends	72 (4%)	34 (5%)	4 (2%)	32 (5%)	2 (<1%)	14.92	0.002**
Disappoint teacher	19 (1%)	2 (<1%)	0 (0%)	17 (2.5%)	0 (0%)	22.36	<0.001***
Hurt relationship/chances	343 (19%)	153 (25%)	45 (23%)	105 (16%)	40 (13%)	25.61	<0.001***
Hurt reputation	679 (38%)	199 (32%)	70 (36%)	275 (41%)	135 (45%)	18.87	<0.001***
Hurt family's reputation	107 (6%)	31 (5%)	6 (3%)	56 (8%)	14 (5%)	11.56	0.009**
Potential trouble with law	554 (31%)	236 (38%)	37 (19%)	244 (36%)	37 (12%)	84.28	<0.001***
Potential trouble at school	70 (4%)	37 (6%)	2 (1%)	30 (5%)	1 (<1%)	21.81	<0.001***
Employer might see	352 (20%)	88 (14%)	40 (21%)	140 (21%)	84 (28%)	26.11	<0.001***
Potential embarrassment	491 (27%)	121 (19%)	73 (38%)	159 (24%)	138 (46%)	87.16	<0.001***
Might regret it	577 (32%)	179 (29%)	73 (38%)	197 (30%)	128 (43%)	23.75	<0.001***
Might make people think I'm slutty	169 (9%)	24 (4%)	7 (4%)	110 (16%)	28 (9%)	68.29	<0.001***
I don't know	45 (3%)	22 (4%)	10 (5%)	9 (1%)	4 (1%)	13.62	0.003**
Other (please specify)	142 (8%)	37 (6%)	18 (9%)	51 (8%)	36 (12%)	10.81	0.01*

Notes: * Indicates significance at the $p < 0.05$ level.

    ** Indicates significance at the $p < 0.01$ level.

    *** Indicates significance at the $p < 0.001$ level.

they were sent to', the vast majority of respondents believed that the images were 'mostly' seen by more people than they were sent to (see Table 8.22). This was particularly the case with young females, around 84 per cent of whom agreed or strongly agreed with the statement. As seen in Tables 8.22 and 8.23, these figures are at odds with what sexting participants tell us about how often images are *actually* seen by third parties.

As demonstrated in Table 8.23, of those respondents who had ever sent or received an image or video, it was only a very small minority who reported they had ever sent an image on or shared it digitally. As such, the perception that an image will be shown to a third party seems to significantly outstrip the reported risk of this occurring.

There were, however, some gender disparities in the practice of sharing images or videos, with males significantly more likely to forward on such material than females, as indicated in Table 8.24.

Of those surveyed, 20 per cent said that they had showed others an image/video in person; that is, physically showed rather than having sent the image on. Respondents who were married or in long-term relationships were least likely to have shown images/videos to somebody else, as seen in Table 8.25. For example, only 13 per cent of those in long-term relationships and 14 per cent of those married said they had shown another person images/videos they had received.

Legal consequences

The survey also captured data on respondents' understandings of the seriousness with which the Australian legal system could treat sexting, particularly sexting between or involving young people. Respondents were asked to choose what they believed were the most serious consequences that could result from a particular scenario (see Table 8.26). Specifically, they were asked: 'A 16 year old guy takes a nude picture of his 15 year old girlfriend and sends it to his school mate. What do you think is the most serious thing that could happen to the 16 year old guy?'

Of the sample, 69 per cent selected the most accurate answer – 'he could be charged with child pornography offences and placed on a sex offenders register' – while another 18 per cent chose the second most serious consequence, that 'he could be charged with child pornography offences'. These responses indicate that respondents were generally cognisant of the possible consequences of sending explicit images in this particular scenario.

Table 8.22 Personal pictures/videos usually end up being seen by more than the people they were sent to[a]

	Strongly agree	Agree	Neither agree nor disagree	Disagree	Strongly disagree	Don't know	Total
Male teen	152 (32%)	205 (43%)	51 (11%)	44 (9%)	12 (3%)	11 (2%)	475
Male adult	41 (26%)	70 (44%)	23 (15%)	14 (9%)	8 (5%)	3 (2%)	159
Female teen	263 (45%)	234 (40%)	45 (7%)	31 (5%)	7 (1%)	10 (2%)	590
Female adult	81 (31%)	106 (40%)	40 (15%)	23 (8%)	3 (1%)	10 (4%)	263
Total	537 (36%)	615 (41%)	159 (11%)	112 (8%)	30 (2%)	34 (2%)	1487

Note: [a] Pearson $\chi^2(15) = 55.39$, $p < 0.001$.

Table 8.23 Have you ever shared a sexual picture/video with someone who wasn't meant to see it (by age)?

	13–15	16–18	Adult (19+)	χ^2	p value
Shown somebody in person	87 (20%)	153 (22%)	68 (16%)	7.83	0.02*
Shared online	23 (5%)	41 (6%)	16 (4%)	2.99	0.22
Forwarded (MMS or email)	26 (6%)	57 (8%)	18 (4%)	8.22	0.02*

Note: *Indicates significance at the $p < 0.05$ level.

Table 8.24 Have you ever shared a sexual picture/video with someone who wasn't meant to see it (by gender)?

	Male	Female	Total	χ2	*p* value
Shown somebody in person	168 (25%)	138 (16%)	306 (20%)	21.96	<.001***
Shared online	44 (7%)	34 (4%)	78 (5%)	6.00	0.01*
Forwarded (MMS or email)	59 (9%)	41 (5%)	100 (7%)	11.12	0.001**

Note: * Indicates significance at the $p < 0.05$ level.

      ** Indicates significance at the $p < 0.01$ level.

      *** Indicates significance at the $p < 0.001$ level.

Table 8.25 Have you ever shown (in person) a sexual picture/video to someone who wasn't meant to see it (by relationship status)?[a]

Not in relationship	Just started seeing someone	Casual/ dating	Long-term Relationship	Married	Other	Total
148 (21%)	30 (25%)	40 (29%)	46 (13%)	6 (14%)	15 (29%)	285 (20%)

Note: [a] Pearson $\chi^2(5) = 23.31$, $p < 0.001$.

Table 8.26 What do you think is the most serious thing that could happen (consequences of sexting between teenagers)?[a]

	Male teen	Male adult	Female teen	Female adult	Total
Nothing	6 (1%)	2 (1%)	4 (<1%)	1 (<1%)	13 (<1%)
Suspended from school	4 (<1%)	2 (1%)	15 (2%)	7 (3%)	28 (2%)
Formal police caution	18 (4%)	15 (9%)	26 (4%)	14 (5)	73 (5%)
Police could force to remove social media page	7 (1%)	0 (0%)	1 (3%)	3 (1%)	27 (2%)
Could be charged with child pornography	95 (19%)	27 (17%)	108 (18%)	56 (20%)	286 (18%)
Could be charged with child pornography and placed on sex offenders register	353 (69%)	114 (70%)	431 (70%)	178 (66%)	1076 (69%)
Could face life in prison	16 (3%)	0 (0%)	13 (2%)	6 (2%)	35 (2%)
Other	15 (3%)	3 (2%)	3 (<1%)	4 (2%)	25 (2%)

Note: [a] Pearson $\chi^2(21) = 41.97$, $p = 0.004$.

Conclusion

This chapter has presented the data from an online survey conducted with a large sample of young respondents. While this survey was not a representative sample, its size and balance allows us to take some important implications from the data.

First, it indicates that a significant proportion of young people have engaged in sexting; that is, they have either sent or received sexually explicit images or videos. Second, the young people we sampled lived lives in which being 'online' and networked was a normal part of their lived experience. Practices around sexting need to be understood in this context. Third, a number of key demographic variables indicate the need for further analysis of this data. For example, in some key areas there are significant differences in practices around sexuality, age and gender. Fourth, there are significant differences in perceptions about why young people engage in sexting and their stated motivations for doing so. This again requires further analysis and will be taken up in subsequent chapters. Fifth, most young people reported being aware of the laws around sexting and their potential to fall foul of these. This indicates that many of those who engaged in the practice knew the risks they were taking. Despite this, there is a high prevalence of sexting among young people, which indicates that criminalisation may not be the best way in which to reduce sexting behaviours. Sixth, while all gender and age cohorts reported that pressure from others was a relatively low level motivation for sexting, young women were more likely than other cohort groups to to report pressure as a motivation. Finally, those who do engage in the practice of sexting tend to do so with people they 'trust' – often within some kind of relationship. Thus, sexting needs to be understood as an increasingly 'normalised' activity that very often takes place within a romantic setting.

The next two chapters detail the results of our focus group interviews. These interviews serve to illuminate further the motivations and perceptions discussed in this chapter and add further depth to this data. This is followed by an analysis of the findings from both the survey and focus groups.

9
Perceptions and Practices of Sexting

Introduction

This chapter and the following detail the responses of young people in focus group interviews about sexting. Eight focus group interviews were conducted with young people aged 18 to 20. Respondents were drawn from the student body of the University of Sydney, University of Western Sydney, and a Technical and Further Education (TAFE) NSW Institute. These institutions represent a broad cross section of educational establishments across NSW and constitute a sample that is of mixed class and social status. This and the following chapter detail and thematise the responses of this diverse group of 54 young people which is constituted of 34 females and 20 males. The present chapter focuses on participants' perceptions and practices of sexting as expressed in the focus groups. Through the use of semi-structured interview schedules several key themes were explored in the focus groups including: how respondents conceptualise and negotiate their online identity; how they define sexting; where their knowledge about sexting originates from; their overall reflections on sexting practices, as well as their personal and second-hand experiences of sexting; the role of age and gender in sexting; and motivations for sexting. The following chapter will explore focus group participant responses to criminal justice interventions around sexting. The focus groups provided an important forum for the examination of young people's views on diverse sexting scenarios and on the legal response to sexting. It also canvassed their views on what would constitute an appropriate response to the issues posed by sexting. In this way, the focus groups provided a way of exploring the themes that emerged from the different arms of our research, including the survey material, media discourse analysis, legal analysis and evaluation of educational responses.

Throughout this arm of the research, data gathering, transcription and analysis occurred in alternating sequences in accordance with a grounded theory approach (see Strauss and Corbin 1998). Through this approach, data was analysed as it was gathered, which in turn had an impact upon subsequent data collection, leading to the refinement of the analysis, which fed back into data collection and so on. Interview data was transcribed and anonymised before being imported into the qualitative analysis program, nVivo, which enabled us to code specific lines or segments of text. This approach is defined by Strauss and Corbin (1998) as the breaking down, naming, comparing and categorising of data, a process in which hypotheses or theories are generated directly from the data, rather than through a priori assumptions or existing theoretical frameworks. A coding matrix was developed from the initial interview data that was then used to inform and refine the structure of subsequent interviews in order to maximise the quality of the data gathered.

Young people and information technologies

Conceptualising online identity: the role of information technologies in young people's emotional and sexual lives

As the existing research and responses to our survey have already demonstrated, information technologies play an important role in young peoples' lives. This was confirmed by focus group participants. Whether for learning, socialising, maintaining existing relationships, meeting potential sexual partners or exploring sexuality, the internet has become a virtual space where young people 'hang out' and live their lives. Given this, it is hardly surprising then that the online world plays an important role in the identities of young people, particularly when it comes to their emotional and sexual development.

Sexual content on the internet and across social media, as one focus group participant noted, is 'uncensored and everywhere. It's so casualised' (Female, UWS FG2). For young people, access to social media sites and sexually explicit content is not overly hindered by the age restrictions settings. The age safeguards imposed on these websites are easily bypassed, and adult content is often available for anyone to see. As one participant related:

> I go on Reddit, and they have Argon Wild, Lady Boners, Space Dicks, I don't go on them, but there are specific forums for consenting

adults. When I say consenting adults it's a loose term, because a lot of people can lie about their age and look older. So basically it's just nude photos of themselves posted up for people to admire. (Female, UWS FG2)

Unsurprisingly perhaps, given how integrated technology is in young people's lives, the internet has become especially important in the maintenance of intimate relationships, especially in long distance relationships. As one respondent told us:

I go online a lot especially for internet messaging, because my boyfriend lives all the way in Gold Coast and that's our means of communication, other than mail which takes days to reply. But with instant messaging we can reply straight away. (Female, UWS FG2)

The online interactions, however, are often fraught. As one participant noted, they can also 'make it or break it. So much drama happens online, so many relationships have been destroyed that I've seen, just from social media. It's sad' (Female, USyd FG3). In this way, the internet, and social media in particular, has become an important space in which relationships are played out. As some focus group participants stated, Facebook plays a role in validating and making relationships 'official':

[W]hen I was dating with my boyfriend and we weren't officially together, it was like everybody knew but it was not official, and then they say yeah you should put it on Facebook then it's official. So it's official only when I put it on Facebook. (Female, USyd FG3)

In this way, the terrestrial relationship status is inextricably linked to Facebook. However, as another participant explained, occasionally young people keep their relationship status away from social media, even though this impacts on the 'validity' of their real-life relationships:

If it's on Facebook that means it's official...There are some people that I know that are going out but they don't necessarily post it on Facebook and make it official so that's on their privacy terms. And I think good on you for doing that, because you don't need everyone to know unless you want them to know what their relationship status is. (Female, TAFE)

Negotiating online identity: risk, surveillance and privacy

Negotiating online risks is an important task young people must consider and/or perform on a daily basis. For the young people we spoke with, the online environment is a 'memory in a digital format' that 'cannot be forgotten' (Female, UWS FG2), thus warranting their attention. One focus group participant described her role as a former 'internet researcher'; her job was 'pretty much to find people's information on Facebook and send it to other people' (Female, USyd FG3). The risk that potential employers might be checking their digital identities resulted in young people's well thought out and carefully managed social media presence. For many focus group participants then, minimising risks while online was considered an important task. As one participant explained:

> I'm really worried about it...I personally make sure there's not an inappropriate photo of me being taken. I still want to look professional; I try not to curse as much, just in case you never know who's going to see...it's better to be safe than sorry. (Male, USyd FG3)

According to participants, young people often engage in thorough self-censoring:

> I'm not going to put photos of me disgustingly off my face from last Saturday night on Facebook. That can stay private. You only put out what you feel comfortable people seeing and consider the consequences of where the photos end up. (Male, UWS FG1)

Privacy and surveillance were major concerns identified in the focus groups. A number of participants related cases where employers had requested potential employees log into their Facebook account during job interviews (Male, USyd FG3). Some reported agreeing that such an invasion of privacy might be necessary depending on a job you are applying for (Female, USyd FG3). Others thought that such surveillance by a range of social actors (such as school teachers monitoring students' use of social media) as 'a bit much, it's really none of your business' (Female, USyd FG3).

Similarly, cyberstalking was not something that was taken lightly by participants. As one female commented with regards to her experience on Instagram:

> I get random notifications from people liking all the photos and think okay they're stalking me. You can tell because they're looking through all of them. A photo that has been there for two months or

so, you think okay they're just looking at my profile now. You sense a bit of stalking happening. (Female, TAFE)

For some participants, one way of managing issues of privacy and reputation online was to change their name on Facebook (Female, USyd FG3), or abstain from posting on their Facebook timelines. As one focus group participant noted, 'I just consider anything on Facebook is no longer private. If you want to message someone's Inbox, that's private. Anything else is not' (Male, TAFE).

Conceptualising and defining sexting

When it came to sexting, focus group participants had very clear ideas and understandings about the practice. Participants defined sexting as 'nudes' (Male, TAFE), 'sexually explicit images over the phone or explicit texts' (Male, UWS FG2), 'makeshift porn' (Female, UWS FG2), 'inappropriate texting' (Female, USyd FG2), 'attention whoring' (Female, UWS FG2) or 'dirty talk' (Female, USyd FG2). The term 'sexting' was reportedly rarely used by young people; they were 'pretty much taught that it was called sexting' from other sources (Female, UWS FG2). Despite the lack of use of the term by young people themselves some were familiar with the term 'sext' and used it in their interactions with peers (Male, UWS FG2).

Focus groups participants conceptualised sexts as inclusive of both visual and textual messages, acknowledging that the development in phone technology (especially in relation to high-resolution pictures and video capabilities) and the relative affordability of photo-sharing services was likely directly related to the increase in prevalence of sexting (Male, UWS FG2; Male, TAFE).

The negative context of sexting practices was verbalised by some female participants who, when asked to define sexting, stated that sexting was 'potentially ruining [sexters] psychologically and socially because [the picture] is still there. Even if they get rid of it, it's still in the public arena and it can affect them later on' (Female, UWS FG2).

Young people's understandings of and knowledge about sexting, including the definition of sexting, drew heavily on content delivered within high school curricula and educational campaigns about sexting. Such content was delivered mostly through the subject PDHP (personal development, health and physical education) subject with some participants noting that, as a part of high school curriculum, they were provided with:

A book lent from the government, I can't remember the exact name of it but yeah, [it was] just about protecting yourself and protecting others, being careful of sexual harassment even if it's inadvertent kind of stuff.' (Male, UWS FG2)

As focus group participants saw it, the key message sent to young people through such educational materials was 'generally not to do it, in the event that it does lead into someone else's hands, and in case it does get misconstrued. So basically be on your guard more or less' (Male, UWS FG2). To reinforce such messages, focus group participants stated they were provided with 'extreme [case studies and examples], because we were at that age and [adults] didn't want us to get into the whole sexting thing' (Female, UWS FG2). In some schools 'teachers were really grilling students... you can get in serious trouble. ... [t]eachers were very adamant on [boys] not having any possession of pictures. It was pretty serious at my school' (Female, USyd FG3).

Unsurprisingly, another important source of information driving young people's understanding and conceptualisation of sexting was the media. The role of tabloid and teenage-content media was seen as especially crucial in emitting (often gendered) warnings about perils and risks of sexting:

The first time I heard the term sexting was through a newspaper article about the rise in teenage girls taking part in sexting to their boyfriends. It was in the *Daily Telegraph*, so that was the first time I'd heard of it. (Female, UWS FG2)

Participants were also alerted to sexting via popular forms of teen media:

[T]he first time I ever read the word sexting was in *Dolly* magazine and then in recent years I've just been reading lots of articles about it, about kids at high schools who have had to transfer because of bullying that was initiated from sexting. (Female, UWS FG1)

While most of the focus group participants acknowledged that sexting was prevalent among their peers, they pinpointed the role the media play in creating the 'sexting problem' (Male, UWS FG2). For some, media focus on the issue of sexting was potentially a catalyst for some young people's engagement in the practice:

I didn't hear about it occurring until it became something big in the media, and I felt like seeing it in the media gave people ideas. So instead of seeing it and being 'oh that's obviously really bad', it gave them the idea to go out and do it. (Female, USyd FG4)

Motivations, prevalence and acceptability of sexting among peers

Most focus group participants believed sexting was a common practice among their peers. At the same time, while still images taken and distributed via mobile phones are predominant, focus group participants indicated that other avenues of sexual communication using online technologies are gaining traction. As one female participant argued, 'I think there wouldn't be as much of still images of young people flashing their bits and bobs out there to see. I think they might have a more discrete way of doing it, maybe through Skype' (Female, UWS FG2). This practice is directly related to young people's online risk management as 'they don't see Skype as as big a danger as taking a photo of yourself. They'd probably just flash themselves momentarily and that's it' (Female, UWS FG2).

Discussing motivations for sexting behaviour among their peers, participants identified a wide range of incentives for sending sexts, ranging from boredom and naivety to attention seeking and explorations of sexuality. There also appeared to be a gendered nature to, and double standard in, the perceptions of motivations for sexting. Experimenting with sexting was seen as peer-acceptable behaviour for young men, but not for women, as they are expected to protect their modesty. As one focus group participant pointed out, sexting is 'a normal part of being young and growing up just to joke around in that kind of way. Especially for guys more so than girls' (Male, UWS FG2). Young men 'sext, 'cause it's so funny' (Male, UWS FG2). At the same time, young women 'are expected to be modest and not prancing around with their bare legs and cleavage popping out and whatnot' (Female, UWS FG2). When asked to elaborate on why girls' and guys' sexting practices might be seen differently, one respondent explained that young men often use sexts as a joke and send them to their male friends, 'saying I want to rape you or something really foul, but it's funny because it's so foul and wrong' (Male, UWS FG2). Focus group participants also claimed that men tended to send sexts for attention, especially gym and bathroom selfies (Male, TAFE). Young women, on the other hand, were perceived to send sexts 'out of like courtesy pretty much' (Female, TAFE).

For focus group participants, sexting in relationships could be clearly differentiated from sexting outside relationships. Focus group participants argued that sexting was '[m]ore a relationship [thing] ... nine out of 10 times maybe, because they can trust that person' (Male, USyd FG3). For some, sexting in a 'loving relationship' was considered desirable, as 'sex can be a very personal thing for most people' (Female, UWS FG2). Sexting was also seen to play a very important role in maintaining long-distance relationships (Male, UWS FG3) and in that context sexting was viewed as an extension of a loving, committed 'real-life' relationship. For some young women, sexting their boyfriends was a way that their boyfriends could 'visualise them, rather than I don't know, girls in Playboy or whatever' (Female, USyd FG3). Importantly, as one participant explained:

> [F]or a woman it's this really personal thing to reveal herself to a man in this private setting and on that basis of that devotion, yes you can have it, it's like a gift. (Female, USyd FG2)

Another participant, relating a friends' story, stated:

> She thought it was this loving thing, like a gift, she was enabling his sexuality and making sure it was directed towards her. (Female, USyd FG2)

While sexting in relationships was normalised, sexting outside relationships was linked to a lack of self-confidence, particularly among young women:

> I think it's self-confidence...Can I see your tits? Oh crap, my tits aren't that good. Should I do it, should I do it? And they go around asking, and their friends being silly as they are, say you should show him your tits. If you're insecure while you're doing it, it's more likely to pop up in the future, and you become more and more pressured by people going wow you were such a slut. (Female, UWS FG2)

> [Girls are] especially at high school at a vulnerable stage in their life, their self-esteem is very based on what other guys think of them, so I think a lot of the time it's that pretty much trying to impress them, trying to feel good about themselves. (Female, USyd FG3)

While seen as more relevant to girls, the link between self-confidence and sexting was identified in relation to boys as well, with focus group respondents relating that men too face questions over 'how should a real man look? What's an ideal man? How do I get girls? Am I good looking enough?' (Female, UWS FG2).

Interestingly, the notion that young people might be sexting for monetary gain was mentioned in one focus group. Two female participants explained:

> There is no blanket explanation as to why all these young people are sending nude pictures of themselves to each other. It could be for

monetary gain, prostitution through the internet kind of thing, both males and females it does happen. (Female, UWS FG2)

Because if they had the whole sexting thing as a monetary thing they can say you want more pay for a premium membership or something. Yeah pay $50 to see my tits, pay $100 if you want to see me masturbate, or pay $150 for you to see my whole body and you know, masturbate as well in one go. (Female, UWS FG2)

Motivations for and prevalence and incidence of sexting among focus group participants

Many participants admitted to either engaging in sexting behaviour themselves, or receiving sexts from others:

Other people send pictures of themselves to me, and I just say something like LOL or something. Like I'd never engage in a full blown sexually explicit record, because I know like you were saying before, the record gets out so you don't want to say anything too harmful to yourself or others. I just kind of laugh it off and move on. (Male, UWS FG2)

The negative repercussions of sexting were identified as the reason why some (mostly female) focus group participants decided not to engage in phone-sexting behaviour:

I think it's a really bad idea to do it because you don't know who they're showing it to and you don't know who's going to see it these days, they could show it to whoever they want. (Female, USyd FG2)

[I]n my opinion, it's sort of like, well if you want your boyfriend or whatever to see you naked or whatever, well then go and get a room and just be... you sort of have that privacy kind of thing, where not everyone's going to see, 'cause you don't know where it's going to end up, even if he is your boyfriend'. (Female, USyd FG3)

Such concerns were seen as the driving motivation behind young peoples' decisions to use alternative social network websites for sexting (such as R-Creepshots[1] or Skype) under the assumption that anonymity and privacy would be assured. Sexting practices, thus, were seen by focus group participants as not simply limited to mobile phones (phone-to-phone) or traditional social networking websites (phone-to-internet; Facebook and Instagram). Innovative opportunities for sexting practices instead flourish through platforms such as 'Deviant Art', a site 'where artists and art lovers can meet up and artists can post their artworks and then people can comment on it' (Female, UWS FG2). As explained by one focus group participant, herself an active participant on one of many alternative platforms for sexting, they are 'non-relative because typically those photos would be shared around way too many times for normal people to go back to the source of it' (Female, UWS FG2). At the same time, participants reported that Facebook and other traditional social networking websites were increasingly being avoided and/or not used for sexually explicit purposes. As one participant related:

> I just don't like the fact that people can look me up in that way and then trace me down, call me or message me or play games with me and that kind of stuff. So I just try to avoid it. (Male, UWS FG2)

While ready to explore new avenues for sexting, young people who participated in focus groups were also familiar with the risks associated with these and other new online file-sharing forums, arguing that such websites have 'a lot of implied paedophilia...and child pornography' (Female, UWS FG2), due to the open nature of access.

Intersectionalities: age, gender and sexting

Peer pressure was also identified as an important factor in young peoples involvement in the erotic digital economy. Some focus group participants acknowledged that such pressures can be felt by both girls and boys, as often 'they're too quick to trust the other partner' (Female, UWS FG2). A majority, however, agreed that peer pressure to sext applies more to young women. Such pressure is especially pronounced if the young woman in question is dating 'an older guy':

> I think it's pressure from a partner, like if a girl is going out with an older guy and he says I want to see your titties, she'll think to herself – like if she's really young like 14 or something, she'll think oh well he's my first boyfriend and if I don't do it for him he's going to break up with me, so they get pressured into it. (Female, UWS FG2)

For these females, however, there can be some negative consequences for submitting to this pressure. As one participant explained, '[g]irls do eventually get bullied for showing themselves to people on the internet' (Female, UWS FG2). In this way, gender inequalities play an important role when it comes to the consequences of sexting. When young women send sexts they are perceived as 'whores' and 'sluts' (as opposed to being called 'prudes' if they refuse to sext), while guys are called 'studs' (Female, USyd FG3).

Commodification and sexualisation of young women in the media and pop culture has been identified as another important element to the sexting debate, and a potential contributor to sexting. Young people we talked to identified that the commodification of young women has led to them being viewed as only suitable for 'friends with benefits', girls that you 'just do and leave' (Female, UWS FG2). The causal link between a sexualisation of public space and sexting is thus clear:

> [T]he media always seem to promote that you've got to wear short skirts and you've got to have half your cleavage on display and stuff. ... So it sometimes sends a bad message to girls that they need to act like that for guys to notice them, and when a guy has noticed them and says I want you to sext me, they think oh yay I'd better go sext them. (Female, UWS FG2)

> I think it's a media thing ... a lot of teen role models now are things like Keisha, Lady Gaga, Rhianna ... Like I look at them and I'm like really? And you've got little kids singing ridiculous lyrics, like do you know what that means? And they're looking at these video clips and going I want to do that because if I act like this then I'll get the attention. I think it's a lot with the media, more than ourselves. (Female, USyd FG3)

Similarly, the sexualisation of men's bodies was also identified as an important factor to consider in understanding sexting practices. The desired, hypersexual and masculine image is an ultimate goal for many men, and, as such, images that depict these ideals are often shared with peers and potential/actual sexual partners to illustrate these masculine credentials:

> I used to go [to the gym] with my mum because there was a little child care thing. I never saw teenagers. I always just saw people my mum's age. But now I see heaps of young people, like they look 12 or 13 and they're on arm machines and I'm like what are you doing? (Female, USyd FG3)

As one female focus group respondent put it in regard to peer acceptance:

> Their (boys) self-esteem is based on what other guys think of them, so I think a lot of the time it's that pretty much, trying to impress them, trying to feel good about themselves. (UWS FG1)

This is an important insight and is echoed by many respondents, reinforcing the notion that for many young people sexting is not just about impressing an individual's sexting partner. Rather, it is also about one's own sexualised credentials in relation to peers and friends.

Trust, consequences and impact of sexting

Young people's responses indicate their awareness of the complexities of sexting practices, and the impact sexting might have on the participants, their families and society more broadly. They are familiar with cases/instances when sexting has resulted in expulsion from school, not getting a job, criminal justice implications and suicide. While most of the cases that focus group participants described resulted in consequences relevant to young people's education (such as expulsion from school for both girl and boy sexters, moving schools and so on), punishments through the criminal justice system[2], as well as the suicide of victims, were identified as the most damaging consequence of sexting. For these most serious of outcomes, gender was seen to play an important role:

> I don't know why it's always girls that get looked down on. If a girl sends a nude picture of herself, of say her breasts to her boyfriend, with both parties consenting and they break up and the boyfriend releases that picture online or something along the lines, the girl is seen as attention whoring, as in she's begging for attention, when she's saying no I don't want this, this is between me and my ex not online, kind of thing. (Female, UWS FG2)

> I think even for me like I hate it, but what I think about it is gosh, you know Jessie took a picture of herself and she sent it to him, she was willing to take naked pictures of herself and give it to this guy, gosh, how could she do that. But what I should be thinking is oh my gosh, so this guy got broken up with, and he decided to ruin this girl's life by sending these around. (Female, USyd FG2)

However, some participants pointed out that the popularity of young girls and boys at school has some significance when it comes to the impact of sexting:

> [I]t depends on who you are. If it was me that sent it in high school I'd probably have the shit kicked out of me by someone. But because this guy was 'up there', nothing happened to him, it was just like oh yeah sick man! (Male, TAFE)

Trusting someone not to circulate or abuse sexts was seen in focus groups as the foundation that underpins much of the sexting behaviour engaged in by young people.

Occasionally, however, this trust is breached and sexts are distributed, occasionally for revenge. As one participant explained:

> I'm thinking of more relationship problems when you got dumped ... and you are thinking why are you doing this to me, even though I'm being a horrible person to you. I'll get you back even worse. I'll post up all your private information, your personal stories that were meant for me only and have everyone laugh at you. So it's kind of petty revenge, but it can end in something very serious. The other person committing suicide, or you get sent to gaol. (Female, UWS FG2)

Beyond this, however, distributing sexts could also have a different intent, such as the garnering of popularity and attention among young men's mates (Female and Male, USyd FG3) – 'look how hot my girl-friend is' type of behaviour (Female, USyd FG3). Regardless of motivation, focus group participants were acutely aware that the consequences of sexting were many and serious.

The focus groups findings confirmed the notion that sexting practices are considered to be more harmful when they involve minors, who are often held to higher account than adults. While focus group participants reinforced the notion that sexting among adults is perceived as safe and acceptable behaviour (Weisskirch and Delevi 2011), they reported that alarm bells among policymakers and in the general public start to ring when teenagers engage in sexting. In this context, disparities between sexting in adult relationships, sexting among teenagers of approximately same age and sexting *between* adults and teens was emphasised by many of the young people who participated in the focus groups. This will be further discussed in the next chapter.

Differences too were distinguished between the types of exchanges that occurred. Text messages, for example, were seen as less harmful than photo messages. Focus group participants were quick to identify the potential for ongoing, permanent harm as a consequence of image-based sexting:

> [Sexting] can add to insecurities. Sure if you don't get caught then fine, whatever [is] good for you. But you'd be thinking pretty much every day, what if we break up tomorrow, is he going to post it on Facebook or something like that. (Female, UWS FG2)

> I think it can be humiliating because a girl sent a picture of herself naked to her boyfriend and then he uploaded it onto Facebook when they broke up, 'cause it kind of sticks around forever once you send a text or an image. (Female, USyd FG3)

While focus group participants argued that there are some platforms that can be identified as potentially 'more safe' for exploring sexuality than others, they agreed that there is no such thing as safe sexting practice, echoing many of the educational campaigns outlined in Chapter 6:

> I think regardless of what media they use, I think they forget that anything can be – like even Skype they can record any chats that you have just for monitoring the quality of stuff and it might come up as some kids flashing and stuff. (Female, UWS FG2)
>
> You should just be aware when you take those photos that there's a possibility of everyone in the world seeing them, and if you're not willing to accept that then you should never do them. (Female, USyd FG2)

Nevertheless, young people overwhelmingly agreed that their peers will continue to engage in a variety of (relationship and non-relationship) sexting practices.

Conclusion

The findings from focus groups highlight the importance of understanding the broader context of online interactions when considering sexting. Young people's digital identities are carefully crafted and maintained, while they use digital technologies to maintain, validate or annul their terrestrial relationships. At the same time, youth are aware of risks and challenges their non-terrestrial identities bring to the fore, including risks of surveillance and limited privacy, and often engage in carefully planned and executed self-censoring practices.

When it comes to sexting, focus group participants outlined that both themselves and their peers do sext, and they do it for a range of reasons and motivations. While they do not use the term 'sexting', their understanding of the practice draws on educational campaigns, school curricula and the media. They clearly differentiate sexting practices that occur while in a relationship from those that occur outside of a relationship setting. Focus groups participants also acknowledged that young people seek out alternative avenues for sexting, as traditional forms (such as mobile phones and Facebook) are increasingly deemed inadequate. These young people acknowledged issues around intersectionalities when it comes to sexting, such as the gendered context around pressures to sext, and gendered inequalities in relation to the consequences of sexting. Finally, the aftermath of sexting (especially in the context of the distribution of sexts) can be grim, and focus groups participants acknowledged that. However, regardless of potential harm, they were clear in stating that sexting is here to stay. The following chapter looks at focus group participants' views on criminal justice responses to sexting.

10
Perceptions of Legal Responses to Sexting

Introduction

Sexting is a phenomenon that has 'outstripped' (Richards and Calvert 2009, p. 3) and 'outpaced' (McLaughlin 2010, p. 137) the law, with little agreement among legal scholars and academics on how to deal with sexting cases both before and after they find their way to the courtroom. As Richards and Calvert (2009, p. 3) put it, prosecutors are often 'trying to jam square pegs into round holes', stuck between inadequate legal responses to sexting and the diversity of sexting practices. In Chapter 4 we discussed how child pornography laws have been or are potentially used to address sexting, as well as the legal ramifications for those engaged in sexting behaviour. While the objective of policymakers and legislators is to protect minors from sexual abuse, in previous chapters and elsewhere (Salter et al. 2013; Crofts and Lee 2013) we have demonstrated how criminal justice interventions in this area can cause more harm. As a consequence of sexting, young people risk finding themselves on a sex offender registry, for example. Importantly, the voices of young people – those whom these legal interventions are aimed at protecting, their thoughts on legal interventions pertinent to such behaviour are largely absent in decision-making realms in Australia and beyond. As Leigh Goldstein (2009, p. 1) suggested, 'it is virtually impossible to hear a child's voice on the subject of sexuality'.

This chapter gives youth a voice, analysing the responses of focus group participants in relation to criminal justice interventions in sexting cases in Australia. Specifically, focus group participants were asked to comment on two real-life sexting scenarios: one involving an adult inviting/pressuring a person under 16 to sext (for which charges were laid for inciting a person under 16 to commit an act of indecency and a possession of child pornography – the case of Damien Eades); the other concerning the sharing of sexts in a relationship and their distribution following its break-up (i.e., the creation and transmission of child pornography). Participants were asked to comment on the circumstances surrounding the case studies, including the social and moral culpability of those involved, legal responses (charges laid) and the (administered and desired) punishment in such cases.

Young people's analysis of these case studies was diverse, indicating their awareness of the complexities that sexting has for those engaging in the practice and their families. Key themes that emerged from focus groups were: the significance of the age (as well as age difference) of those involved in sexting practices and/or the distribution of sexts; the accountability of participants for the emotional, social and legal consequences of sexting; the notion of trust and its abuse between sexting partners/participants in sexting; the proper identification and acknowledgment of harm in the context of sexting; and the notion of an appropriate – or just – punishment for sexters.

On crimes: inciting to sexting and distribution of sexts

Sexting, age, morality and blame: the case of Damien Eades

As discussed in the previous chapter, sexting practices are considered more dangerous when they involve minors, and minors are held to a higher standard than sexting adults. Concerns that sexting is a gendered practice particularly harmful for young women (Ringrose 2010), a feature of problematic practice of sexualisation of childhood (Greenfield 2004; McLaughlin 2010), or an abusive process often instigated by adults (Davidson and Gottschalk 2010) locate the age of sexting participants firmly in the focus of the sexting debate.

Disparities between sexting in adult relationships, sexting among teenagers of approximately the same age and sexting *between* an adult and a teen were emphasised by focus group participants, reinforcing the notion that sexting among adults is normalised, safe and acceptable behaviour (Weisskirch and Delevi 2011). As one participant noted:

If you're long married with your husband and you're really happy and you have like kids, you live in a big house and you're sending him a photo of you naked. Like is your husband going to send it around? I think that's more acceptable. It is more acceptable just to send it to your husband, than for some 13 year old girl to send it to some guy she's barely met. (Female, UWS FG3)

By comparison, participants felt that when teenagers engage in sexting (whether or not there is an age difference between the parties involved), concerns are raised and intervention follows:

I imagine if people are over 20 and they're sending stuff to each other I don't think anyone would really care, I think it's when it comes to the under 20 age group that people give a toss. Like if they're married, no-one cares what they do, but it's when they're younger there should be some social policy. (Female, USyd FG3)

In order to explore these issues first, focus groups were presented with the landmark case of Damien Eades – the first attempt to prosecute sexting in Australia – in which age of participants played an important role in the criminal justice outcomes.

Damien Eades, aged 18, was working in a fast-food outlet in Sydney's western suburbs in March 2009. There he met a 13-year-old girl, whom he started exchanging text messages with. In one of the exchanges Eades asked the girl to send him naked photos of herself, which she eventually did. The girl's father soon discovered the messages and reported Eades to the police. He was charged with inciting a person under 16 to commit an act of indecency and possession of child pornography under the *Crimes Act 1900* (NSW), the maximum penalty for which was two years imprisonment. Eades was initially found not guilty at Penrith Local Court, with magistrate Daniel Reiss determining that the photo the girl sent was not indecent. The magistrate noted that while there was 'a sexual aspect behind his request', there was no evidence that the relationship ever progressed beyond friendship (McClymont 2010). The Director of Public Prosecutions appealed the decision and the matter was reheard at the Ryde Local Court in 2010. The magistrate found that the indecency offence was proven, but did not record a conviction against Eades (Danks 2010; McClymont 2010).

In the case of Damien Eades, in addition to attention generated by the fact that one of the participants in sexting behaviour was under the age of consent, there was also a significant age gap between the two parties. When presented with the case, focus group participants echoed Temple et al. (2012, p. 6), who argue that 'while juvenile-to-juvenile sexting may come to be understood as part of adolescents' repertoire of sexual behaviors, this understanding should not be applied to sexting between teens and adults'.

The vast majority of focus group participants identified the age gap in the case of Damien Eades as too excessive; they had trouble understanding 'why an 18 year old would be texting 13 year old' (Female USyd FG2). Moral transgressions of adult-teen sexting were emphasised along the lines that young adults should not engage in (real-life or virtual) sexual exchanges with prepubescent or pubescent teenagers:

> [T]hinking an 18 year old approaching a 13 year old, you're thinking – you would say why do you think – like do you not have a life, you have your own age friends, why would you go for a 13 year old sort of thing. (Female, TAFE)

The power imbalance generated by the age difference, according to focus group participants, makes these cases similar to child sexual abuse. This was exemplified in one focus group when the mostly male cohort cheered loudly when a male in the group called Eades a 'paedo' (Male, TAFE).

The vulnerability of young people in their teenage years to such encounters was especially prominent in focus group discussions about the case. As one participant pointed out: 'That's quite a big difference. You're not talking about a 23 year old and a 28 year old because it's different in the next decade, like the five year gap' (Female, UWS FG1). According to focus group participants, like child sexual abuse, such transgressions in sexting should invoke a strong moral condemnation, as well as social and criminal accountability, with the adult being the wrongdoer in this scenario, someone who should know better:

> [The blame is on] him, she's only 13, she doesn't know anything in regard to adult [hood]– this is kind of an adult thing. (Female, USyd FG3)

As another participant commented:

> Even though in the transcript she quite clearly seems to be going along with it and on board there's still the degree of there's a five year age gap. He's older. I think he should have been the responsible and the sensible one. ... I think if you're both the same age it could get out of hand but you're both equally, well you'd think on a similar – you both understand what you're doing or you both have a similar grasp on what's happening. Whereas this age gap, yeah he should know that that's not on. (Male, UWS FG1)

The age difference was also associated by focus group participants with bullying and abuse of power (Kowalski et al. 2012). As an adult, Eades was expected to act maturely; his request for nude photos was a negation of that, for which he was perceived as solely responsible:

> I think the fact that he's 18. He is an adult. It's an abuse of power I think. (Male, UWS FG1)

> He did incite a person under 16 to commit an act of indecency. He was requesting the photos. It would have been a little bit different if she had just sent it without him asking for any. ... Well it's very obvious that he encouraged her, from this transcript whereas if he hadn't requested those photos then that would kind of mitigate his involvement in having child porn. (Female, UWS FG1)

This led many participants to conclude that he deserved to be punished:

> Yeah, I think he deserves ... the charge of indecency. ... I think it's an abuse of power. (Male, UWS FG1)

Similar to debates around rape and sexual assault (Ehrlich 2002), the issue of consent in sexting – or, more precisely, one's capacity to give consent – was identified as central in debating the moral and social appropriateness of sexting behaviour. Focus group participants acknowledged that in the Eades case there was no possibility for an underage person to actually give consent:

> [L]ike she's not mature enough I don't think. So she's consenting the action of it, but it's not consent. (Male, USyd FG4)

> Even if it's consensual – it's not really consensual at that age because psychologically their brain hasn't developed yet. There's an area of the brain called the pre-frontal cortex. That's to do with decision making and for children it hasn't developed yet so they're not able to connect what they're doing with the consequences. (Female, UWS FG1)

> It wasn't like a consensual relationship ... The massive age difference is just ridiculous. (Female, USyd FG4)

> [S]he was only 13, I know this sounds a bit belittling but she hardly knows what she wants or who she is, and she's obviously going to be coerced more easily by an 18 year old. (Female, USyd FG1)

In this way, for focus group participants, coercion was implied, rather than overt. Yet, while the majority of participants in focus groups negated that consent could be given, arguing that Eades was 'an idiot' who 'should have known she was underage' (Female, UWS FG3), they later acknowledged potential difficulties in establishing someone's age, especially if their acquaintance was recent:

> I think you ask the age after the relationship has already progressed. Oh by the way how old are you? That's how I find. You talk to people and then you're like – it wouldn't even cross my mind and after a while it will be like, 'How old are you?' but it's not the first thing you bring up in a conversation. You'd be like, 'How are you? What area do you live in?' but you don't really talk about age until after a while which can be a problem. (Female, UWS FG1)

Focus group participants also noted that identifying one's age might not be so straightforward in such situations as young people often do not tell the truth about how old they are:

> Yeah but you have to consider all factors, like she might have lied about her age. She could have told him that she was a lot older than what she was. (Female, UWS FG3)

> We cannot tell the age of the person just by looking at them. For young people in their 20s, 30s and particularly nearing their late teenage years, they all kind of look the same. People don't know that, they go oh wow, you've got great tits or nice ass or whatever, strong arms and whatnot, but you don't really know their age. People lie about their age every day. (Female, UWS FG2)

Regardless of these challenges, however, Eades' accountability was unquestioned by participants, as for them the young woman at the centre of the case would 'have to be a pretty mature looking 13 year old to be able to pass as even 16, the age of consent' (Male, UWS FG1).

When teen-to-teen sexts go 'viral': intimacy, trust and betrayal

Harmful consequences of sexting are especially highlighted in the context of non-consensual distribution of sexts (Walker et al. 2011; McLaughlin 2010; see also Chapter 6). The second case study presented to focus groups was the case of a man added to a sex offenders' registry for distributing two pictures of himself and his former girlfriend. The pictures depicted them having sex when they were both 17, but were distributed to friends after the break up, and after the teen turned 18. The girl found out and reported him to police. Although the pictures had been deleted, the man was charged one count of making child pornography and two counts transmitting child pornography online. He pleaded guilty, was fined $1000 without conviction and placed on good behaviour bond. However, his conviction put him on the sex offenders' registry for eight years (Brady 2012).

The key observation that emerged from focus groups debating this case was the lack of understanding many young people have with regards to sexting, both legally and socially. As one participant stated:

> I don't get why children are charged for child pornography. I thought the whole idea of child pornography was like children being exploited in this power play with an adult and maybe it was a teacher or an employer or something, but when it's like oh we were both 17, it was a pretty stupid thing to do it's not like he's exploiting a child, he was a child. (Female, USyd FG2)

While Eades' case was immediately linked to narratives around sexual predation and exploitation, the language that participants in focus groups used to describe the participants in this case study was dramatically different; they mostly talked about 'immature' (Male, TAFE) and 'intrusive' behaviour (Female, TAFE), not crime:

> It just seems to me for a teenager at 17 to be angry over a break up and then do something stupid is kind of normal. (Female, USyd FG4)

The age of those involved in sexting was again identified as an important starting point in debating sexting behaviour. As one focus group participant noted, in this case both actors 'were legally allowed to have sex' (Male, USyd FG4) removing many of the moral transgressions identified in Eades' case:

> There's no abuse of power. Well it is but at least she's an adult. It's not a child [photo] you're sending. (Female, UWS FG1)
>
> Yeah it wasn't as though it was illegal, it wasn't a pedophilia example because they were both the same age. (Female, USyd FG4)
>
> It's bad in a different way. The scenario of ... [consensual sexting of people same age with photos getting out], it doesn't seem malicious to me, just really inappropriate and ill thought out. (Female, UWS FG1)

I think the fact that they were 17 as well, I don't know you're not officially an adult but you're at that point where you are an adult, so you're able to make that consensual decision. (Female, USyd FG4)

Privacy violations when sexts go 'viral' and the breaking of trust that is supposedly the basis of intimate relationships has been comprehensively explored in the sexting literature (see, e.g., Arcabascio 2009–10; Walker et al. 2011). Focus group participants confirmed that such violations must be considered when debating moral and social wrongdoings of sexters:

[U]sually when you're in a relationship you don't think about you're going to break up, because you don't know what's going to happen. But you should think again and be like, yeah if you send those photos. (Female, TAFE)

I guess at the end of the day it's your choice for what you do, so say with a girlfriend and boyfriend, I guess she wants him to love her and all that stuff, and if the worst was to happen one day, I guess if the guy really did love her he wouldn't do it and you'd just pray that – I don't know. (Male, UWS FG3)

Participants argued that, though the sex was consensual, the girl in the case study did not consent to pictures being sent to others. Although they called the offender 'a creep' (Male, USyd FG2), focus group participants acknowledged the importance of the fact that he tried to get rid of the images and that the young woman was not identifiable in the photos. This led some in the focus groups to conclude that the harm caused by distribution of photos in this case was minimal, and that the wrongdoer redeemed himself by trying to rectify the consequences of his actions:

Yeah but he tried to get rid of it and it says that they're not identifiable in the image. And the things were deleted, they couldn't find the photo, all they had was him being honest and saying yeah I did this, and 15 years on the sex offender register. (Female, USyd FG4)

Similar to Eades' case, and paralleling feminist debates on pornography (Hayward 2012), young women's willing participation in creating sex tapes/sexts was scrutinised; as one male participant noted, they don't 'speak very highly of her character' (Male, USyd FG4):

If you send it to someone, you have to send it thinking this could get around. And if they send it, being stupid thinking no-one will ever see this then it's their fault but if it's unwillingly taken, like they're getting changed and someone takes a photo. (Female, UWS FG3)

If someone sends a naked photo around of someone I just think, no offence, but sucked in, you sent the photo. (Female, UWS, FG3)

If it was against your will. But if you fully did it and knew the consequences, it's your fault. (Female, UWS FG3)

Interestingly, the vulnerability of a female victim and the gender of an offender in mainstream sexting cases was also perceived as selective justice, with an 'ideal victim' and an 'ideal perpetrator' (Christie 1986) unmistakably outlined in criminal justice interventions:

> Yeah but shouldn't she have taken some responsibility at the same time for taking that action, knowing that he could have done anything with it? So I don't know, I think there's an unfair balance of responsibility here, that because he's the guy and she's vulnerable – I'm not saying she's not vulnerable, I'm saying there's this betrayal that because she's the woman she's the one that needs to be taken care of, whereas he's the one that needs to be punished. (Female, USyd, FG4)

> So you think if she was the one who sent the picture she wouldn't be charged? (Male, USyd, FG4)

> Not as severely at all. (Female, USyd FG4)

On punishment: who to penalise and how?

The age disparity between sexting parties and the power imbalance generated by such disparities guided focus group participants' thinking on appropriate punishment in the case of Damien Eades. An extreme response came from a small group of young people in two focus groups, who argued that Eades was a paedophile 'that could grow into a bit...It could scale up into something else' (Male, TAFE). This selection of focus group participants perceived Eades as a sexual 'predator' (Female, USyd FG2), regardless of the fact that the photo in question was not obtained by force or deception, and had not been distributed. For these focus group participants, the criminal justice response needed to be severe:

> This guy should have been treated so much more harshly than [the offender discussed in a second case study]. The age difference is such a massive thing. Thirteen is so young and what was he, 18? The girl was probably looking for attention – I don't know but she was so

young and then for him to be 18, he should have known better. (Female, USyd FG2)

However, a majority of participants acknowledged that, while some form of punishment was needed, Eades' behaviour did not warrant a prison sentence. Punishment was perceived as necessary in order to eliminate the risk of future transgressions and send a message to other potential offenders – to achieve both general and specific deterrence:

> Yeah but if you did charge this one person then other people that are doing are going to realise oh well, there is ways I can get caught, this is the punishment that I'm going to get. Do I really want to risk having a naked photo just so I can have it? (Female, UWS FG3)

> I think the fact that like he had to go to court and face a judge would have been a huge deal, and I think he probably – hopefully learned his lesson that way. I think if people get taken to that level, I think they're so scared out of their socks and they don't – I don't think – especially 18, they don't need to go to gaol necessarily, because I think even just having to go to court I reckon would scare them silly and that's sometimes enough. (Female, USyd FG3)

Yet, similar to educational campaigns that aim to deter young people from sexting (see Chapter 6), the outcome of such interventions is questionable. As Day (2010, p. 8) points out, '[a]lthough the threat of criminal sanctions is considered a strong deterrent, its deterrent effect on kids is minimal, if nil'. As we noted in Chapter 5, both the policy and academic literature on sexting identify harm caused to (mostly white, heterosexual, middle-class female) victims as one of key motivations for regulating sexting (see also Karaian 2012; Parker 2009; Wastler 2010). Likewise, some focus group participants maintained that appropriate punishment should depend on the consequences sexting had on the female victim (Female, UWS FG3). Arguing that the harm caused by Eades was negligible, a majority of focus group participants called for a non-custodial sentence. By claiming that 'if he gets some help hopefully he'll get straightened out' (Male, TAFE), they identified 'counselling or something [similar]' (Male, TAFE), community service (Male, USyd FG1; Female, UWS FG2) or restorative justice as more appropriate interventions in such cases:

> [S]tudies show that sort of therapeutic and restorative justice works better than throwing a person into prison, especially at a teenage age like that. (Male, UWS FG2)

It also shows how inflexible laws can be. For example these are really young people they're dealing with, if you send them to gaol or send them for prosecution you're basically ruining their lives and not giving them a chance. Perhaps maybe counselling and then putting them on probation and then probably checking them would be a better option, because they've not really had a chance to develop their personalities as such, so you can't really label them as sex offenders, that will just make the whole thing worse. (Female, USyd FG4)

Yeah the thing is now – he definitely would no doubt have a criminal record that's going to affect him for the rest of his life. It's going to affect his job, it's going to affect his ability to leave the country, it's going to affect all kinds of things in his life and over what, just an 18 year old getting horny [laughs]. (Male, UWS FG2)

Young people who send images and who are convicted of child pornography may – depending on the jurisdiction – find themselves placed on a sex offender's register (see also Ostrager 2010; Richards and Calvert 2009). This issue polarised the participants in discussing this case; some argued that participants should be added to a registry if they distribute or take images of someone else without their knowledge, or when the age difference is too excessive:

I think that's why the sex offender list is there because when you go look for a job or whatever you can't get one if you're on the sex offender list. (Female, UWS FG3)

I think it's only if it's unwillingly taken or .... (Female, UWS FG3)

Or spread around. Because if you ruin someone's life by spreading it, it's the same thing. (Female UWS FG3)

If you followed this sort of precedent in terms of real physical relations – like if an 18 year old guy asked a 13 year old girl to expose herself in front of him would that be seen as sexual harassment, even if he didn't touch her? So if we transfer that to like this digital medium, it doesn't seem as bad in the digital format but if it was in person it would be a lot worse, wouldn't it? Let's say they didn't touch each other at all – he's still an 18 year old and she's still under age. So it doesn't seem so bad. It seems like a very harsh thing for him to be termed as a sex offender but I think it fits the description. (Female, UWS FG1)

I'm not sure about in a circumstance like this. It is an abuse of power and those sort of things. I think putting [Eades] on a sex offender list might be a little bit extreme because there doesn't seem to be any malice behind it other than he's an idiot. It doesn't seem to be malicious in that he is trying to take advantage of her. Yeah, it seems a thing that needs to be taken case by case. (Male, UWS FG1)

The age difference was yet again identified as a key factor that must be taken into consideration when debating the penalty for sexting. When asked whether the punishment would be different in a scenario where participants are teenagers of a similar age, focus group participants indicated that if distribution of images does not occur, neither side should be punished (Female, UWS FG3). At the same time, while Eades was predominantly identified as the sole wrongdoer, several focus group participants indicated that the young girl in the case study should bear some responsibility as she 'was edging him on...she was reciprocating it...not trying to avoid him at all costs, even though of course she was under 16' (Male, UWS FG2):

[S]he's an idiot, she should be charged as well because she was 'Yeah, I'll send you it', blah, blah, blah. So it's not just his fault I think she should take part of the blame. (Female, UWS FG3)

But at the same time she sent the photo herself, it's not like he forced her, so I suppose there's two ways of looking at it. (Female, USyd FG1)

I think he's more at fault, but I don't think she's completely off the hook. Obviously 13 is not a full mature adult by any means, but he didn't go spread it round or anything, it got to his phone, but he's still the instigator. So I think he's at fault. (Male, USyd FG3)

Similar to findings by Ringrose et al. (2013), and educational sexting campaigns outlined in this book, the inherent responsibility for sexting is located within the body in the image, rather than in the act of pressure to sext. The consequences for violation of 'age appropriate' sexual expression (Ringrose et al. 2013) in the case of Damien Eades, as suggested by one female focus group participant, could be criminal charges against the young woman in question. A more common standpoint, however, was that she should participate in education programs that would teach her that girls of her age should not engage in sexting with adults:

I think it's just the father being outraged, his little girl 13 years old sending nude pictures, it can't be her fault, it must be the boy's fault.

I think the fault lies at both. The girl needs to be taught better, don't send nude pictures of yourself, especially he's 18. (Female, UWS FG2)

The young woman's age was, nevertheless, considered a mitigating factor as she 'might not have known that it's illegal because she's so young. It might have just been the fact that she wanted to be cool' (Female, UWS FG3). In this context, some female participants identified the notion of young girls exploring their sexuality via sexting as important when discussing the case. Sexual awakening and a changing notion of privacy for Generation Y (highlighted in Chapter 9) are identified as potential drivers behind sexting behaviour, especially for young girls:

I guess you can see both sides. Like you wouldn't know what that 13 year old would be thinking at that age, because she's young, she's probably exploring how the older people are. Some younger girls do like older [guys]. I don't know, you don't know what they've been through, what they're experiencing at that time, then you think okay this 18 year old has the opening of a 13 year old approaching him and stuff. So it's not every day you see a 13 year old sending nudes to an 18 year old. In this generation now you think it's normal because the younger generation like 13 and 14 year olds are open to the older guys and stuff like that. (Female, TAFE)

While policymakers argue that the rationale for criminal sanctions in sexting are in the best interests of young people and society (Angelides 2013), charging young people for child pornography in this case was seen as unwarranted and overly punitive. Participants noted that such interventions created harm rather than protecting the vulnerable, which was the supposed intention of policymakers. The 'ticking the boxes' approach was not seen to acknowledge the context in which sexting practices occur, nor the impact of placing an offender on a sex offenders' registry, something heavily criticised by focus group participants. As Corbett (cited in McLaughlin 2010, p. 169) argues, a balance between punishment and sensibility needs to be attained. In the second case study, participants held that the registry was an extreme penalty for a behaviour that occurred a long time ago, when participants were teenagers:

But if you were talking about this person's name is on the sex offender list, you would not likely think that was the case. You would likely think he was having sex with a 14 year old girl or something, very recently. You wouldn't think that that was the case, that that's what he was going to be punished for, so there's that stigma which doesn't actually match what he did by any means. (Female, USyd FG4)

I think the fact that if two consenting under 16 year olds are engaging in sex or sexting or whatever, I find the fact that one of them can be put on the sex register completely wrong. (Male, UWS FG2)

It seems like the law was pretty insensitive in that case, like that he would be treated the exact same as a man who took a picture or used a picture of a six year old being raped or something, that would be probably a similar consequence and yet they were 17. I don't know if it should have been treated as a child porno case. (Female, USyd FG2)

It seems like with these cases, in law it seems – like to prosecute something you have to prosecute them with something, and this case the guy is like I agree I did the wrong thing, and I don't know about sex offender, but something. But the law kind of has to put in within a framework, if you tick X amount of boxes then you're a sex offender and if you've broken the law in that respect then you're a sex offender. You need the law to be that stringent and that set in stone so people can't get out of it, but it's annoying because it doesn't appreciate the complexities of the situations, it just kind of labels him. If any company sees, oh sex offender, they're not going to think he just posted a pic of him and his girlfriend having sex, they're going to think child pornography, child molester, rapist, and that's a whole lot worse than two 17 year olds. (Male, USyd FG4)

The impact of placing an offender on a sex offenders' registry was assessed as both disproportionate and permanent (Richards and Calvert 2009):

He's on the sex offender list now. He can't work as a teacher, he can't work with children, he can't do anything. His whole career is gone. His whole life is screwed up because of one thing he did when he was... His name's in the sex offender list which is where rapists are as well. You can't work with children. You can't live near children. You can't live near a school. So much consequences and people don't even know that. (Female, UWS FG1)

Dissenting voices among focus group participants were rare when it came to entry onto a sex offenders' registry as the consequence of sexting in this case. One male participant, however, was vocal in expressing his disapproval of such behaviour and thought that the punishment was appropriate. Such punishment, he argued, would be a warning sign that future sexters would not be able to ignore:

Think about sex offence, it's like some type of sex, act of sex which offended someone. He offended the girl pretty brutally in my opinion by sending out naked pictures of her. I think he should be a sex offender, I don't know about for 15 years, but I think his initial punishment was fair....I mean it's a pretty tough punishment, but one way to solve it, just don't do the act. I mean it shows that this guy makes rash decisions, pretty harsh ones. I wouldn't want him to work for me...He sent out naked pictures of him having sex with a girl, that's pretty incriminating in my view. (Male, USyd FG4)

Conclusion: rethinking criminal justice interventions

Two decades ago, Catharine MacKinnon (1993, p. 36) argued that 'sex pictures [should be] legally considered as sex acts' that harm the children in the pictures. However, it must also be considered in sexting cases between young people that criminal justice intervention might be equally, if not more, harmful for young people than the production and distribution of images. While legal scholars and criminologists alike have been debating criminal justice responses to sexting for some time (see McLaughlin 2010), there is a notable absence of young people's voices in the debate.

As Heath et al. (2009) noted, understanding sexting from the perspective of young people is essential if we wish to develop criminal justice and other strategies that prevent the potential harm generated by sexting practices. What emerged from the focus groups was that young people rejected a 'one-size–fits-all' criminal justice approach to sexting, instead, calling for more nuanced understandings of sexting practices. They drew our attention to the importance of participants' ages and issues around consent, highlighting that adult-teen sexting requires both moral and social condemnation, accountability of adults in question and appropriate criminal justice interventions. Focus group participants also called for more refined interpretations of gender in sexting, in terms of (mostly female) victims and (mostly male) offenders, responsibilisation of female victims, and the role sexting plays in exploring female sexuality.

Young people also believed that criminal justice responses were inappropriate, with the law trailing technological advancements in communication. Struggling to catch up with social media and new technologies, those applying the law simply translate old rules onto new 'crimes':

[A criminal justice response in Damian Eades' case] is just entirely disproportionate. I think the issue is that because of the internet and social media and stuff like that, it's such a recent phenomenon that existing laws still haven't been able to adapt to put them. So using standards for pre-existing laws that you can't apply to this huge new phenomena [sic]. ... But they're suggesting that it could be a friendly relationship, and I mean common sense, no-one would actually think that based on the technicalities, and I think it's just because laws still haven't been able to adapt to the new technology. You can put them in a framework but it's impossible to make them accurate to what is done because it doesn't exist yet. (Female, USyd FG4)

In addition to setbacks embedded in the legal system, a combination of media hype and demands for authorities to create precedents was identified as an underpinning force behind harsh and disproportionate punishments applied in case studies discussed in the focus groups. Similar to findings by Podlas (2011), focus group participants linked media hype about teenage sexuality and/or vulnerability and 'legislative outbreaks' on sexting:

Yeah if you look at the dates, the first one was 2010 ... I don't know when all this media hype started, but I think it was more like 2011, and it seems like the first one he read, he was more of an example of the law and it was too harsh. (Male, USyd FG4)

But it's hard to regulate and it's hard to get these cases out, so when something does come up they obviously want to make an example of it and how serious it is, so they go hard on them. (Female, USyd FG2)

Importantly, most young people held that locating teen sexting within child pornography offences was exaggerated and unnecessary (even in the case of Damien Eades). Focus group participants called for improved balance between punishment and sensibility, while identifying distributing pictures as a greater infringement of rights than receiving or inciting people to send pictures (unless there is a significant age difference, such as in Damien Eades' case). The notion of harm caused to victims was identified as a crucial factor that needed to be considered in administering criminal justice interventions (Richards and Calvert 2009). Punishment, including placing offenders on a sex offender registry – an extreme penalty with lasting consequences – needed to be appropriate to the harm caused to victims of sexting transgressions. Finally, focus group participants held that non-custodial, less retributive criminal justice mechanisms needed to be deployed in sexting cases.

The following chapter draws together and analyses the findings of the survey and focus groups. In this chapter we piece together the complex socio-legal tapestry that situates sexting, and we deconstruct and analyse the various elements and meanings of sexting, as per our research findings.

11
Making Sense of Sexting

Introduction

> There is no blanket explanation as to why all these young people are sending nude pictures of themselves to each other. (Female, UWS FG2)

Taking our qualitative and quantitative evidence together, we can identify many contradictions, qualifications and conflicted meanings around the perceptions and motivations of sexting for young people. It is clear that in public discourse, as demonstrated by our media analysis, and in legal discourse, sexting behaviours have provided a significant challenge to existing normative moral and legal frameworks, and to the capacity of the criminal law to deal with this emerging phenomenon. This chapter begins with an analysis of our empirical research data in order to better understand the perceptions and motivations of sexting, before moving on to discuss how this situates sexting within contemporary legal and media discourses.

Lives online: the private becomes public

> But if you disconnect now, you are so out of the loop. Like I have a friend who isn't on Facebook and she's fallen off the face of the planet. We don't know what she's doing, I had to go to her house and be like hey, and she's like yeah I'm working now I don't go to uni. I'm like what? I don't know this because you're not on Facebook. (Female, USYD – FG3)

One prominent theme to emerge from the focus group research is that of how to negotiate what we might see of the collapse or blurring of the public and private spheres of life. As our research confirms young people increasingly live their lives online, but they are aware of the risks this brings to their identity and privacy. This has particular implications for the creation, maintenance and the nature of social and intimate relationships. While they may have different perceptions of identity and privacy from earlier generations, they still report a need and desire to retain a private self. This means care has to be taken to clearly establish the impact of new technologies on the lives of young people and not overstate or simply assume a complete disjuncture between young people today and previous generations.

It has long been argued that technologies – not just the internet or social media – have seen a merging of the public and private worlds. Indeed, the diminishment of an almost fabled public sphere as a space for active democratic action was noted decades ago by Habermas (1989). Habermas suggested that the public sphere of communicative action, once the realm where publicity was about submitting political action and activity to critical scrutiny, had been invaded by private interest groups undermining its democratic potential. While Habermas's idealised version of a public sphere has long been criticised by feminists (Frazer 1990), postmodernists (Deleuze and Guatarri 1972), and others, much less attention was given to the changing nature of the private sphere. Richard Sennett (1977) foresaw the kinds of changes facilitated by social media when he suggested a new 'tyranny of intimacy' was developing where the 'fall of public man' indicative of political consciousness and democratic rhetoric of a public sphere gives way to the publicity of private lives. Deleuze and Guatarri (1972) also noted the way in which the traditional split between public and private has been challenged by late capitalism, producing a supersaturated space of immediate presence and media scrutiny, with no better example than social media. As our research respondents indicated, negotiating this supersaturated space is an ongoing and dynamic process that entails balancing expectations of a public social media identity with potential risks (both dangerous and pleasurable).

> If you think about it, it's the same as being in a public situation with a group of friends. You make sure that you don't say something that's going to offend anybody, it's the same online. Although sometimes I worry when you personal message people, people can print that stuff out and all that sort of stuff... That sometimes worries me, but that's not the system, that's the people. (Female, USYD FG1)

With the advent of social media and digital technology, the split between public and private has blurred even further. According to

Boyd (2007, p. 3), the 'internet lacks walls'. Social media is an obvious example of how this blurring has occurred, with private selves being formed and performed through publicity – 'a networked public' (Boyd 2007). Facebook, for example, turns the private outwards for reaffirmation though self-subjectification in a networked public sphere – the dramaturgy of once private selves seeking public affirmation – a publicity. Sennett would no doubt see the ubiquity of the 'like' function on Facebook replacing the theatre of the public realm. In this sense, online normative behaviours form through mutual reinforcement; approval from 'friends' produces, and indeed places limits upon, subject formation.

As our survey indicated, almost all young people use some form of social media; 98.4 per cent of our respondents have a social media profile. Many of these young people live their private lives in public. As focus groups respondents noted, so much drama happens online; relationships are made and unmade on social media – 'put it on Facebook then it's official' (Male, USyd FG3). Selfhood is thus constituted through social media, and social media representations come to constitute truths about users. Constructing selfhood via social media is inherently risky because when private lives occur in public, 'publicity' (negative and positive) is only a mouse click away:

> I think with our age group too everything is so accessible, what is one click away you can find out anything you want. You can find out if they're single, you can find out what school they go to. (Female USYD FG2)

Our focus group participants noted the double-edged nature of this engagement with social media. A key theme to emerge from the data was that of the negotiation of online identity and its mundane, 'casualised' use. Young people identified the risk of the digital footprint they may leave and the possible future harm(s) that could occur. As their private lives leak into the public realm, most take some measures to guard against the possible embarrassment of publicised private moments going viral. As Boyd notes:

> The inherent replicability of bits and the power of search make most walls temporary at best. This is why most participants in networked publics live by 'security through obscurity' where they assume that as long as no one cares about them, no one will come knocking. While this works for most, this puts all oppressed and controlled populations (including teenagers) at risk because it just takes one motivated

explorer to track down even the most obscure networked public presence, (2007, pp. 3–4)

This 'security by obscurity' at its most banal is illustrated in the recent distribution of celebrity nude images through the hacking of cloud computing platforms such as iCloud, where being famous is the key to the currency of the image. Media reports indicated that such celebrity nudes were selling as encrypted files for as much as $350 per image (D'Amato 2014). This episode not only illustrates the relative ease with which images thought to be secure can be circulated, but it also confirms the value of certain people's images, and types of images, over others. However, this value is also contextual. As Boyd suggests in the quote above, the veil of obscurity can easily be lifted in a context where the subject is under scrutiny or some other form of observation. A number of our focus group respondents noted the ease with which information on individuals can be gathered:

> I used to be an internet researcher, and my job was pretty much to find people's information on Facebook and send it to other people. ...So you message this number, ask someone's name and within a few minutes they write back and say so and so lives at, these guy friends...people think it's amazing, they think it's some sort of tracking machine or something. It's actually not, it's heaps of internet researchers researching people on Facebook, and all their Facebook friends. (Female, USYD FG3)

Experimentation with sexuality has always been a part of coming of age. It is therefore unsurprising given the uptake of new technologies by young people, that the performance of private selves in public can also become sexualised. Our focus group respondents confirmed that even expressions of sexuality, often assumed to be a relatively private practice, may also be publicised via social media.

This is not of course limited to young people. As we have argued, adults use sexting as a way of adding excitement, risk and variety into their sex lives. For young people growing up with their online selves being such an important part of their identities, sending a sexy image to a romantic interest is not necessarily a great departure from their normal online activities. Moreover, if we follow the logic of the analysis above, the sexualisation of the online self is presumably reinforced as a norm for many young people through the number of 'likes' received from their networked friends. 'Breasty' images of young women, and young men with 'six-pack' abs, reflections of celebrity success, become markers of successful selfhood, liable to attract numerous 'likes'. As our focus group respondents put it:

> You need to be ripped, that's all you...like how many boys go to the gym now? Like all my friends go to the gym but they never used to before. (Male, USYD FG3)

As such, specific normative expressions of selfhood are thought to be attractive to prospective partners and in the eyes of peers, and these are often reflections of portrayals of masculinity and femininity on a range of media platforms:

> I think it's just what pop culture can sometimes do. It's like the media always seems to promote that you've got to wear short skirts and you've got to have half your cleavage on display and stuff. For example with Delta's costume on *The Voice*, how it's got cleavage all the way down here. (Female UWS FG2)

Risky information about sexting

As our survey indicated, most young people first heard about sexting type practices through friends or the media. This is not surprising given the media saturation of the practice as demonstrated in the media analysis in Chapter 3. Importantly too, more than 10 per cent of survey respondents first heard of the practice through schoolteachers, and the focus groups spoke with familiarity of the discourses of sexting that they had heard in school education campaigns. Many of the cautionary tales recited by focus group participants were reminiscent of the current generation of educational campaigns aimed at reducing sexting behaviour by demonstrating the negative outcomes such practices can have – especially for young women (see Chapter 6). It was clear that many young people had been party to an enormous amount of information about sexting. Even taking into account the explosion in media reporting of sexting over the past five years (see Chapter 3), sexting has become part of everyday discourse. It has, in a sense, been normalised.

This everyday discourse around sexting is framed primarily around risk. However, risk in this sense also has two very different elements. On the one hand, in the adult world, sexting is constructed as an exciting romantic activity, albeit risky and risqué, where consumers are given advice on how to engage in 'sexy pre-play', as exemplified in the popular women's magazine *Cosmopolitan* (Nagi 2011). Indeed, adults can find tips on sexy texting in any number of mainstream lifestyle magazines, on websites, or though social media. In this sense, teen sexting is simply a subterranean expression of mainstream adult values (Matza and Sykes 1961; O'Malley 2010). Risk-taking has thus become more acceptable in the contemporary period where leisure industries and leisure activities – even gambling – have become governmentally sanctioned. Taking risks is seen as exciting and is encouraged.

On the other hand, adolescent sexting poses a negative risk that is framed as problematic for young people by policymakers, educators, parents and other 'adult' figures. This negative risk model also has multiple modalities. Under a largely public health model discourse, sexting is coupled with a range of negative practices, most specifically with underage sexual activities (e.g., Dake et al. 2013). Conversely, education campaigns focus more on the negative consequences to young people's reputation and damage to future prospects. Yet for young people, sexting is truly a 'risk-taking' activity in both respects. Most understand the negative risks but many revel in the excitement of such risk. Indeed, sexting could be seen as a form of resistance, a rejection of control, even a celebration of the carnivalesque: '[a] refusal to conform with a liberal utilitarian discipline imposed by the respectable middle classes' (O'Malley 2010, p. 53). To use Lyng's term, sexting can be a form of 'edgework' (2005), a way of bringing risky excitement into otherwise relatively mundane lives. Several of our focus group respondents noted that sexting was the result of boredom, for example: 'I think people just do it when they get bored' (Female, USYD FG1) and 'It's just a boredom kind of thing' (Female, USYD FG3). Others noted that it may be exciting within a relationship: 'in the context of a relationship it could be just a sex thing, be sexually thrilling to do' (Male USYD FG2).

Much sociological research has documented the social pressure for conformity among peers, as well as the pleasure of experimenting with risks, which underpin risk-taking behaviour (Lupton 1999). While as our focus group respondents indicate some risks need to be avoided, risk-taking is also a key developmental process through which we can learn coping mechanisms, independence, and individual responsibility (Coleman and Hendry 1999). Yet the focus of public attention (and inter-vention) around childhood sexuality has been on taming the risk-taking behaviour of young people. Such a focus also obscures 'risk-imposing' factors for young people (Ratcliffe et al. 1984), such as poverty, aliena-tion, peer pressure, or the corporate promotion of unhealthy products and lifestyles. That is, the focus and panic about young people's online activities can serve to divert our attention from more pressing issues of which negative risk taking may just be a by-product.

There is also a clear paradox in the regulation and legislation that has sought to govern and repress sexting by young people. The over-criminalisation of the activity has, as is obvious given the proliferating discussion about the practice in popular culture, incited the practice further into public discourse – with more of our respondents having heard of the practice though the media. This 'mainstreaming' allows sexting to be considered something of a legitimate activity – and so it is for adults. As Fishman (1982) noted in his history of childhood sexuality, moral concern of theologians, and other moral crusaders in the 19th century to repress childhood masturbation, may have had similarly perverse or paradoxical outcomes:

> Children whose hands and minds were so zealously guarded, may have searched more ardently for covert time and space to indulge their sexual impulses. The conspiracy of adults and their institutions to prohibit child sexuality may even have produced unusual examples of sexual precocity and prowess. Obsessive efforts to control behaviour often beget determined and ingenious violators. (1982, pp. 278–9)

As such, the desire to suppress teenage sexting has in fact led to a proliferation of discourse around the practice, as it is increasingly rendered a risk-taking pleasure or leisure activity. As Foucault might put it in a different context, the attempt at suppression of this particular sexual practice has resulted in the production of a new pleasurable activity with an equally pleasurable nomenclature – sexting can thus induce 'perpetual spirals of power and pleasure' (Foucault 1990, p. 45).

Prevalence and practice

Our survey provides strong evidence of the ubiquitous nature of sexting: 38 per cent of young people between 13 and 15 and 50 per cent of those between 16 and 18 surveyed reported having sent a sexual image of themselves. Even accounting for the fact that our survey may have over-sampled those actively engaged in sexting, these figures suggest that sending and receiving sexual images is not a marginal activity. However, these prevalence figures tell us little about motivations or actual practices. Indeed, as discussed in Chapter 8 they may well obscure the reality of the way in which young people sext and may even be misleading in terms of prevalence. There is, for example, a vast difference in terms of risk and motivation between those who have sent sexts to only one person in their life or in the past 12 months (as was the case with many of our respondents), those who have sent numerous sexts to multiple partners, and those who might use sexting as a form of cyberbullying.

While large numbers of young people have sent and received sexts, our evidence suggests the majority do not do it often and generally send to only a few partners. So while sexting may have become a somewhat accepted way of expressing sexual selfhood, it is not a practice that most young people necessarily take lightly, or partake in with multiple partners. In fact, the majority of young people who had sent a sext reported sexting with only one partner or not at all in the previous 12 months. Moreover, most who reported having sent a sext had been in a relationship at the time they sent the image. So, although social media may be loaded with publicly accessible images of young people in somewhat sexualised poses, we should be wary of jumping to the conclusion that sexting is a simple extension of these public expressions of sexual selfhood. Rather, most (but certainly not all) sexting by young people appears to be specifically targeted, and is very much an expression of life in the private sphere – even while there is the real risk that it could be publicised. Sexting practice is for the most part not a public expression of selfhood, but much more a traditionally private one that sometimes finds its way into the public sphere. As these two female respondents put it:

> F1: That's true, but it's meant to be private, even though it may be in a text message it's meant for that person it's not meant for everyone.
>
> F2: But you do it with such a public medium.
>
> F1: Exactly that's why it's so risky. (USYD FG1)

In this way, private exchanges occur through public networks, where risk is inherent.

One way in which we might understand the normalised nature of sexting is to explore the most prolific demographic group of sexters. While our sample of those identifying as gay men was small, 81 per cent of these respondents across the age groups (including adults) reported sending a sexy image. The ubiquitous nature of the practice through apps such as Grindr, Scruff and numerous other online dating and 'hook up' platforms often sees a sexual image as the first contact between gay sexting partners (Gudelunas 2012). This practice among gay men undermines a notion that sexting is a hetero-normative activity reflective of only gendered power relations. Rather, it suggests the power relations involved, from the socio-cultural to the biographical, are much more multifaceted. Nonetheless, it also suggests the commodification of self-made pornographic images is widespread and that men, even gay men, may need to conform to different standards in terms of the gendered expectations that sees women's involvement in sexting much more negatively than men's.

Perceptions of sexting

This gendered double standard comes into stark relief when we turn to our data on perceptions of sexting by young people. On one level our focus group respondents identified that young females whose sexting practices became public were likely to be judged more negatively than young males. As this respondent clearly demonstrates:

> I don't know why it's always girls that get looked down on. If a girl sends a nude picture of herself, of say her breasts to her boyfriend, with both parties consenting and they break up and the boyfriend releases that picture online or something along the lines, the girl is seen as attention whoring. (Female UWS FG2)

And another notes:

> Well he sent it to his mate so it's a sense of pride. That's what I said before in the society we live in, it's sort of that women are seen as different to men in the sexual aspect when it come to things like this. So women are victimised, where men see it as pride. (Male USYD FG1)

One young male confirmed that if an image of him went public, there would likely be very few negative ramification compared to if he were a young women:

> Yeah but I don't think it would be a massive issue, it would be like oh there's [me], sans clothes. And then everyone forgets about it a fortnight later. (Male USYD FG2)

Indeed, young women suggested that if they were to send photos on to third parties this would not only have few negative ramifications for most young men, but that it may even boost their egos and their status:

> To me if you sent things from the guys that would sort of boost their ego somehow, I've got that mentality that they'd go oh well now all these girls have seen kind of thing, and I feel like that wouldn't achieve anything. That's not revenge, that's just helping. (Female USYD FG1)

But such double standards cut both ways. Thus while they may serve to normalise sexual exploration by young males they can also operate to deny young women agency to explore their sexuality:

> Yeah definitely, I think it's because growing up you always hear boys are obsessed with sex and girls aren't supposed to be as sexual, boys think about sex every 30 seconds, which is not really true. Girls are just as sexual as boys are, but for some reason our culture, boys are thought to be more sexual, kind of like the boys are just being boys and the girls it's like why are you so sexual, it's almost taboo. (Female USYD FG1)

As noted in Chapter 8, when our entire pool of respondents were asked about why they thought young women send sexts, they suggested it was to show off, or because of pressure, or to get a person to like them. In contrast, the same pool of respondents judged young men's behaviour quite differently. For boys, the perception was that sexting was about being noticed and showing off and getting attention. Specifically, there was a tendency not only to judge young women's behaviour more negatively, but also to suggest a lack of agency on the part of young women. That is, while boys were seen as active sexting participants, girls were constructed as reluctant participants; often lacking self-esteem and/or driven by a desire for a better self-image. This is perhaps best illustrated by those focus group participants who had the self-awareness to suggest they were buying into the discourse themselves. As this focus group respondent commented in relation to her response to a sexting incident at her school:

> That's what happened to that girl in my high school it went viral. I felt bad for her. But you see it and the first thing I thought was oh she's a slut whatever, then I realised I did the same thing I was talking about. Now I've realised that must have been so embarrassing, terrible. (Female USYD FG2)

Thus, while focus group respondents were able to clearly identify a gendered double standard in relations to girls who sexted, they were unable to easily break from either the discourse of the double standard, or the reality that young women would be judged differently, and so should act more prudently.

In contrast to general perceptions of why young people sext, those who have actually sent an image of themselves reported very different motivations. Our motivation data indicated that most sent an image to be 'fun and flirtatious', or to give a 'sexy present'. Indeed, pressure was rarely expressed as a motivation for sexting by those who had sent an image or video.

Understanding motivations

> [F]or a woman it's this really personal thing to reveal herself to a man in this private setting and on that basis of that devotion, yes you can have it, it's like a gift. (Female, USyd FG1)

One clear theme from both the focus group and survey data was that sexting constituted a type of gift giving. Senders of images reported in the survey that such images were very often 'sexy presents' for boyfriends or girlfriends. Meanwhile, focus group participants also suggested the intimate nature of such images often constituted (particularly for young women) the gifting of something quite special to a trusted intimate – as the quote above illustrates.

As discussed in Chapter 2, Marcel Mauss (1990) dealt specifically with the nature of gifting and gift economies. A gift, according to Mauss, is not simply an object, but a part of oneself because 'the objects are never completely separated from the men [or women] who exchange them' (1990, p. 31). Sending an image of oneself might then on the face of it be a clear example of gifting – giving something intimate of the self. There is much to say here about the idea of the image. Images are not static or fixed in meaning. They are context specific, and open to alterative readings and interpretations. But sexts are also images of subjects. Sexting is usually a self-subjectification; the images are literally of the self ('selfies'), providing interpretations of the self, with the purpose of particular decoding by the receiver (Hall 1980). For example an image sent to an intimate can be read as a romantic and sexy present. Yet, this same image when forwarded to unintended parties may be read (or decoded) very differently; it may be seen as pornographic, embarrassing, exploitative, or even trivial. This is why, as we argue below, such images can have divergent meanings in different configurations of the gift economy.

Gender

As we have seen, some researchers have concluded that girls feel pressure or coercion to sext. But the self-image of young women that completed our survey does not suggest this: As we saw, very few actually reported being pressured. Another – potentially more fruitful – way of understanding sexting starts with Mauss' notion that there is always some pressure to gift. As Mauss puts it, 'one must give, there is an obligation to give' (1990, p. 41). In the case of sexting this might mean, given that young people today live digital online lives, that once they become romantically active there is a general pressure to gift a romantic partner. Here it is important to remember that most active senders of images in our study sent images while in some form of relationship. Sexting is a very easy way for young people in a romantic relationship to gift – particularly in the context of their online lives. This general pressure may see them produce and send a sexual photo of themselves to a romantic interest. Of course the various (often gendered) biographical, peer and social pressures discussed in Chapter 2 are likely to intersect with the general pressure to gift, so no two examples of sexting will necessarily follow identical dynamics. As one of our focus group respondents suggested:

> A lot of guys see young girls as very easy to get things out of, and of course they're naïve so they trust you. Like wow, he's willing to give this to me and I'll give it to him, it's this romantic exchange. (Female USYD FG2)

So such romantic exchanges can have vastly differing dynamics and as the following focus group interaction indicates, there is debate around just where any pressure comes from:

> M1: I think the pressure is inner-built pressure, if a girl's going to want to send a photo she's going to do it because she feels he really wants it, like she wants to be liked by him or approved by him, almost looking of his satisfaction. I don't know how to put it, I don't think it's necessarily a cultural thing, it's more like individual pressure.
>
> F1: To make sure the boyfriend's happy so he stays with you.
>
> M2: That kind of pressure.
>
> F2: I think there's pressure. I think especially if you're younger, if a boy can get 10 pics of topless girls then he's going to be popular, he'll be cool or whatever, and I think there's some pressure there.

Previous research has also noted how images of young women can be collected and exchanged between young men (Ringrose et al. 2013) – as indicated in the above exchange. Our research also finds evidence of this. As one female focus group respondent put it: 'Yeah, I know these guys who have like a folder of naked photos' (UWS FG3). This could be seen to support Irigaray's (1985, p. 170) position that the reproduction of patriarchal society 'is based on the exchange of women'. We are not suggesting that sexting is always produced or reproduced by structured gendered relations as Irigaray might, although it can be in particular circumstances. Rather, the power relations between sexting participants is much more complex and multifaceted than this. These image-gifts have a value not just between sender and receiver, but also between peers and beyond. This has potentially important implications in terms of the ways in which images can be circulated beyond the original sender and intended receiver but still be part of a broader gift economy.

Thus, the idea of gifting provides an analytical tool for understanding the range of behaviours that tend to be classified as sexting – from those we might consider as agentive, to others we see as pressured or coercive; from those where young girls experience some sense of sexual empowerment in giving and receiving a gift, to those where the subject of the photo is objectified as a pure gift and whose image becomes a commodity in a gift economy which bolsters the social status of others (usually, but not always, boys or men).

As Pyyhtinen (2014, p. 110) suggests, 'women are not merely objects being circulated, they also have a more active and autonomous role'. He notes that, in contemporary Western societies overall, 'women are more active givers than men' (Pyyhtinen 2014, p. 110) in that women often purchase, choose and wrap gifts. This need not suggest full agency on the part of the giver and, even where the practice may be seen as agentive, it is never completely so. And, as with giving in the market economy more generally, as all the large-scale surveys on sexting indicate, more young women send more images and videos than young men (although in the case of our survey this difference was not statistically significant).

If we accept that, in this gift economy, images of young women generally have more currency, we might expect an excess of young women producing and sending images of themselves. But to understand the dynamics, we must look more closely at the way in which status relates to gift giving and also intersects with gender.

Status

According to Jacques Derrida (1995), no gift is ever given completely freely or altruistically (indeed, such a pure gift is an impossibility); the gift has inscribed within it not only an expectation of some form of reciprocation (which actually annuls the idea of pure gift) – discussed below, and also effectively suggested by Mauss – but also the self-gratification and enhancement of the sender. It is an exercise in power.

According to our data, the most popular motivation for sexting was that sexting is 'fun and flirtatious'. Being 'fun and flirtatious' not only aligns the sender with a set of positive normative expectations, but also becomes a mark of individual self-empowerment – the sender is 'fun'. The second most common reason young women sent was 'as a sexy present'. So, in this scenario, who is sexy? It is as much for the sender (whose self-image is affirmed as sexy when the gift is acknowledged) as for the receiver. Potentially this is about the sender's status enhancement, although there are caveats as we will see. The third most popular motivation for young women was 'to feel sexy and confident'. Here the gift is almost completely motivated by self-enhancement. Although this 'self-image' may be a particularly sexualised one already based on the social construction of young women as sexualised objects.

This gift economy analysis holds not just for consensual senders, but for those who send images of others without consent, or who forward images on to third parties. The gift of sending is one aimed at the status enhancement of the on-sender in front of their peer group. This explains why there is an inclination to on-send or show images in some instances. But young women send images not only to young men; they also gift other young women in their peer group – to look 'hot' in front of (not for) other female peers. Keep in mind, the third most common reason young women sent images was 'to feel sexy and confident'. This is not just about confidence in relation to the self, but confidence and status within a peer group. Of course young men engage in similar activities, sending semi-naked images amongst friends either as 'jokes' or to demonstrate a particular form of masculinity. Again, this is all about the status of the sender.

However, as Mauss points out in relation to the giving of gifts in traditional societies, how the gift is *received* – and whether it will be reciprocated – also depends on the status of the giver.

Receiving

The second most common reason young men send sexts is that they have received one. As this male focus group respondent noted:

> If I have a girlfriend, I feel there's more pressure, a girl can be like oh if I did this you should do this for me, they have a reason for it

because it's your significant other. I don't think guys are just randomly sending – at least from my experience. (Male USYD FG3)

Again, Mauss' model seems to account for this. He notes that, as you accept a gift, you take 'a gift on the back' (1990, p. 40). The receiver is obligated to prove himself or herself worthy through some form of reciprocation. Because of this relationship between giver and gift, the act of giving creates a social bond with an obligation to reciprocate on the part of the recipient. To not reciprocate would be to lose honour or status. However, this obligation to reciprocate can also be overridden or ignored if the sender lacks status. So reciprocation is not assured.

As we have outlined, one particularly problematic element of sexting is when the receiver of an image passes the image on without consent. But here again the image operates as a gift enhancing the status of the secondary sender among peers, creating an obligation in these peers to reciprocate at some point – for example, a pressure on young men to engage in this gift economy by reciprocating and sending another girl's image back to a friend. This is a relatively neglected element of the current scholarship on the topic: any real analysis of the masculine codes that might pressure young men to sext.

On-sending also potentially undermines the status of the original sender, which from a Maussian point of view might not have been powerful enough to gift in the first place. There is a potential gendered double standard here as well where, not only is the image of a young women worth more in this gift economy, but a young woman's status is more fragile than a young man's. However, it is not a given that on-sending will diminish the status of the original sender; it is also possible that on-sending can bolster the status of the original sender. How this is experienced will depend on the status of the original sender and how the image is subsequently decoded. A 'hot' young woman's reputation may be enhanced by on-sending, but a young man pictured with a small penis might be humiliated. These spirals of power and pleasure, to quote Foucault (1990), are complex.

What all this suggests is that for young people today who live their lives online there will be a general pressure to engage in sexting as part of a romantic attachment – for both young men and women. This pressure is general, but will have gendered characteristics and link into broader gendered social relationships. However, status will also have a role to play – perhaps a more important one. For example, the way in which a young man's sexualised image is read among his peers (and by young women) will depend on his status – and this may well in turn depend on physical characteristics. He may be celebrated or humiliated depending on this, as might a young woman – but gender may not always be a key predictor. That is, status may be more important.

Gift giving is an act that sets up and feeds into a set of socio-cultural and biographical power relationships mediated through the intersectional context of gender, sexuality, class, ethnicity and the normative expectations that follow. In sending sexual 'selfies' 'as a sexy present' – as many of our respondents did – young people are entering into a gift economy that potentially enhances status and self-image, and where there is usually an expectation of reciprocity. However, there is also a risk (with both the negative and positive connotations) that the receiver has a number of options in regard to how to respond to the gift, based around his or her own status and power. In most cases, as our respondents attest, the gift is reciprocated, as is the expectation. But there is also the possibility of non-reciprocity or even exploitation. The danger of a digital image is that it is the gift that 'keeps on giving'.

Childhood sexuality

As we saw in Chapter 2, the problematisation of childhood sexuality, and how to suppress and/or regulate it is not new (Fishman 1982); the regulation of childhood sexuality has always been about something more than childhood (Foucault 1990). Applying this historical framework to sexting, it is interesting to note the apparent willingness of many jurisdictions to conflate sexting with child pornography, and the reluctance of legislators to untangle and distinguish between the two. This speaks to a broader set of questions in relation to the regulation of adolescent sexuality and its discursive construction in terms of abuse, vulnerability and risk. Brownlie (2001) identifies the profound impact that renewed public awareness of child sexual abuse since the 1980s has had on the reconceptualisation of childhood. The social construction of children has been reshaped not only by increased concern relating to victimisation, but also through an enhanced awareness of children as potential perpetrators of abuse. As the origins of adult offending were increasingly traced back to abusive behaviours in childhood, a new category of the sexually 'deviant' child emerged from within 'risk' discourses and practices. This focus on risk has been buttressed by tendencies of sex education programs and campaigns to address youth sexuality in terms of 'risk factors' for particular negative outcomes, such as pregnancy or sexually transmitted disease infection (Shoveller and Johnson 2006). This public health framework is problematic in relation to sexting. Simply viewing sexting as a risk factor for engaging in underage sex misses the point about the way in which young people go about sexting. On the one hand, it is not surprising that young people who have sex might also be sexting, but sexting can also be a way for young people to experiment with sexuality without sexual physical contact. This is something the public health risk paradigm simply cannot account for.

With the popularisation of pseudo-scientific claims about the 'adolescent brain', a range of 'psy-' experts have called for an expansion of adult control and surveillance over children (and an expansion of the category of childhood itself) on the basis that young people are biologically prone to risk-taking and poor decision-making well into their twenties (Bessant 2004). There is a group of professions and experts on childhood whose professional standing and influence is based on the characterisation of young people as unruly and lacking true agency or selfhood; a view of children that has strong cultural antecedents in Western societies (Scott et al. 1998).

It has been argued that, in late-modern societies, the self is viewed as a project that serves as the focus of what Foucault (1988) termed 'technologies of the self', or the practice of continual self-appraisal, maintenance and renewal. In the case of children and adolescents, parents have a particular investment in passing on 'technologies of the self' that result in the presentation of an appropriately governed, regulated, civilised subject who can perpetuate the cultural and class norms upheld by the family. It might be argued that anxieties over sexting and teenage sexuality have less to do with potential harms to teenagers, and more to do with concern over the development of the child into an appropriately self-regulating, self-censoring citizen.

Conclusion

The analysis of our data suggests that the sending and receiving of sexual images is quite widespread amongst young people. However, it also suggests that while there are a range of differing motivations for sexting, most young people conceptualise their own behaviour positively. While a small proportion of young people – particularly younger females – report feeling pressured to send images, these are a clear minority. Nonetheless, perceptions of why young people send images are replete with gendered double standards that conceptualise young women as either being pressured to send images or as having no agency in the behaviours they undertake.

Our analysis of sexting using Mauss' conception of gifting suggests there is always some pressure to gift, and that sexting provides an exciting and relatively easy method through which young people can gift in a romantic context. Indeed, as we saw in the earlier chapters, those dating or in a relationship (other than marriage) were most likely to engage in sexting. Mauss also indicates to us how the online digital economy of sexting can operate. Here there is an expectation of reciprocity when one receives a sext – again backed up by our survey findings. And while gender no doubt mediates some sexting behaviours Mauss' model tells us that status intersecting with gender and a range of other factors may be more important. The model also suggests that the forwarding of sexts can be seen as a form of gifting to peers that operates to enhance status – often at the expense of the original sender.

None of this is to suggest that sexting is not a risky behaviour for young people. We are certainly not suggesting that sexting is completely unproblematic and should be encouraged. However, we also need to understand sexting risks both positively and negatively. That is, it may be the attraction of this risk taking that draws young people to engage in the practice. In this sense our attempts to suppress sexting my indeed be inciting sexting behaviours in young people. It is perhaps worth noting, as one of our focus group participants did very cogently, that most of the sexting incidents we hear about are when things go wrong:

> [I]t's not something people really talk about so we only see it when it does go wrong. I'm sure there are plenty of people are entertaining each other in any way they want with mobile phones. (Male USYD FG2)
>
> Yeah I think the majority of time it's not going to be a problem. (Female USYD FG2)

In the final section of the book we look more closely at the possible responses to sexting and begin to articulate alternative models for responding to sexting by young people.

Part IV
Futures and New Directions

12
Developing Responses to Sexting

Introduction

While discourses around the legal response to sexting have tended to centre on the appropriateness of the application of child pornography offences, as discussed in Chapter 4, sexting is a complex behaviour that cannot be reduced to simplistic (legal, social, media) narratives. Taken in their entirety, the results of our research demonstrate that young people's practices and motivations for sexting rarely fit the rationales for child pornography offences that so often lead debates on appropriate legal responses to sexting. Furthermore, prosecution under child pornography laws has the potential to cause more harm to young people than was caused by the original sexting behaviour. While our research shows that young people are generally aware of the potentially serious legal consequences of sexting, such legal consequences have not been enough to deter many young people from sexting. Although we cannot truly know all of the complex reasons why individuals choose to sext despite these legal risks, our findings suggest that some young people do not think that what they are doing – largely consensual sexting – is a form of behaviour that would or should be prosecuted. Beyond this, young people are more prone to take risks and act impulsively without necessarily thinking through potential future consequences. Moreover, the very risks involved (legal and reputational) may in fact incite or excite young people to engage in the practice.

This chapter explores how law and policy might best accommodate and respond to sexting by young people. It begins by drawing on existing research discussed in Chapter 7 and our research contained in Part III to argue that sexting should generally not be regarded to be child pornography. Following this we critically discuss what mechanisms might be adopted to remove or restrict the application of child pornography offences to sexting by young people, including: raising the age of criminal responsibility; introducing defences to child pornography offences; creating procedural barriers to prosecution and greater reliance on diversion. We then consider what alternative legal and non-legal measures could be employed to address sexting by young people. Here we assess what other legal provisions may be appropriate including existing offences, the development of sexting specific offences and civil law provisions. In considering the law, it is important to remember that legal change is only part of the solution and that legal change without social change is unlikely to be effective. We therefore end this chapter considering non-legal measures, such as administrative mechanisms and holistic educational programs that might appropriately address sexting by young people.

Sexting generally is not child pornography

Our research suggests that the child pornography framework that has dominated the legal regulatory approach to sexting in many jurisdictions is inappropriate for dealing with the many and varied practices that amount to, or have been labelled, sexting. In the vast majority of cases, prosecution under child pornography offences would be seriously misaligned with the behaviours undertaken and the motivations for such behaviours. As Chapters 7, 8 and 11 have shown, the motivations for sexting are often to have fun or to flirt, and to provide a sexy gift to a boyfriend or girlfriend. They are largely not exploitative. And even where pressure or coercion might take place this rarely accords with the motivations of adults who have a sexual interest in children.

In many ways, sexting is not new behaviour. New technologies are merely providing novel and potentially exciting modes for young people to begin to explore their sexuality – and with these new mechanisms come new risks. Sexting may well be positive, in that it allows young people a relatively safe online space in which to explore their sexuality, rather than in the physical world with its associated dangers. Online they can safely adopt and explore certain subject positions (see, eg Buckingham 2008, Cupples & Thompson 2010, Simpson 2013). As such, behaviours associated with sexting may actually foster positive risk taking experiences for many young people and reduce the negative risks associated with physical sexual exploration.

Alongside these positive experiences of risk taking are negative risks: sexters may later regret their sexting and this can lead to low self-esteem and depression (Joint Select Committee on Cyber-Safety 2011, [4.60]). A further risk is that initially consensually shared images may be distributed more widely without consent – although this in itself may not necessarily always be perceived as a negative risk either, and could be part of the attraction of sexting for some. As we discussed in Chapter 11 forwarded sexts may in some circumstances enhance the status of the forwarder and the subject of the image, despite the gendered double standards evident in attitudes towards sexting. More serious risks are that such images can be used as a tool for cyberbullying, to harass, to threaten or to blackmail a young person (see Keeley et al. 2014). What is clear from our research is that generally young people are aware of such incidents either in their immediate circles or via media reports, but that for these young people – as the research of others has also found (Livingstone and Smith 2014) – such risks were not common. As Livingstone and Smith note:

> Prevalence estimates vary according to definition and measurement, but do not appear to be rising substantially with increasing access to mobile and online technologies, possibly because these technologies pose no additional risk to offline behaviour, or because any risks are offset by a commensurate growth in safety awareness and initiatives. (2014, p. 635)

Recent research also finds that young people perceive traditional forms of bullying to be more hurtful than cyber bullying (Corby et al. 2015). This in no way means that there is not a need to address such behaviours – and our research does not suggest that either. But it does suggest that it may be inappropriate to conceptualise sexting and cyberbullying and harassment as causally related or motivationally connected. This book thus argues that a single legislative or policy approach to such varied behaviours and scenarios is unlikely to be effective. Where the behaviour is part of a consensual exploration of sexuality or mere playfulness, there is likely no need for any legal intervention at all. Rather, holistic sexual education strategies aimed at empowering young people to understand and ethically deal with a range of behaviours that might include sexting are more likely to be more productive. At the other extreme are those instances where a sext is the product of a criminal act (for instance, where the image is taken of a sexual assault) or where it is used as a tool of cyberbullying. In such circumstances, a legal (civil or criminal) response may be necessary.

Our research confirms that there is a need to develop strategies (which may include no response at all) that can be applied to a variety of behavioural scenarios associated with sexting. It is therefore appropriate that legal mechanisms are developed to ensure that child pornography offences are only used against young people as a last resort for the most exploitative forms of behaviour or where the behaviour is motivated either by maliciousness or by a conscious distribution to significantly older adults who sexualise, or may sexualise, the image. As the Law Reform Committee of Victoria (2013, p. 73) noted, 'child pornography laws were created for the purpose of protecting children from predatory sexual behaviour. ... [they] were not designed to capture this type of behaviour'. Despite this, there generally appears to be a reluctance to totally exclude young people from the ambit of these offences. For example, the Law Reform Committee of Victoria noted that it received submissions, which it agreed with, recommending that genuinely exploitative behaviour by young people should not be 'exempted from the full force of the child pornography laws' (2013, p. 135). Given that it appears unlikely that young people will be totally removed from the reaches of child pornography offences the following discussion explores the mechanisms which might restrict the application of such offences to only aggravated cases.

Reducing the scope for prosecution under child pornography offences

Raising the age of criminal responsibility

The age levels of criminal responsibility have been discussed in Chapter 5. As noted many common law countries have a relatively low minimum age level of criminal responsibility. While young people may begin experimenting with sexting between the ages of 9 and 14 (Law Reform Committee of Victoria 2013, p. 69) the rate at which they send sexts increases from 38 per cent for 13 to 15 years olds to 50 per cent for 16- to 18-year-olds (see Chapter 8). This means that depending on the jurisdiction current age levels of criminal responsibility may provide some protection for the young but not for those at ages where they are more likely to engage in sexting. Consideration could be given therefore to increasing age levels of criminal responsibility to protect young people from a child pornography conviction. While the United Nations *Convention on the Rights of the Child* calls for nations to establish a minimum age 'below which children shall be presumed not to have the capacity to infringe penal law' (art. 40.3), it does not mention what age that should be. However, the *Standard Minimum Rules for the Administration of Juvenile Justice* (Beijing Rules), Rule 4.1 does state that 'the beginning of that age shall not be fixed at too low an age level, bearing in mind the facts of emotional, mental and intellectual maturity'. In 2007, the United Nations Committee on the Rights of the

Child stated in line with the recommendation contained in Rule 4 of the Beijing Rules that it considered 'a minimum age of criminal responsibility below the age of 12 years... not to be internationally acceptable' (2007, [32]). It therefore recommends that State parties should set the age of 12 years as an absolute minimum, but continue to work towards a higher minimum age level.

When the minimum age level is set at 12, consideration should also be given to retaining and increasing the higher flexible age period where criminal responsibility depends on an assessment of whether the young person understood the wrongfulness of his or her behaviour. There is much research that suggests young people are not fully cognitively nor emotionally developed until they reach their early twenties (see, e.g., Cauffman and Steinberg 2000; Fried and Reppucci 2001; Steinberg and Scott 2003; Monahan et al. 2009). Moreover, these developmental factors are likely to influence the level of value young people place on risk-taking behaviours. As a report by the Sentencing Advisory Council on sentencing of young people in Victoria notes:

> The frontal lobe, which governs reasoning, planning and organisation, is the last part of the brain to develop. This is likely to contribute to adolescents' lack of impulse control, although their attraction to risk and the high value they place on the immediate rewards flowing from risky behaviour, as well as their heavy 'discounting' of the future costs of this behaviour, also contribute. Adolescents are very vulnerable to peer pressure (which in turn can strongly affect their risk-taking behaviour), in part due to the importance they place on peers and in part due to neurological and hormonal changes. Scott and Steinberg conclude that although adolescents have roughly the same ability as adults to employ logical reasoning in making decisions by early to mid adolescence, adolescents have far less experience using these skills. (2012, p. 11, references omitted)

If we accept these developmental factors, consideration should be given to setting a flexible age period of criminal responsibility at the age of 16 or even 18. These are the ages at which the young take on other rights and responsibilities. This would be in line with the Beijing Rules as the following commentary on Rule 4.1 of the Beijing Rules notes:

> The modern approach would be to consider whether a child can live up to the moral and psychological components of criminal responsibility; that is, whether a child, by virtue of his or her individual

discernment and understanding, can be held responsible for essentially anti-social behaviour. ... In general, there is a close relationship between the notion of responsibility for delinquent or criminal behaviour and other social rights and responsibilities (such as marital status, civil majority, etc).

A problem with this approach, however, is that it may not necessarily filter out cases of consensual sexting because, in such cases, a young person may nonetheless understand that it could amount to child pornography and that it is wrongful to make, send and possess naked or sexualised images of a young person. In fact, our research confirms that 87 per cent of young people recognised that sexting could lead to a child pornography conviction (although this might not equate with understanding the wrongfulness of the behaviour). Thus, raising the minimum age of criminal responsibility (in jurisdictions where it is below 12) and setting a flexible age period of criminal responsibility at a higher level could be only part of a broader strategy to the address the liability of young people for conviction of criminal offences more generally. A more targeted approach would therefore be to consider the development of defences to child pornography laws specific to young people.

Defences to child pornography offences

As noted in Chapter 5, there are examples of existing defences to child pornography offences for young people in various jurisdictions, such as the Australian states of Tasmania and Victoria and in England and Wales. The Law Reform Committee of Victoria investigated the defences in Australian jurisdictions. They were critical of the defence existing in Victoria and recommended the development of a defence along the lines of the Tasmanian approach, which essentially applies to a minor where the image depicts lawful sexual activity. This reform proposal was taken up by the Victorian Government and defences to child pornography offences have since been included in the *Crimes Amendment (Sexual Offences and Other Matters) Act 2014* (Vic), s 8, inserting s70AAA into the *Crimes Act 1958* (Vic). Accordingly, a defence will apply to a minor for the offences of production and possession of child pornography and procurement of a minor for child pornography.[1] It is a defence if an image depicts the minor alone or with an adult, or where it depicts the minor with another minor(s), and at the time of the offence the minor is not more than two years older than the youngest minor depicted, or the minor believes on reasonable grounds that he or she was not more than two years older than the other minor. However, this defence does not apply where the image depicts an act that is a criminal offence punishable by imprisonment. It is designed, as the example provided in the Act shows, to cover images of consensual acts between minors within two years of age.

A defence also applies to a minor where the image is one that depicts child pornography and is an offence, but the minor is the victim of that offence. Furthermore, a defence applies to a minor where the image is child pornography but does not include the minor, provided that it does not depict a criminal offence punishable by imprisonment and he or she is not more than two years older than the youngest minor depicted. If the image does depict an offence but the minor believes on reasonable grounds that it does not the defence still applies. Similarly, if the minor is more than two years older than the youngest subject of the image the defence will still apply provided that he or she believes on reasonable grounds that he or she is within two years of age. The example provided in the Act is that the image depicts a minor being sexually penetrated and the minor to which the defence applies believes on reasonable grounds that he or she is not more than two years older than the minor depicted. Interestingly, in all instances where the defence applies, if the minor believes a certain fact (e.g., that he or she is no more than two years older), that minor has the burden of proving that fact on the balance of probabilities.

The Law Reform Committee of Victoria was in favour of a requirement that the parties should be close in age because it felt that where the age gap between the sexting parties is significant this could be an indication of exploitation. In such a case the sexting behaviour should be seen as criminal behaviour on the part of the older person. Young people we talked to in focus groups and who completed our survey also recognised the importance of age difference in addressing sexting. As we saw in Chapter 9, in our focus groups some respondents expressed concern about the scenario where age differences between participants were greater – as in the Eades case. Importantly, they considered that scenario more problematic and potentially harmful, voicing both moral condemnation and the potential need for criminal justice intervention (see Chapter 10).

These legislative reforms would seem to appeal to our respondents' concerns, given that the parties must be aged within two years of each other and the behaviour must not amount to a criminal offence. However, requiring such a rigidly close age level between the parties may be overly restrictive and may fail to protect many for whom our respondents would not see sexting as problematic. The assumption that a larger than two year age gap may indicate exploitation or a problematic interest in a child, while appropriate in cases of adult interactions with young people, does not necessarily apply in situations in which both parties are minors. It has long been established that young people mentally and physically develop at vastly different and inconsistent rates. Thus, the biological age of a child does not necessarily represent a fixed level of intellectual and/ or social development. This means that a biologically older child will not necessarily be developmentally more mature than a younger child. Similar concerns arise in relation to the existing defence to possession of child pornography which can only apply to a young adult who is not more than two years older than the young person depicted (*Crimes Act 1958* (Vic), s 70(2)(d)). Again, our focus group respondents were only concerned where age difference was quite significant and where the minor involved might be presumed to have a much lesser capacity to understand the consequences of their actions.

A focus on the context and intention of the creation, possession and distribution of an image, particularly where the image could be otherwise innocent (i.e., show no sexual activity or context but mere nudity/ semi-nudity), is important in determining whether prosecution should be pursued. This could compliment a more flexible approach to age difference, allowing a more context specific legal evaluation. As research indicates, law enforcement agencies are generally determining whether to prosecute under child pornography laws based on aggravating factors (Wolak et al. 2012, p. 4) and/or whether there is an intention to possess or procure child pornography (Law Reform Committee of Victoria 2013, p. 139). Such intention may be indicated by how many images are collected, how they are sorted, how often a person has viewed the images and so on (see, e.g., Taylor and Quayle 2003; Krone 2004).

Even in the minority of cases where there is non-consensual and malicious creation and distribution of images, the motivation may not necessarily fit the rationale for prosecuting child pornography offences; instead, it may be for the purposes of bullying, harassment or blackmail. In such cases, rather than using child pornography offences, there are more appropriate legal sanctions that might be used, including existing criminal offences (such as those prohibiting stalking, harassment, blackmail and so on) and, in some jurisdictions, non-consensual sexting-specific criminal offences. It is important that behaviours are prosecuted under appropriately developed and labelled offences if confidence is to be maintained in the criminal justice system and offenders punished in proportion to their wrongdoing. As our research found in Chapter 3, the media has shifted to reporting with concern about the inappropriateness of young people who sext being prosecuted under child pornography laws with the potentially harsh consequences that follow. This is especially of concern given that, in many jurisdictions, a child pornog-raphy conviction carries with it a listing on a sex offender register with all the labelling consequences that follow.

Procedural barriers to prosecution

During debate in the Australian Commonwealth Parliament in 2011 on amendments to the *Criminal Code Act 1995* (Cth) to strengthen child pornography laws, the issue arose of whether it was appropriate to apply child pornography offences to young people. It was acknowledged that these offences were generally not designed to capture young people who engage in sexting, but that there was a need to retain the possibility of prosecution for aggravated cases, such as where there was malicious, non-consensual distribution of images (Explanatory Memorandum 2010). Furthermore, it was argued that there was a need to deter young people from engaging in such behaviour (Simpkins 2010, p. 2046). Thus, rather than developing a defence, it was suggested that a more appro-priate method of generally removing young people from the reaches of child pornography laws was to introduce a requirement that the permission of the Attorney General be sought before commencing any proceedings for a child pornography offence for a person under 18 years of age. This has the advantage of placing the decision of whether to prosecute at a higher level and therefore should make decisions easier to review. However, while the exercise of discretion is a fundamental element of most criminal justice systems, in this case without clear guid-ance it leaves the prosecution of young people possibly open to inap-propriate political and cultural whims (Ericson 1982). The role of the Attorney General in Australia combines a policy, legal service and public interest function (Ray 2008). Prosecutorial practice is liable to change with developments in public attitudes, political opinion, operational constraints and so forth, particularly in relation to morally controver-sial behaviours or where the subjects are seen as particularly vulnerable. In this case concerns about young people exploring their sexuality and their susceptibility (actual or real) to exploitation could readily drive a more punitive approach.

In Australia the Attorney General's permission is only required for prosecutions for Commonwealth (federal) offences. This leaves open to police the capacity to bring charges under State or Territory legislation to circumvent the oversight of the Commonwealth Attorney-General or to bring charges for other criminal offences. This means that the likely outcome of sexting cases is reliant on the exercise of discretion at a range of levels – from police through to the Attorney General in Australian jurisdictions. Thus the gateway to prosecution for child pornography offences lies in the discretion generally exercised by police deciding whether to prosecute young people (Hogg 1991; Chan 2005; Rowe 2007). As noted previously, police already exercise such discretion not to proceed with charges in cases of 'experimental' sexting (e.g. Wolak et al. 2012). However, while this may be appropriate in cases where it is working to exclude young people unless there are aggravating factors (as appears to be the case in Victoria and New South Wales), this does not necessarily lead to a consistent or coherent approach. As the research of Wolak et al. (2012) in the US demonstrates, in around 18 per cent of cases young people were arrested for 'experimental sexting'. They conclude that '[t]his suggests that some youth may be facing exposure to criminal treatment in cases that might be better handled informally by families and clinicians' (2012, p. 9). Such an approach can lead to factors determining whether or not a young person is prosecuted for a child pornography offence that are unrelated to the sexting incident. Furthermore, as discretion within the police force is broadest at the lower ranks, it is difficult to review and address.

The opaqueness of such prosecutorial practice can mean that police and/or prosecutors are selectively applying child pornography laws without clear public criteria guiding which cases are appropriate for prosecution. As Tallon et al. (2012, p. 19) comment in the Australian context, 'while this unofficial policy may provide a useful rubric for police, and may have implicit public approval, it does not provide a great deal of certainty or transparency to young people'.

One method of increasing clarity is to introduce guidance on the factors to be considered by the Attorney General, police or prosecutors in relation to decisions about whether to pursue prosecution (Chan 2005). As discussed in Chapter 5 various jurisdictions have adopted guidance on factors to be considered when determining whether to prosecute young people for sexual offences against other young people. Given the vastly different behaviours that are viewed as sexting the development of specific guidelines would be appropriate. Such guidance in relation to child pornography offences could focus on factors which are the basis for the criminalisation of child pornography, such as whether the sexting indicates that a young person was exploited, an adult was involved, or the sexting was done for financial gain.

Diversion

The use of discretion can lead to a young person being diverted from formal criminal proceedings. It is a vital principle of juvenile justice that young people should be diverted from formal proceedings wherever appropriate and desirable (*UN Convention on the Rights of the Child*, art 40(3)(b) and the *UN Standard Minimum Rules for the Administration of Juvenile Justice*, Rule 11; see also Australian Law Reform Commission 1997, [18.35]–[18.62]). Australian Police are generally aware that entry into the criminal justice system can lead to a cycle of offending and therefore diversion is preferred so far as is possible and appropriate (Paterson 2012, p. 16). However, the commitment of police to diversionary measures depends on the requirements and accessibility of such alternatives and whether police feel that there is adequate flexibility. Aside from informal warnings, police may give formal warnings (often called 'cautions'). Cautions are often not available for severe offences and so may not be available where sexting falls under a child pornography offence. This is the case in Victoria, where the Police Manual notes that a caution may only be given in exceptional circumstances for sexual or sexually related offences (Victoria Police 2012, p. 2).

Other more formal diversionary mechanisms that may be available include juvenile justice teams, whereby the young person is diverted from formal court proceedings on the condition of satisfactory completion of an agreed program. In relation to sexting, a diversionary program combining educational elements focusing on ethical sexual practices might be an appropriate option where a warning or caution is an insufficient response, but prosecution for child pornography (or any other applicable offence) is thought to be too harsh. Such a program was recommended by the South Eastern Centre against Sexual Assault (2012, pp. 2–3) in its submission to the Law Reform Committee of Victoria:

> A diversion program needs to be created for the under 18 year olds who forward on a message or image without knowledge or consent of the person who originally sent it and this transmission has come to the notice of the authorities....There needs to be early intervention in such instances and referral into a program that will conduct an assessment of risk. If it is assessed that this was a one off offence, and there is no risk, the young person can be dealt with by attending an information session about sexting and the law, etc. If it is assessed that this young person is high or medium risk they would attend a program about respectful relationships, offending and issues around technologically facilitated offences for 6–12 months, depending on the assessment.

Alternatives to child pornography offences

Existing offences

Although debate surrounding sexting has centred on the applicability and appropriateness of child pornography offences, there is a range of existing offences that may apply to sexting behaviours in various jurisdictions. However, to date little attention has been paid to prosecution of young sexters under other existing offences.[2] A narrow focus on child pornography offences may be advantageous in the sense that young people are being diverted out of formal proceedings unless the case is a severe one, for example, involving exploitation. However, it may mean that other less severe, more appropriate offences are missed where there is problematic behaviour associated with the sexting such as harassment, bullying, coercion or threats.

Just drawing on the example of one jurisdiction, in this case the Australian State of Western Australia, reveals the range of offences that can apply to sexting. Where a sext is shown to a young person, this could amount to the offence of showing offensive material to a child under 16 (*Criminal Code* (WA), s 204A) or using electronic communication to procure, or expose to indecent material, a child under 16 (*Criminal Code* (WA), s 204B). If a person obtains an image that depicts a young person's naked genitalia or the young person in a sexual pose or engaging in sexual activity and then threatens to distribute the image to others, this could amount to the offence of threats (*Criminal Code* (WA), s 338B). Stalking (*Criminal Code* (WA), s 338E) would apply where there is repeated communication, for example sending of sexts, with the intention to intimidate or where the behaviour could reasonably be expected to intimidate and does intimidate. Furthermore, other offences such as procuring a person to have unlawful carnal knowledge (*Criminal Code* (WA), s 192), as well as procuring, inciting or encouraging a child to engage in sexual or indecent behaviour (*Criminal Code* (WA), sis 320(3),(5), 321((3),(5)), may apply.

This example jurisdiction demonstrates that there can exist offences which may be better fitting problematic forms of sexting. The question of whether police and prosecutors are charging for such offences in appropriate cases requires further investigation.[3] If such alternative offences are not applied often, police and prosecution agencies may need to rethink the framing of sexting and prosecution policies, setting out what might be the most applicable offences/responses to varied sexting scenarios.

Sexting-specific offences

Alongside the range of existing offences that could apply to sexting, in some jurisdictions there has been a move to create new offences specifically to cover non-consensual sexting. Our research confirms that the harm associated with sexting stems primarily from the non-consensual distribution of the image to third parties. In such instances, a child pornography offence may be too harsh, but there might be a need for some other form of criminal law response. A sexting-specific offence can appropriately target the non-consensual distribution of images and attach an appropriate label and penalty to that action. This has been done in 19 US States (see Duncan 2014) and in the Australian State of Victoria.

In North Dakota, the distribution or publication of a sexually expressive image with the intent to cause emotional harm or humiliation to the person depicted in the image, and who has a reasonable expectation of privacy, is a crime (North Dakota Century Code § 12.1–27.1–03.3(1)(b)). This offence is not specific to young people and criminalises on the basis of the intention of the offender. It is also an offence to surreptitiously create or wilfully possess a sexually expressive image without the consent of the subject of the image and where there the subject has a reasonable expectation of privacy (North Dakota Century Code § 12.1–27.1–03.3(1)(a)). Acquiring and knowingly distributing a sexually expressive image that was created without the consent of the subject of the image is also an offence (North Dakota Century Code § 12.1–27.1–03(2)). In all these instances, the person must know the character and content of the image.

In Victoria, new offences of 'distribution of an intimate image' and 'threat to distribute an intimate image' have been created (*Summary Offences Act 1966* (Vic), ss 41DA, 41DB inserted by *Crimes Amendment Sexual Offences and Other Matters) Act 2014* (Vic), s 25), signalling a potential way forward for other Australian jurisdictions. It is an offence to intentionally distribute an intimate image of another person in a way that is contrary to community standards of acceptable conduct. A defence applies if the person depicted is not a minor and expressly or impliedly consented or could reasonably be considered to have consented to the distribution of the image or the manner in which it was distributed. There is no defence of consent in the case of a minor because of 'their greater vulnerability and need for protection' (Crimes Amendment (Sexual Offences and Other Matters) Bill 2014, Explanatory Memorandum, p 39). An intimate image is defined as one that shows sexual activity, a sexual context or the genital or anal region of a person or, in the case of a female, the breasts. The requirement that distribution is contrary to community standards of acceptable behaviour is a recognition that what may be contrary to such standards in one case may not be in another and provides 'a safeguard against overreach by the new offence' (Crimes Amendment (Sexual Offences and Other Matters) Bill 2014, Explanatory Memorandum, p. 39). It requires a court to have regard to the nature and content of the image, the circumstances in which it was captured and distributed, the relevant circumstances of the person depicted, including his or her age, intellectual capacity and vulnerability, and the degree to which distribution affects the privacy of the person depicted (*Summary Offences Act 1966* (Vic), s40). These are exactly the sort of factors that our focus group respondents identified as determinants of whether a criminal response was appropriate for sexting (see Chapter 10). It is also an offence for a person to threaten to distribute an intimate image in a way that would be contrary to community standards and to intend the subject of the image to believe that the other person will carry out the threat.

For young people, one danger of such sexting specific offences is that they could lead to net-widening, with increased prosecutions of young people for sexting. As we have seen, at present, because child pornography offences are generally seen as an inappropriate response for most cases of sexting, police are choosing not to charge young people and to divert them from formal criminal proceedings. Because of this, a new offence that is appropriately labelled and fits the scenario of non-consensual distribution of intimate images may be seen as the correct response to sexting and may result in increased prosecutions. Such concerns were raised by Neil Paterson, Acting Commander of Victoria Police (2012, p. 16), who argued that police discretion was a useful way of dealing with sexting. Others, however, do not view increased prosecutions as necessarily a bad thing. As Judge Grant noted in evidence before the Law Reform Committee of Victoria:

I am not that happy with an approach that says that every single case should be cautioned unless you get the really serious ones that go into court. There has to be a recognition that there are some areas in between here, and they probably have to be recognised by the creation of a specific offence. (2012, p. 26)

The advantage of the approach taken in jurisdictions such as North Dakota and Victoria is that there is consistency in addressing the major source of harm associated with sexting: the non-consensual distribution of images. However, the Victorian legislation does not allow for the consent of a young person to excuse the distribution. Instead, the requirement that the distribution or threat of distribution be done in a way that is contrary to community standards should allow a flexible approach to whether a young person who sexts should be charged with this offence.

A further advantage of these sexting offences is that the offences apply equally to adults – who, as we have seen, are generally more prolific sexters. In doing so, they reduce the apparent hypocrisy of young people facing more severe consequences for behaviour that adults engage in with apparent impunity.[4]

Consideration of the principle of fair labelling (or 'representative labelling') also supports the creation of a new offence of non-consensual distribution of intimate images. The importance of offence labels lies in the central censuring function of the criminal law (see Ashworth and Horder 2013, p. 1). Criminal law is a tool of social control, warning citizens about behaviour that should be avoided and the consequences that will ensue if that behaviour is not avoided. Offence labels communicate the wrong committed by the offender and they stand as a 'moral and legal record, as a testimony to the precise respect in which the defendant failed in her or his basic duties as a citizen' (Horder 1994, p. 339). This is important for the victim and the offender. From the perspective of the victim (or the victim's family) the offence label is important because 'she deserves to have her suffering reflected by an offence of appropriate seriousness' (Chalmers and Leverick 2008, p. 238). For the offender the offence label lets him or her know exactly how his or her behaviour has been classified by the justice system and why he or she is being punished in a certain way (Chalmers and Leverick 2008, p. 229); thus the punishment is seen as meaningful to the offender and not just arbitrary and harsh (Simester and Sullivan 2007, p. 31). This is particularly important in cases of sexting because a child pornography offence does not accurately capture the wrongfulness of the behaviours in the majority of these cases. Such a conviction carries the message of exploitation and abuse of children – motivations that, as we have seen, are rarely present in sexting scenarios. In the case of sexting, a conviction for a child pornography offence may be regarded as an overreaction and an unjust outcome. This is evidenced by our research, which shows that media reports increasingly focused on the inappropriateness of such a conviction for sexting and the disproportionate harms that follow from such a conviction (see Chapter 3). Our focus group respondents similarly felt that prosecution for child pornography offences and placement on the sex offender register was inappropriate as the following responses indicate:

> But if you were talking about this person's name is on the sex offender list, you would not likely think that was the case. You would likely think he was having sex with a 14 year old girl or something, very recently. You wouldn't think that that was the case, that that's what he was going to be punished for, so there's that stigma which doesn't actually match what he did by any means. (Female USYD FG4)
>
> If any company sees, oh sex offender, they're not going to think he just posted a pic of him and his girlfriend having sex, they're going

to think child pornography, child molester, rapist, and that's a whole lot worse than two 17 year olds. (Female USYD FG4)

In contrast, a sexting-specific offence that targets the non-consensual distribution of an intimate image communicates exactly where the wrongfulness and harm in sexting scenarios lies. This also feeds into another wider and perhaps more fundamental aspect of fair labelling – that offence labels have a symbolic and educational function in society. Seeing offenders convicted according to the perceived wrongfulness of the behaviour communicates society's core values and confirms in the public's mind the wrongfulness of the behaviour (Mitchell 2001, p. 398). An appropriately labelled offence is important because, '[a] criminal provision is better able to communicate the boundaries of socially acceptable behaviour if it packages crimes in morally significant ways' (Wilson 2007, p. 162). Thus, a sexting-specific offence can have an educative effect, communicating that the wrongfulness of sexting lies in non-consensual distribution.

Civil law

Legal debate about how to appropriately respond to sexting has tended to focus on criminal law. This may be explained by the social significance of criminal law as a tool of social control and by the potentially severe consequences that may follow conviction, particularly for a child pornography offence. Aside from criminal law, a range of civil laws may be applicable to sexting or may be developed to address sexting. The disadvantage of civil law is that it lacks the censuring, broader symbolic function of criminal law. Importantly, civil law remedies are not limited to monetary compensation for damage suffered but can also include a range of other remedies which may provide effective relief where images are distributed without consent, such as an injunction (an order compelling a person to do or not do certain acts).

Civil laws that could be applicable to sexting scenarios include intentional infliction of emotional harm, breach of confidence, invasion of privacy, defamation, breach of copyright law or sexual harassment laws. Intentional infliction of emotional harm is an action that is generally only available in extreme cases of causing emotional harm. This is because of concerns that it can be difficult to confirm the existence and extent of such harm (see Hiestand 2014, p. 231). In the United States, the Restatement (Third) of Torts: Liability for Physical and Emotional Harm §46 (2012) states that this action is available where a person 'by extreme and outrageous conduct intentionally or recklessly causes severe emotional harm to another'. Non-consensual creation of an image may amount to extreme and outrageous conduct. There are cases in the

United States where adults have taken pictures consensually of sexual activity and then the images have been distributed upon the break-down of the relationship with derogatory comments attached. This has been found to amount to the intentional infliction of emotional harm (see Hiestand 2014, pp. 232–6 for a discussion of relevant cases). Such extreme and outrageous conduct must be done intentionally or reck-lessly and the subject of the image must suffer emotional harm that is 'so severe that no reasonable [person] could be expected to endure it' (Restatement (Third) of Torts: Liability for Physical and Emotional Harm §46 cmt J (2012), cited in Hiestand 2014, p. 238). Being upset, embar-rassed, disgusted, very depressed, or angry is not enough (see Hiestand 2014, p. 239 for a discussion of relevant cases).

In Australia, the case of *Giller v Procopets* [2008] VSCA 236 illustrates that the tort of intentional infliction of mental distress (the *Wilkinson v Downton* [1897] 2 QB 57 tort) is currently severely limited, but may be in a state of flux (see Witzleb 2009). Presently, recovery is only available where there is 'harm going beyond embarrassment, injury to feelings, humilia-tion or psychological distress and constituting a psychiatrically cognisable injury to mental health' (*Nationwide News Pty Ltd v Naidu* [2007] NSWCA 377). Given the restrictive approach taken to this tort in Australia, it will only be available in sexting cases in the rarest of situations.

The tort of invasion of privacy is designed to protect a person's private life. It may therefore seem to be a suitable cause of action in sexting cases involving the non-consensual distribution of images that are highly private (Hiestand 2014, p. 240). In the United States, the Restatement (Second) of Torts §652D (1977) states that this tort is available where publicity is given to a matter concerning the private life of another where the publicity would be highly offensive to a reasonable person and is not of legitimate concern to the public. Alternative forms of privacy include intentional intrusion upon a person's seclusion (§652B), appropriation of a name or likeness (§652C), and publicity placing a person in a false light (§652E) (see Hiestand 2014). Other jurisdictions, such as Australia, do not provide for such a cause of action (*Australian Broadcasting Corporation v Lenah Game Meats* Pty Ltd [2001] HCA 63; *Giller v Procopets*) and the issue of whether a similar tort should be recognised is the subject of much debate. The Law Reform Committee of Victoria noted that the law at present in Australia is not suffi-cient to protect victims of non-consensual sexting (Law Reform Committee of Victoria 2012, p. 177) and it therefore recommends the development of a tort of invasion of privacy (2013, p. 188). This follows recommendations for the development of such a tort by the Australian Law Reform Commission (2008), the New South Wales Law Reform Commission (2009) and the Victorian Law Reform Commission (2010). In the absence of a tort of invasion of privacy in Australia, privacy-like actions may be brought for breach of confidence (see *Giller v Procopets*). This requires that the information (in a sexting case, the image) is of a confidential nature, the circumstances of receiving the information import an obligation of confidentiality, and there is actual or threatened use of that information.

Civil law focusses (primarily) on redressing the harm done to the complainant rather than punishing a wrongdoer. It may therefore have a significant role to play alongside criminal law sanctions or where a criminal law response is considered unnecessary.

Administrative mechanisms

Mobile phone providers and social networking sites may have an important role to play in addressing sexting behaviours. As the Law Reform Committee of Victoria notes, most providers and sites require users to adhere to terms of service that allow appropriate measures to be taken where those terms are breached (2013, p. 189). For instance, mobile phone contracts generally allow termination of the contract if the service is used for illegal purposes and some prohibit conduct that is offensive, defamatory, indecent, menacing or obscene (see 2013, p. 190). As the Law Reform Committee of Victoria notes:

> Approaching the mobile phone provider to take action against someone who is misusing their phone service may provide a means to dissuade that person from engaging in such conduct, without having to take the more serious step of going to the police. (2013, p. 190)

Similarly, social networking sites also have terms of use and can remove content and terminate use if those terms are breached. A concern expressed by the Law Reform Committee of Victoria is that, given the sheer volume of complaints, providers may not respond with sufficient speed. The Law Reform Committee of Victoria therefore recommends that a body be created 'that can hear and determine complaints about offensive and harmful online content quickly, inexpensively and effectively' (2013, p. 197).

Education/ethics

While there are multiple ways in which the law can play some part in the regulation of sexting by young people, education is key to approaching sexting behaviours. This was a point not lost on our focus group participants many of whom voiced similar ideas to the respondent below:

> I think it's all about education and it's all about informing people before it happens. (USYD FG1)

As the Law Reform Committee of Victoria notes, while legislative change is important, 'most of the gains from effective government policy in this area will be achieved through effective education about the social and personal effects that sexting can have on children and adults and the legal ramifications of sexting' (2013, p. 53). Education about sexting should not become a stand-alone topic, it should form part of a broader approach to education about cybersafety that needs to focus on 'developing positive practices for engagement with the online world' (Law Reform Committee of Victoria 2013, p. 53). Clearly our focus group respondents also understood this need:

> Yeah education is the most – you have to educate young kids about this these days with the media, because the media's already out of control, Twitter and Facebook and all that, and who knows how it's going to be in five years. (Female USYD FG2)

However, another respondent talked about the need to integrate education about sexting into other areas such as personal development and health education:

> I think there needs to be a lot more discussion about it in PDHPE and health and stuff from Year 7 onwards, if there was a lot more discussion I think it would really benefit people the way they think about it. (Female USYD FG2)

As much research has already shown, young people now live in a digital world and as the Joint Select Committee on Cyber-Safety notes, '[t]he online environment is an essential tool for all Australians, including children' (2011, p. 1). Indeed, as Arcabascio argues, '[i]t is unlikely that today's teenagers recognize or recall a world without cellular phones and texting' (2009–10, p. 5).

With this in mind, and as we stated at the beginning of the book, our research suggests that the context in which we conceptualise sexting is crucial. Through the analysis of focus groups conducted with young people, we found that young people have a significant online presence. Perhaps unsurprisingly then, young people are becoming increasingly savvy about the virtual world they live in and how to manage their online presence/identity. Our research (both qualitative and quantitative) also suggests that young people do engage in sexting and that the practice of sexting is widespread, despite the dominance of a risk management approach to preventing sexting, in which the key message is 'there is no such thing as safe sexting'. Thus, consideration must be given to the appropriateness, as well as the effectiveness, of the abstinence-style model favoured in education campaigns discussed in Chapter 6. As our research suggests, such a model does not speak to the needs or strategies of young people when it comes to sexting specifically, or online presence more broadly. As one respondent noted:

> Instead of threatening you they should educate you. They need to let you know what are the possibilities, don't do it you'll get in trouble. You know, just don't do it because look what happens. (USYD FG2)

Rather, such models, as is often seen in general sex education approaches that take the abstinence approach, can potentially create resistances, leading to more sexting, rather than less, as was backed up by our focus groups.

> Well young people are told not to have sex either. They still do it. I think you have a discussion about why it's bad but if you say just don't do it they rebel. That's what young people do. (Female UWS FG1)

The 'worst-case scenarios' presented in abstinence models do not correlate with real-world experiences of young people to whom they speak. While it is often the case that in these campaigns, as well as in the media, we are likely to hear when things go bad, what is not being told is when things work.

Yet, while there may be some problems with the approach of many current education campaigns (see Chapter 6; Salter et al. 2013), they can assist young people to be more aware of risks associated with online communication and to develop methods to reduce those risks. The most effective education campaigns will be responsive to the voices and experiences of young people, rather than a reflection of the moral panics fostered by the mass media. The development of a sexual ethics around sexting should be a key strategy of education. As we have noted, technology in this area has moved ahead of manners, expectations and, importantly, ethics. While many education campaigns tell cautionary tales of the possible negative outcomes of sexting, this does not equate with the reality of many young peoples' experiences. Moreover, the focus should not be on the outcomes for the 'victim' in sexting exchanges gone wrong. Instead, as with contemporary sexual assault campaigns which problematise the actions of the perpetrators rather than the 'imprudent' actions of victims, the focus should be on the unethical behaviour of the young person who breaches the trust of his or her sexting partner(s). As Moira Carmody (2013) puts it:

> In talking with young women and men aged 16–25 years of age from across NSW, we found that many young people felt let down by their sexuality education at school or at home. Few felt well prepared to negotiate issues around sexual consent or how to manage issues around sexual negotiation, pressured or coerced sex in casual or ongoing relationships. They felt the messages they received from school and families were primarily negative about sex, focusing on risk and danger and excluded positive skills for ethical intimacy.

We could hardly better capture the situation in regard to sexting. Negative campaigns, and a lack of preparation as to how to really negotiate consent, context and coercion – in short, to negotiate the rules of any sexting exchange – have been at the epicentre of anti-sexting education campaigns so far.

New education campaigns, thus, need to focus on ethics that might extend from understanding when a person is being coerced, or when a person might be applying pressure to a sexting partner. They need to explain the various scenarios of sexting, and the pros and cons in terms of outcomes that can flow from each. They also need to clearly explain how sexting might affect reputation or self-esteem into the future, and teach strategies of agency and resistance. Importantly, campaigns must equip young people with tools to discuss the ground-rules of any sexting exchange with a prospective partner. Of course, such strategies are not going to mean every sexting exchange is undertaken safely, or that no young person is ever coerced or humiliated by such actions. However, they would speak to young people in a language they relate to, and would reflect the reality of online sexual exchanges, rather than denying them or wilfully ignoring the reality that young people will always experiment with their sexuality.

Conclusion

Clearly there is no one size fits all way to address sexting by young people into the future. Technological change as well as changes in practices and etiquette will mean that law and educative strategies will always struggle to keep up. However, our research provides some clear implications for future attempts at regulation and legislation, which we draw together in the following closing chapter.

13
Conclusion

Over 160 years ago, Harvey Kellogg outlined what he saw as the dangers of a childhood sexuality out of control. Some contemporary political statements and educational campaigns on childhood sexuality echo him:

> [A] new danger arises to children from corrupt communication of companions, or in the boy from an intense desire to become a man, with a false idea of what manliness means. The brain, precociously stimulated in one direction, receives fresh impulse from evil companionship and evil literature, and even hitherto innocent children of ten are drawn into temptation. (John Harvey Kellogg as cited in Egan and Hawkes 2008, p. 353)

Childhood sexuality has long been constructed as a problem. Concern about sexting is a contemporary manifestation of our impulse to regulate and problematise overt expressions of childhood sexuality, compounded by risks associated with new technologies.

While the harms of sexting are real, we need to make sure that anti-sexting interventions do not exceed the harm caused by sexting itself. As we have demonstrated, the criminalisation of sexting by young people under child pornography laws is, in almost all cases, an unnecessarily harsh response. Moreover, it does not correspond with the motivations that lead to such behaviours, nor does it reflect that, for the most part, such behaviours do not result in harm to either sexting partner. Most harms do not flow merely from young people creating and distributing images of themselves and, even where there are harms, such as regret, humiliation and low self-esteem, criminalising a person for distributing his or her own image adds further unnecessary harm. It is also overly harsh to criminalise a young person for mere possession of an indecent image that has been consensually transmitted to him or her. Given that, as our research and other research (see, e.g., Law Reform Committee of Victoria 2013, p. 136) shows, sexts are often sent by young people as part of a relationship, it is problematic to criminalise the possession of an image that may show behaviour that young people may lawfully engage in. Possession of an image of a young person by another young person does not in itself necessarily reveal an unhealthy sexual interest or an exploitative motive. Rather, as the Law Reform Committee of Victoria notes, this may be part of a normal phase of human development and 'their motivation is to obtain explicit images of people in their age group, at a similar stage of physiological and psychological development, and with similar interests' (2013, p. 139).

Media reporting of sexting by young people has done much to bring the practice into the public domain. As our survey and focus groups suggest, most young people first hear of sexting either from friends or through the media. However, as we discussed in Chapter 3, sexting debates in the media have been driven by anxiety about the harms to which young people have been exposed. Media focus on sexting by young people as a risky behaviour, and one that has explicit harms associated with it, has done much to raise alarm about the practice in public discourse. Moreover, such a discourse of risk may have also provided an incitement to young people to engage in sexting – given many young people's attraction to risk-taking activities. Nonetheless, as we have demonstrated, many media outlets have also been instrumental in raising concern about the possibility of young people being criminalised under child pornography laws.

In addition, when it comes to sexting, we have seen too much research (Kelly 2002) about sexting that focuses on the perceived (im)morality of the practice. As we argue in this book, the moral component of sexting indeed dominates the debate, and is something we have to reconsider. We need to problematise a dichotomy of (desired and welcome) adult sexting versus (deviant and dangerous) teen sexting. Clearly, young people engage in sexting because new technologies have facilitated an activity that was not possible as recently as ten years ago. However, exploration of sexuality by young people is not new. Rather, new technology is offering up new opportunities to explore things that young people have always explored with new mediums opening up spaces for creative new practices. However, as already noted, the evidence suggests that when sexting is consensual, it is largely an extension of existing relationships. Moreover, when it is coercive, it is often an extension of coercive activities already existing in peer groups, school, or particular socio-economic or demographic groups. Additionally, sexting, while sometimes offering up examples of the increasing encroachment of the public sphere by the private sphere, is perhaps only an extension of the way television and other mediums have already eroded or collapsed this somewhat problematic divide. There are thus a range of continuities and discontinuities that can be teased out in regards to sexting. It may well be that sexting provides some young people with a relatively safe environment in which to explore their sexuality, rather than simply producing new risks. That said, there are certainly risks associated with young people and sexting, and these should not be downplayed.

What our research suggests is that most young people experience sexting as something they enter into voluntarily. The vast majority, both young women and men, do not report being pressured or coerced. Rather, they report being motivated by the will to give a partner some kind of sexy gift, to be fun and flirtatious, or because they received an image from someone else. As we have suggested, they have entered into an online gift economy. However, as our perceptions data indicates, they are judged much differently by others – even peers – compared to the way in which they judge themselves. That is, the perceptions of others are often that young women are pressured into sexting, and young men do it to show off. This double standard in the way young women in particular are judged is perhaps the most negative element of sexting and reinforces a set of gendered power relations through which young women's behaviour is problematised, and through which humiliation can occur when things go wrong.

Our research and the research of others confirms that the concept of sexting can cover a vast range of behaviours and motivations and, as such, a one-size-fits-all approach cannot be an appropriate response to sexting. We have therefore argued in this book that the conceptualisation of sexting as a form of child pornography must be reconsidered and a broader focus should be placed on other criminal laws and civil laws, as well as non-legal measures. Of fundamental importance is education that allows young people to navigate the pros and cons of sexting; education that enables them to make informed decisions, understand when they may be being pressured, and negotiate the terms under which they engage in sexting. There is great 'temptation' for young people to engage in sexting. The technological advances that facilitate the practice cannot be undone. Rather, they must learn to navigate this technology, and their online sexual practices, in the safest and most ethical ways possible. In providing such a framework, we must ensure that the agency and citizenship of young people is an important part of the debate, as their voices must be heard in order to develop more effective and more nuanced responses to sexting.

Appendix

The Sydney Institute of Criminology at USYD, along with UNSW and UWS is asking Australian young people to share their views on sexting. This survey will include questions about sexual pictures (like pictures sent to a boyfriend/girlfriend). We would like to know your honest thoughts about this. All responses are anonymous – no one will know you have participated and no one will know which answers are yours. The survey will only take 10–20 minutes.

If you are not comfortable sharing your opinions, please exit the survey now. By continuing, you are giving your consent to participate in the survey.

1. **Would you like to continue?**

   O   Yes

   O   No

2. You indicated you do not want to continue with the survey. Please confirm that you want to exit the survey.

If you choose to continue, you may change your decision at any stage of the survey and exit. Your responses prior to exiting will be used for research and will remain anonymous.

O I do not want to participate

O I would like to continue with the survey

3. Are you:

○   Male

○   Female

○   Other (please specify)

```
[                                                              ]
```

4. How old are you? *Please select <u>one of the following</u>:*

○   Under 13

○   13–15

○   16–18

○   19–21

○   22–24

○   25 and above

Please answer about your use of technology generally.

5. Do you:

	Yes	No
Send/receive text messages	O	O
Have a social networking profile (like on Facebook, Twitter, Instagram, MySpace etc.)	O	O
Have a profile on a dating or singles site	O	O
View profiles/pictures on a social networking site	O	O
View profiles/pictures on a dating/singles site	O	O

If this survey has made you feel uncomfortable or distressed we encourage you to call Kids Help Line 1800 551 800 (free-call) or visit their website by clicking here: www.kidshelp.com.au.

Please answer about your use of technology generally.

6. Do you:

	Yes	No
Write/update a personal blog (like Tumblr or Flickr)	O	O
Read/view blogs	O	O
Send/receive/share pictures (MMS) or videos on your mobile/smart phone	O	O
Send/receive/share pictures or videos on a computer	O	O
Post/upload/share photos (like on YouTube, Facebook, Instagram, Snapchat etc)	O	O
Post/upload/share videos (like on YouTube, Facebook, Instagram, Snapchat etc)	O	O

If this survey has made you feel uncomfortable or distressed we encourage you to call Kids Help Line 1800 551 800 (free-call) or visit their website by clicking here: www.kidshelp.com.au.

Please answer about your use of technology generally.

7. Do you use the internet on a computer or tablet (like an iPad) without adult supervision?

O   Yes

O   No

8. Do you have access to a mobile phone without adult supervision?

O   Yes

O   No

If this survey has made you feel uncomfortable or distressed we encourage you to call Kids Help Line 1800 551 800 (free-call) or visit their website by clicking here: www.kidshelp.com.au.

Throughout this survey, it is **IMPORTANT** that you understand what we mean so that we interpret your answers correctly. Please keep the following in mind as you read and answer each question:

- Any time that we ask about "**sexual pictures/videos**", we are only talking about sexually suggestive, semi-nude, or nude personal pictures and/or videos (like nudes, naked selfies, banana pic etc) – and not those found on the internet (like unwanted mail, images, videos or text from someone you don't know).

- If you hover your cursor over this phrase, a definition will appear to remind you what we mean. Please note this won't work on an ipad/tablet or mobile devices.

9. Sexting is the sending and receiving of sexual images. Where did you first hear about it? *Please tick <u>one option</u>.*

O   School teachers

O   Friends

O   Police officers visiting school

O   An information/prevention web-site

O   A parent or guardian

O   A brother or sister

O   Social networking (like on Facebook, Twitter, Instagram, MySpace etc.)

O   The media (TV, radio, newspapers etc.)

O   This survey

O   Other (please specify)

If this survey has made you feel uncomfortable or distressed we encourage you to call Kids Help Line 1800 551 800 (free-call) or visit their website by clicking here: www.kidshelp.com.au.

10. How common do you think each of the following is among people your age?

	Not Common At All	Common	Very Common	Don't Know
Asking someone for sexual pictures/ videos	O	O	O	O
Sending of sexual pictures/videos of oneself to someone else	O	O	O	O
Posting/uploading of sexual pictures/videos of oneself online	O	O	O	O
Sharing/showing of sexual pictures/ videos with people other than the one(s) they were meant for	O	O	O	O

If this survey has made you feel uncomfortable or distressed we encourage you to call Kids Help Line 1800 551 800 (free-call) or visit their website by clicking here: www.kidshelp.com.au.

11. Do you think each of these activities is more common among guys, girls, or both the same?

	More Common Among GUYS	Both the Same	More Common Among GIRLS	Don't Know
Asking someone for sexual pictures/videos	O	O	O	O
Sending of sexual pictures/videos of oneself to someone else	O	O	O	O
Posting/uploading of sexual pictures/videos of oneself online	O	O	O	O
Sharing/showing of sexual pictures/videos with people other than the one(s) they were meant for	O	O	O	O

If this survey has made you feel uncomfortable or distressed we encourage you to call Kids Help Line 1800 551 800 (free-call) or visit their website by clicking here: www.kidshelp.com.au.

12. Why do you think <u>girls</u> send sexual pictures/videos? Please tick <u>*up to 3 reasons only*</u>:

- ☐ Get or keep a guy/girl's attention
- ☐ Boyfriend/girlfriend pressured them to send it
- ☐ As a sexy present for a boyfriend/girlfriend
- ☐ To feel sexy or confident
- ☐ Get a guy/girl to like them
- ☐ Pressure from friends
- ☐ To get compliments
- ☐ To be included/fit in
- ☐ To be fun/flirty
- ☐ To get noticed or to show off
- ☐ Because she received one
- ☐ I don't know
- ☐ Other (please specify)

If this survey has made you feel uncomfortable or distressed we encourage you to call Kids Help Line 1800 551 800 (free-call) or visit their website by clicking here: www.kidshelp.com.au.

13. Why do you think guys send sexual pictures/videos? Please tick *up to 3 reasons only*:

☐ Get or keep a girl/guy's attention

☐ Boyfriend/girlfriend pressured them to send it

☐ As a sexy present for a girlfriend/boyfriend

☐ To feel sexy or confident

☐ Get a girl/guy to like them

☐ Pressure from friends

☐ To get compliments

☐ To be included/fit in

☐ To be fun/flirty

☐ To get noticed or to show off

☐ Because he received one

☐ I don't know

☐ Other (please specify)

If this survey has made you feel uncomfortable or distressed we encourage you to call Kids Help Line 1800 551 800 (free-call) or visit their website by clicking here: www.kidshelp.com.au.

14. How strongly do you agree or disagree with the following statements? Sexting is:

	Strongly Agree	Agree	Neither Agree nor Disagree	Disagree	Strongly Disagree	Don't Know
Flirty	O	O	O	O	O	O
Gross	O	O	O	O	O	O
Hot	O	O	O	O	O	O
Lame	O	O	O	O	O	O
Stupid	O	O	O	O	O	O
Dangerous	O	O	O	O	O	O
Exciting	O	O	O	O	O	O
Fun	O	O	O	O	O	O
Harmful	O	O	O	O	O	O
Immoral	O	O	O	O	O	O
Bold	O	O	O	O	O	O
Slutty	O	O	O	O	O	O
Cool	O	O	O	O	O	O
Immature	O	O	O	O	O	O
Desperate	O	O	O	O	O	O
Wrong	O	O	O	O	O	O
Daring	O	O	O	O	O	O

If this survey has made you feel uncomfortable or distressed we encourage you to call Kids Help Line 1800 551 800 (free-call) or visit their website by clicking here: www.kidshelp.com.au.

The following section will ask you personal questions. Remember this survey is anonymous.

If you are not comfortable sharing this information, then we encourage you to stop the survey now.

15. Would you like to continue?

○   Yes, I want to continue the survey

○   No, I do not want to continue this part of the survey

16. A 16 year old guy takes a nude picture of his 15 year old girlfriend and sends it to his school mate. What do you think is the most serious thing that could happen to the 16 year old guy? *Please tick <u>one option</u>.*

O He could be charged with child pornography offences and placed on a sex offenders register

O Nothing

O Police could force him to remove his social media pages

O He could face life in prison

O He could be suspended from school

O He could receive a formal police caution

O He could be charged with child pornography offences

O Other (please specify)

```

```

If this survey has made you feel uncomfortable or distressed we encourage you to call Kids Help Line 1800 551 800 (free-call) or visit their website by clicking here: www.kidshelp.com.au.

17. Have you ever sent a sexual picture/video of yourself?

○   Yes

○   No

*If this survey has made you feel uncomfortable or distressed we encourage you
to call Kids Help Line 1800 551 800 free-call)
or visit their website by clicking here: www.kidshelp.com.au.*

18. Who have you sent a sexual picture/video (of yourself) to? Please *tick all that apply*.

- ☐   Boyfriend/girlfriend
- ☐   Someone I have dated or hooked up with
- ☐   Someone I just met
- ☐   Someone I wanted to date or hook up with
- ☐   One or more personal friends
- ☐   Someone I only knew online
- ☐   Someone I didn't know
- ☐   Other (please specify)

If this survey has made you feel uncomfortable or distressed we encourage you to call Kids Help Line 1800 551 800 (free-call) or visit their website by clicking here: www.kidshelp.com.au.

19. Why did you send a sexual picture/video (of yourself)? Please tick _all that apply_.

☐ Get or keep a girl/guy's attention

☐ Boyfriend/girlfriend pressured them to send it

☐ As a sexy present for a girlfriend/boyfriend

☐ To feel sexy or confident

☐ Get a girl/guy to like them

☐ Pressure from friends

☐ To get compliments

☐ To be fun/flirty

☐ To get noticed or to show off

☐ To be included/fit in

☐ Because I received one

☐ I don't know

☐ Other (please specify)

If this survey has made you feel uncomfortable or distressed we encourage you to call Kids Help Line 1800 551 800 (free-call) or visit their website by clicking here: www.kidshelp.com.au.

20. In the past 12 months, how many people have you sent a sexual picture/ video to?

O   No one in the past 12 months

O   One person

O   2 – 5 people

O   More than 5 people

If this survey has made you feel uncomfortable or distressed we encourage you to call Kids Help Line 1800 551 800 (free-call) or visit their website by clicking here: www.kidshelp.com.au.

21. Have you ever received a sexual picture/video?

  O   Yes

  O   No

*If this survey has made you feel uncomfortable or distressed we encourage you
to call Kids Help Line 1800 551 800 (free-call)
or visit their website by clicking here: www.kidshelp.com.au.*

22. Who have you ever received sexual pictures/videos from? Please *tick all that apply*.

- ☐ Boyfriend/girlfriend
- ☐ Someone I have dated or hooked up with
- ☐ Someone I just met
- ☐ Someone who wanted to date or hook up with me
- ☐ One or more personal friends
- ☐ Someone I only knew online
- ☐ Other (please specify)

If this survey has made you feel uncomfortable or distressed we encourage you to call Kids Help Line 1800 551 800 (free-call) or visit their website by clicking here: www.kidshelp.com.au.

23. In the last 12 months, how many people have you received sexual pictures/videos from?

   ○ No one in the past 12 months

   ○ One person

   ○ 2 – 5 people

   ○ More than 5 people

If this survey has made you feel uncomfortable or distressed we encourage you to call Kids Help Line 1800 551 800 (free-call)
or visit their website by clicking here: www.kidshelp.com.au.

24. Have you ever:

	Yes	No
Shown (in person) a sexual picture/video to someone who wasn't meant to see it (for example, shown your phone to someone at school)	O	O
Shared a sexual picture/video with someone online who wasn't meant to see it (for example, on Facebook)	O	O
Sent or forwarded on a sexual picture/video to someone who wasn't meant to see it (for example, MMS or email)	O	O

If this survey has made you feel uncomfortable or distressed we encourage you to call Kids Help Line 1800 551 800 (free-call) or visit their website by clicking here: www.kidshelp.com.au.

25. What might discourage you from sending sexual pictures/videos? *Please tick __up to 3 options only__.*

☐   Already had a bad experience

☐   Could disappoint family

☐   Could disappoint friends

☐   Could disappoint teacher

☐   Could hurt my relationship or chances with someone I like

☐   Could hurt my reputation

☐   Could hurt my family's reputation

☐   Could get in trouble with the law

☐   Could get in trouble at school

☐   Potential (or current) employer might see

☐   Potential embarrassment

☐   Might regret it later

☐   Might make people think I'm slutty in real life

☐   I don't know

☐   Other (please specify)

If this survey has made you feel uncomfortable or distressed we encourage you to call Kids Help Line 1800 551 800 (free-call) or visit their website by clicking here: www.kidshelp.com.au.

26. How strongly do you agree or disagree with each of the following statements?

	Strongly Agree	Agree	Neither Agree nor Disagree	Disagree	Strongly Disagree	Don't Know
There is pressure among people my age to post sexual pictures/videos in their (social networking) profiles	O	O	O	O	O	O
Personal sexual pictures/videos usually end up being seen by more than the people they were sent to	O	O	O	O	O	O
Girls have to worry about privacy (of sexual pictures/videos) more than guys do	O	O	O	O	O	O
People my age are more confident sexually with sexual pictures/videos than they are in real life	O	O	O	O	O	O
Sexting is no big deal	O	O	O	O	O	O
Sexting can have serious negative consequences	O	O	O	O	O	O
My friends have sent sexual pictures/videos to someone	O	O	O	O	O	O
My friends have posted sexual pictures/videos on the Internet	O	O	O	O	O	O
People who exchange sexual pictures/videos are more likely to date or hook up with each other in real life	O	O	O	O	O	O
Sexting makes people feel good	O	O	O	O	O	O

If this survey has made you feel uncomfortable or distressed we encourage you to call Kids Help Line 1800 551 800 (free-call) or visit their website by clicking here: www.kidshelp.com.au.

27. Which of the following best describes how you think of yourself in terms of your sexual preference?

○   Heterosexual/straight

○   Lesbian

○   Gay

○   Bisexual

○   Questioning (not sure if you are straight, gay, lesbian or bisexual)

○   Other (please specify)

If this survey has made you feel uncomfortable or distressed we encourage you to call Kids Help Line 1800 551 800 (free-call) or visit their website by clicking here: www.kidshelp.com.au.

28. Which of the following best describes your <u>current</u> relationship status?

- O Not in a relationship
- O Just started seeing someone
- O In a casual/dating relationship
- O In a long term relationship
- O Married
- O Other (please specify)

[   ]

29. Where do you currently live?

- O ACT
- O NSW
- O Northern Territory
- O Queensland
- O South Australia
- O Tasmania
- O Victoria
- O Western Australia
- O Other (please specify)

[   ]

30. What is the postcode where you live?

[   ]

31. What is the suburb/town you live in?

[   ]

If this survey has made you feel uncomfortable or distressed we encourage you to call Kids Help Line 1800 551 800 (free-call) or visit their website by clicking here: www.kidshelp.com.au.

32. Which of the following best describes where you live?

O   City or suburban

O   Rural or country

33. Are you:

O   Torres Straight Islander or Aboriginal

O   White (Anglo Saxon) European born in Australia

O   Non-white European born in Australia

O   Asian born in Australia

O   South American born in Australia

O   North American born in Australia

O   African born in Australia

O   Pacific Islander born in Australia

O   Middle Eastern born in Australia

O   White (Anglo Saxon) European born outside Australia

O   Non-white European born outside Australia

O   Asian born outside Australia

O   South American born outside Australia

O   North American born outside Australia

O   African born outside Australia

O   Pacific Islander born outside Australia

O   Middle Eastern born outside Australia

O   Other (please specify)

If this survey has made you feel uncomfortable or distressed we encourage you to call Kids Help Line 1800 551 800 (free-call) or visit their website by clicking here: www.kidshelp.com.au.

34. What is your religion?

- ○ No religion
- ○ Christianity
- ○ Islam
- ○ Judaism
- ○ Hinduism
- ○ Buddhism
- ○ Other (please specify)

If this survey has made you feel uncomfortable or distressed we encourage you to call Kids Help Line 1800 551 800 (free-call) or visit their website by clicking here: www.kidshelp.com.au.

Thank you for your interest in the survey. This survey is only for people above 13 years old. You will now be exited from the site.

If this survey has made you feel uncomfortable or distressed we encourage you
to call Kids Help Line 1800 551 800 (free-call)
or visit their website by clicking here: www.kidshelp.com.au.

The team appreciates you participating in our research by providing valuable insight into the subject of Sexting and Young People. If you would like to find out more information about the research, you can visit their website: www.sydney.edu.au/law/criminology.

If this survey has made you feel uncomfortable or distressed we encourage you to call Kids Help Line 1800 551 800 (free-call) or visit their website by clicking here: www.kidshelp.com.au.

To protect your privacy, please close this browser page after you have selected the **Done** button below. Thank you again on behalf of the University of Sydney, University of New South Wales and the University of Western Sydney.

Notes

1 Understanding Sexting by Young People

1. Child pornography offences are sometimes referred to by other labels, such as 'child abuse material' or 'child exploitation material'. Throughout this book, we refer to these offences as 'child pornography offences' unless detailing a specific jurisdictional offence.
2. Throughout this book we generally use the term 'young people' (also young men and young women) to refer to those under the age of 18.

2 Conceptualising Sexting

1. Which, as Coopersmith (2000) points out, has played an integral role in the proliferation of the internet and other media technologies.

3 Young People and Sexting Discourses

1. There are obvious limitations to the retrieval and compilation of content through databases such as ProQuest, not least of which is the potential for important or relevant stories to be excluded from the sample due to the choice of search terms that may limit or narrow the categories of analysis (Jewkes 2011b, p. 250).
2. Wire feeds are news items that come from organisations such as the Associated Press, whose journalists supply news reports to news organisations, such as newspapers, magazines, and radio and television networks.
3. While 'sext text' was first mentioned in the print media in two articles from 2002, the use of the term in these articles was actually in relation to a newly released sex book, as opposed to sexually explicit mobile text messages, and thus their relevance has been discounted in relation to this study.

4 Sexting as Child Pornography

1. See, for example, Law Reform Committee of Victoria 2013, p. 108 which refers to evidence by Paterson, Acting Commander of Victoria Police, noting that while prosecution under child pornography offences is rare the alternative in an incident from 2010 was a caution or no further police action.
2. This case does not fit the paradigm of sexting because the pictures were distributed in hard copy rather than electronically. Nevertheless the principles involved apply to sexting cases.
3. This was confirmed by the Court of Appeal: *Eades v DPP* [2010] NSWCA 241, [33]. Since this case the definition of 'child pornography' has been widened in NSW and now can include depictions of the private parts of a child.

4. This may relate to a case in which certain facts relevant to the decision to prosecute were not revealed. In evidence before the Law Reform Committee of Victoria, Neil Paterson, Acting Commander of Victoria Police noted that:

> There is another person, which is a matter that has been referred to in media articles, where both the victim and the offender were 17 years old when certain footage of them having sex was taken by one of the parties. If you read about the actual nature of the offending, it sounds like a consensual sexual relationship and there is a video and it has been distributed somewhere. It sounds like someone has ended up on the Sex Offenders Registry for something quite minor. The footage was taken when they were both 17, but when the male of the relationship was 19, he then forwarded on to four other people via email the video of the victim and him having sex, so it was not via a text message or sexting sort of process for forwarding the image. But more worrying is the nature of the offending, because in reading the victim's statement it all came about because the offender had threatened the victim that if she did not have sex with him and allow him to videotape it, he would disclose their sexual relationship to her parents – she came from a very conservative and religious background. The relationship continued and then he also threatened that if she did not have oral sex or anal sex with him on numerous occasions, he would then distribute the video that he had already taken on to her friends and family. (Paterson 2012, p. 15)

5. Gillespie (2010a, p. 16) notes that it was not until around the 1970s that concern to regulate child pornography distinct from other obscene material developed.

6. It is acknowledged that some jurisdictions may have more than one age of consent with a higher age level set where there is a position of trust or authority, or for certain sexual acts.

7. See *United States v Dost*, 636 F Supp 828, 832 (SD Cal 1986); see also *United States v Brunette*, 256 F3d 14, 18 (1st Cir 2001) (adopting and applying the *Dost* factors); *United States v Villard*, 885 F2d 117, 122 (3d Cir 1989) (adopting and applying the *Dost* factors).

8. Quoting *Roth v United States*, 354 US 476, 485 (1957).

9. First, because of the physiological, emotional and mental health harms to children associated with child pornography, the states have a compelling interest in the prevention of sexual exploitation and abuse of children. Second, distribution of photographs harms children because they 'are a permanent record of the children's participation' and horrible reminders of prior sexual abuse. Additionally, the only way to decrease production is to close the market for distribution. Third, distribution is an economic motive for production. Fourth, the value of child pornography is 'exceedingly modest, if not *de minimis*'. Fifth, not granting child pornography First Amendment protection is consistent with earlier decisions, which exempted content from constitutional protection when its harm outweighed its benefit (at 756–64).

10. Non-photographic pornographic images of children have been criminalised in the *Criminal Justice and Immigration Act 2008* (UK), s 63.

5 Factors Determining Whether Young People Are Prosecuted

1. Although it should be noted that the abolition of the higher level where there was a presumption of *doli incapax* was not connected with an increase in the minimum age level of criminal responsibility, which had been raised from the common law level of seven to eight through the *Children and Young Persons Act 1933*, s.50 and to ten through the *Children and Young Persons Act 1963*, s.16. The presumption of *doli incapax* applying to young people aged 10 but not yet 14 was abolished through the *Crime and Disorder Act 1998*, s. 34 (see, e.g., Crofts 2002, pp. 65–90).
2. The case name changed due to change of District Attorney while the case was on appeal.
3. Although this tends to be overt, rather than societal coercion. For discussion of forms of coercion, see Chapter 2.
4. Although a recent US study found that in nearly two-thirds of cases, images were confined to mobile phones and were not posted on the internet: see Wodak, Finkelhor and Mitchell, above n 74, 9.

6 Sexting Education

1. We have seen the transfer of this discourse into Parliamentary debate in 2010, in which Senator Simpkins called sexting an 'unhealthy behaviour' (see Lee et al. 2013).
2. This is why we refer to such interventions as 'anti-sexting' campaigns.
3. Many Australian anti-sexting campaigns are either spin-offs or adapted versions of overseas campaigns (especially from the United Kingdom).
4. A rare exception is the educational DVD 'Photograph', which involved teenagers in the production of the movie (Cyber Safe Kids 2010).

7 Review of Existing Research

1. Cox Communications (2009); Dake et al. (2013); Englander (2012); Joint Select Committee on Cyber-Safety (2011); Lenhart/Pew Internet and American Life Project (2009); Peskin et al. (2013); Phippen (2009); Strassberg et al. (2013); The National Campaign to Prevent Teen and Unplanned Pregnancy (2008); Tallon et al. (2012).
2. See Lounsbury et al. (2011, p. 3) for a more expansive critique.
3. Elsewhere, Ringrose and her colleagues have developed nuanced conceptual frames for understanding girls 'schizoid subjectivities' from experiencing pleasure to pressures that provide a useful way of conceiving of girls' array of responses to sexting (Renold and Ringrose 2011; Ringrose and Renold 2012a, b; Ringrose et al. 2013).

8 Sexting: Young People's Voices

1. Triple J is the Australian Broadcasting Corporation's (ABC) national youth radio network. 'Hack' is a Triple J current affairs program aired each weekday afternoon at 5.30 p.m.
2. By active senders we refer to those that had ever reported sending a sext.
3. This data includes the adult cohort due to the lower number of respondents in the younger age cohorts.

9 Perceptions and Practices of Sexting

1. A sub-forum of Reddit 'where redditors share suggestive photos of women taken publicly and without their consent' (Alfonso 2014).
2. Criminal justice interventions are discussed at greater length in the Chapter 10.

12 Futures and New Directions

1. Similar defences will apply to publication or transmission of child pornography: *Crimes Amendment (Sexual Offences and Other Matters) Act 2014* (Vic), s 28, amending s 57A of the *Classification (Publications, Films and Computer Games) (Enforcement) Act 1995* (Vic).
2. This may be because of an all or nothing approach to child pornography offences by police. For instance, Paterson, on behalf of Victoria Police, noted before the Law Reform Committee of Victoria that when police do investigate sexting prosecution for child pornography is rare but the alternative is a caution or no further police action (based on figures in relation to an incident in 2010 (Law Reform Committee of Victoria 2013, p. 108). It is, however, acknowledged that this limited case example may not reflect police practice across jurisdictions.
3. As noted in Chapter 5 this may be due to police operational manuals requiring police to prosecute for the offence most fitting the facts and police seeing child pornography offences as the most fitting offences.
4. For a discussion of revenge pornography and the potential legal responses, see Salter and Crofts (2015).

Bibliography

Aas, KF 2007, *Globalization and crime*, Sage, London.

ABC Ballarat 2010, *Police adopt anti-sexting campaign*, viewed 11 January 2015, http://www.abc.net.au/news/stories/2010/08/30/2997371.htm?site=ballarat.

ABC South West WA 2011, *Underage sex case triggers 'sexting' warning*, viewed 12 December 2014, http://www.abc.net.au/news/stories/2011/01/25/3121304. htm?site=southwestwa.

ACMAcybersmart 2011, *Tagged*, online video, viewed 12 December 2014, http://www.youtube.com/watch?v=TtEGAcLBTTA.

Akdeniz, Y 2008, *Internet child pornography and the law: national and international responses*, Ashgate, Hampshire.

Albury, K 2013, 'Young people, media and sexual learning: rethinking representation', *Sex Education: Sexuality, Society and Learning*, 13, sup. 1, S32–S44.

Albury, K & Crawford, K 2012, 'Sexting, consent and young people's ethics: beyond Megan's story', *Continuum*, 26(3), 463–73.

Albury, K, Crawford, K, Byron, P & Mathews, B 2013, *Young people and sexting in Australia: ethics, representation and the law*, ARC Centre for Creative Industries and Innovation/Journalism and Media Research Centre, University of New South Wales, Australia.

Albury, K, Funnel, N & Noonan, E 2010, 'The politics of sexting: young people, self-representation and citizenship', refereed Conference Proceeding, Australian and New Zealand Communication Association Conference 'Media, Democracy and Change', Old Parliament House, 7–9 July 2010, viewed 12 December 2014, http://www.crr.unsw.edu.au/media/File/AlburyFunnellNoonan.pdf.

Alder, A 2001, 'The perverse law of child pornography', *Colombia Law Review*, 101, 209.

Alfonso, F 2014, 'Creepshots never went away – we just stopped talking about them', *The Daily Dot*, viewed 12 December 2014, http://www.dailydot.com/lifestyle/reddit-creepshots-candidfashionpolice-photos/.

Anderson, L 2009, 'To friend or not to friend? College admissions in the age of Facebook', *USA TODAY*, viewed 12 December 2014, http://usatoday30.usatoday.com/news/education/2009–09–16-facebook-admissions_N.htm.

Anonymous, 2010, 'Kids can be charged under "sexting" laws', *The Daily Telegraph*, 19 March, p. 3.

Anonymous, 2010, 'Court case displays worry of teens sexting each other', *Fraser Coast Chronicle*, 22 October, p. 16.

Anonymous, 2011, 'New protocols for explicit texts', *ABC Premium News*, 5 December.

Angelides, S 2013, '"Technology, hormones and stupidity": the effective politics of teenage sexting', *Sexualities*, 16(5–6), 665–89.

Arcabascio, C 2009–10, 'Sexting and Teenagers: OMG R U Going 2 Jail???', *Richmond Journal of Law and Technology*, 16(3), 1–43.

Ashworth, A & Horder, J 2013, *Principles of Criminal Law*, 7th edn, OUP, Oxford.

Association of Chief Police Officers of England, Wales and Northern Ireland, ACPO Child Protection and Abuse Investigation (CPAI) Group (n.d.), 'ACPO CPAI Lead's Position on Young People Who Post Self-Taken Indecent Images', viewed 12 December 2014, http://ceop.police.uk/Documents/ceopdocs/exter-naldocs/ACPO_Lead_position_on_Self_Taken_Images.pdf.

Atkin, M 2011, 'Anti-sexting campaign branded dull, unrealistic', *ABC News*, viewed 12 December 2014, http://www.abc.net.au/news/2011-04-16/anti-sexting-campaign-branded-dull-unrealistic/2612398.

Attorney-General's Department (Cth) 2009, Criminal Justice Division, Australian Government, *Proposed Reforms to Commonwealth Child Sex-Related Offences.*

Attwood, F 2009, *Mainstreaming sex: the sexualisation of western culture*, London, I. B. Taurus & Co.

Australian Federal Police 2012, 'Submission No. S57', Law Reform Committee, Parliament of Victoria, viewed 12 December 2014, http://www.parliament.vic. gov.au/images/stories/committees/lawrefrom/isexting/subs/S57_-_AFP.pdf.

Australian Government 2010, *Fact Sheet: TXTing/SEXTing*, The Line. On file with authors.

Australian Law Reform Commission 1997, *Seen and heard: priority for children in the legal process* (ALRC Report 84), viewed 12 December 2014, http://www.alrc. gov.au/publications/report-84.

Australian Law Reform Commission, New South Wales Law Reform Commission 2010, *Family violence – a national legal response – Volume 1* (ALRC Report 114; NSWLRC Report 128), viewed 12 December 2014, http://www.alrc.gov.au/sites/ default/files/pdfs/publications/ALRC114_WholeReport.pdf.

Australian Privacy Foundation 2012, 'Submission to the Victorian Parliament's Law Reform Committee on the Inquiry into Sexting', Law Reform Committee, Parliament of Victoria, viewed 12 December 2014, http://www.privacy.org.au/ Papers/VicParlt-Sexting-120607.pdf.

Battersby, L 2008, 'Alarm at teenage "sexting" traffic', *The Age*, 10 July, p. 3.

Bauman, Z 2000, *Liquid modernity*, Polity Press, Cambridge.

Beck, U 1992, *Risk society: towards a new modernity*, Sage, London.

Beck, U, Giddens, A & Lash, S 1994, *Reflexive modernization: politics, tradition and aesthetics in the modern social order*, Stanford University Press, Stanford.

Becker, H 1963, *Outsiders: studies in the sociology of deviance*, Free Press, New York.

Benns, M 2003, 'It keeps getting worse: my affair with Warne stripper reveals all', *Sun Herald*, 24 August, p. 9.

Berg, C 2011, 'One hack of a crime wave, or so they say', *Sydney Morning Herald*, 26 June, available at http://www.smh.com.au/opinion/politics/one-hack-of-a-crime-wave-or-so-they-say-20110625-1gkrf.html.

Berkman Center for Internet and Society 2008, 'Enhancing Child Safety & Online Technologies, Final Report of the Internet Safety Technical Task Force to the Multi-State Working Group on Social Networking of State Attorneys General of the United States', viewed 12 December 2014, http://cyber.law.harvard.edu/ pubrelease/isttf/.

Bessant, J 2008, 'Hard wired for risk: neurological science, "the adolescent brain" and developmental theory'. *Journal of Youth Studies*, 11(3), 347–60.

Birdee 2013, *Sorry, but your dick pic is illegal: new sexting laws for Victoria*, viewed 12 December 2014, http://birdeemag.com/dick-pic-illegal/.

Bita, N 2012, 'Sexting teens risk porn charge', *The Courier Mail*, 1 October, viewed 12 December 2014, http://www.couriermail.com.au/news/national/sexting-teens-risk-porn-charge/story-fndo1yus-1226484895382.

Bond, E 2010, 'The mobile phone = *bike shed*? Children, sex and mobile phones', *New Media & Society*, 13(4), 587–604.

Boyd, D 2007, 'Social network sites: public, private, or what?', *Knowledge Tree*, viewed 12 December 2014, http://www.danah.org/papers/KnowledgeTree.pdf.

Branley, A 2010, 'Kids in net alert', *Newcastle Herald*, 18 September, p. 1.

Brownlie, J 2001, 'The "being-risky" child: governing childhood and sexual risk', *Sociology*, 35(2), 519–37.

Buckingham, D 2008, 'Introducing identity', in D Buckingham (ed.), *Youth, Identity, and Digital Media, The John D and Catherine T MacArthur Foundation Series on Digital Media and Learning*, Massachusetts Institute of Technology Press, Cambridge, pp. 1–22.

Burke, R 2008, *Young people, crime and justice*, Willan Publishing, Devon.

Butler, J 1990, *Gender trouble: feminism and the subversion of identity*, Routledge.

Cann, L 2008, 'Strife of the party', *The Sunday Times*, 16 November, p. 32.

CareerBuilder 2014, *Number of Employers Passing on Applicants Due to Social Media Posts Continues to Rise, According to New CareerBuilder Survey*, viewed 12 December 2014, http://www.careerbuilder.com/share/aboutus/pressreleasesdetail.aspx?sd=6%2F26%2F2014&id=pr829&ed=12%2F31%2F2014.

Carmody, M 2013, *Sex and Ethics*, viewed 12 December 2014, http://www.sexandethics.net/.

Carr-Greg, M 2012, 'Opinion: Oh what a tangled world wide web it can be', *Newcastle Herald*, 30 October, p. 11.

CASA Forum 2012, 'Submission to Inquiry into Sexting', viewed 12 December 2014, http://www.casa.org.au/assets/ReportsPapers/SextingInquiryfinal14612.pdf.

Catholic Education Office Sydney 2014, *Our Schools*, viewed 12 December 2014, http://www.ceosyd.catholic.edu.au/Parents/Pages/our-schools.aspx.

Cauffman, E & Steinberg, L 2000, '(Im)maturity of judgment in adolescence: why adolescents may be less culpable than adults', *Behavioral Sciences & the Law*, 18, 741–60.

Chalmers, J & Leverick, F 2008, 'Fair labelling in criminal law', *Modern Law Review*, 71, 217.

Chan, J 2005, 'Conclusion', in J Chan (ed.), *Reshaping juvenile justice: The NSW Young Offenders Act 1997*, Institute of Criminology, Sydney.

Chibnall, S 1977, 'Press ideology: the politics of professionalism', in C Greer (ed.), *Crime and media: a reader*, Routledge, London, pp. 203–14.

Christie, N 1986, 'The ideal victim', in E Fattah (ed.), *From crime policy to victim policy: reorienting the justice system*, Macmillan, Basingstoke.

Cipriani, D 2009, *Children's rights and the minimum age of criminal responsibility*, Ashgate, Farnham.

Cohen, S 1973, *Folk devils and moral panics*, Paladin, St Albans.

Coleman, J & Hendry, L 1999, *The nature of adolescence*, Routledge, New York.

Coopersmith, J 2000, 'Pornography, videotape and the internet', *Technology and Society Magazine*, 19(1), 27–34.

Corby, EK, Campbell, M, Spears, B, Slee, P, Butler, D and Kift, S 2015. 'Students' Perceptions of Their Own Victimization: A Youth Voice Perspective'. *Journal of School Violence*, 18, 1–21.

'Court case displays worry of teens sexting each other' 2010, *Fraser Coast Chronicle*, 22 October, p. 16.

Cox Communications 2009, 'Teen Online & Wireless Safety Survey: Cyberbullying, Sexting, and Parental Controls', available online at http://ww2.cox.com/wcm/en/aboutus/datasheet/takecharge/2009-teen-survey.

pdf?campcode=takecharge-research-link_2009-teen-survey_0511. Last accessed 24 January 2014.

Crofts, T 2002, *The criminal responsibility of children and young people*, Ashgate, London.

Crofts, T & Lee, M 2013, '"Sexting", children and child pornography', *Sydney Law Review*, 35, 85–106.

Crown Prosecution Service undated, Prosecution Policy and Guidance, Youth Offenders, Child sex offences committed by children or young persons, viewed 12 December 2014, http://www.cps.gov.uk/legal/v_to_z/youth_offenders/#a29.

Cumming, PE 2009, 'Children's rights, children's voices, children's technology, children's sexuality' (Paper presented at Roundtable on Youth, Sexuality, Technology, Carleton University, 26 May 2009), viewed 12 December 2014, http://www.yorku.ca/cummingp/documents/TeenSextingbyPeterCummingMay262009.pdf.

Cupples, J & Thompson, L 2010, 'Heterotextuality and digital foreplay', Feminist Media Studies, 10(1), 1–17.

Cyber Safe Kids 2010, '"Photograph" a film about "sexting" and cyber bullying'. Available at http://www.cybersafekids.com.au/2010/06/photograph-a-film-about-sexting-and-cyber-bullying/.

CyberSmart 2014a, 'So you got naked online …', viewed 12 December 2014, http://www.cybersmart.gov.au/Teens/How%20do%20I%20deal%20with/~/media/Cybersmart/Documents/Documents/So%20you%20got%20naked%20online.pdf.

CyberSmart 2014b, *Teens*, viewed 12 December 2014, http://www.cybersmart.gov.au/Teens.aspx.

CyberSmart 2014c, *Schools*, viewed 12 December 2014, http://www.cybersmart.gov.au/Schools.aspx.

CyberSmart 2014d, *About outreach training*, viewed 11 January 2015, http://www.cybersmart.gov.au/Outreach/about-outreach-training.aspx.

Dake, J, Price, J, Maziarz, L & Ward, B 2013, 'Prevalence and correlates of sexting behaviour in adolescents', *American Journal of Sexuality Education*, 7(1), 1–15.

D'Amato, P 2014, 'Hacked celebrity nude photos are selling online for $350 with hundreds of previously unseen photos and videos for sale', *Daily Mail*, viewed 12 December 2014, http://www.dailymail.co.uk/news/article-2785871/Photos-unreleased-potentially-massive-collection-stolen-celebrity-nudes-bought-online-350.html.

Danks, K 2010, 'Bond for Sydney man "sexting" with teens', *The Daily Telegraph*, 18 December, viewed 12 December 2014, http://www.dailytelegraph.com.au/bond-for-sydney-man-sexting-with-teen/story-e6freuy9-1225972931904.

Davidson, J & Gottschalk, P 2010, *Internet child abuse: current research and policy*, Routledge, London.

Day, T 2010, 'The new digital dating behavior – Sexting: teens' explicit love letters: criminal justice or civil liability', viewed 12 December 2014, http://works.bepress.com/cgi/viewcontent.cgi?article=1005&context=terrI_day.

Declaration and Agenda for Action, 1st World Congress against Commercial Sexual Exploitation of Children, Stockholm, Sweden, 27–31 August 1996, viewed 12 December 2014, http://www.ecpat.net/sites/default/files/stockholm_declaration_1996.pdf.

Deleuze, G & Guattari, F 1972, *Anti-Oedipus*, Continuum, London and New York.

Department of Education and Early Childhood Development 2013, 'Sexting', viewed 12 December 2014, http://www.education.vic.gov.au/Documents/about/programs/bullystoppers/smsexting.pdf.

Derrida, J 1995, *The gift of death*, University of Chicago Press, Chicago.

Director of Public Prosecutions Victoria 2014, *Director's policy: prosecutorial discretion*, viewed 12 December 2014, http://www.opp.vic.gov.au/getattachment/5b830306-a17b-4ada-9078–6982539d44ac/2-The-Prosecutorial-Discretion.aspx.

Dobson, A, Rasmussen, M & Tyson, D 2012, 'Submission to the Victorian Law Reform Committee Inquiry into Sexting', Law Reform Committee, Parliament of Victoria, viewed 12 December 2014, http://www.parliament.vic.gov.au/images/stories/committees/lawrefrom/isexting/subs/S34_-_Dobson_Rasmussen_Tyson_Monash_Uni.pdf.

Draper, N 2012, 'Is your teen at risk? Discourses of adolescent sexting in United States television news', *Journal of Children and Media*, 6(2), 221–36.

Drotner, K 1992, 'Modernity and media panics', in M Skovmand & KC Schroder (eds), *Media cultures: reappraising transnational media*, Routledge, New York.

Duncan, SH 2014, 'Child pornography statutes and new legislation', in Hiestand, TC & Weins, WJ (eds), *Sexting and youth*, Carolina Academic Press, Durham.

Durham, M 2008, *The Lolita Effect: the media sexualisation of young girls and what we cane do about it*, Gerald Duchworth Press, London.

Egan, D & Hawkes, G 2008, 'Imperiled and perilous: exploring the history of childhood sexuality', *Journal of Historical Sociology*, 21(4), 355–67.

Ehrlich, S 2002, *Representing rape: language and sexual consent*, Routledge, New York.

Eleftheriou-Smith, LM 2014, 'Teenagers who "sext" each other could land themselves on sex offenders' register', *The Independent*, 23 July, viewed 12 December 2014, http://www.independent.co.uk/news/uk/home-news/teenagers-who-sext-each-other-could-land-themselves-on-sex-offenders-register-9622340.html.

Englander, E 2012, 'Low risk associated with most teenage sexting: a study of 617 18-year-olds', *Massachusetts Aggression Reduction Center*, Bridgewater State University.

English, B 2004, 'Becks Inc survives sex, slumps and gaffes', *The Daily Telegraph*, 12 November, p. 91.

Ericson, R 1982, 'Reproducing order', extract reprinted in T Newburn (ed.) 2005, *Policing: key readings*, Willan, Cullompton.

Explanatory Memorandum to the Crimes Legislation Amendment (Sexual Offences against Children) Bill 2010 (Cth), viewed 12 December 2014, http://www.austlii.edu.au/au/legis/cth/bill_Em/claoacb2010554/memo_1.html.

Farber, H 2014, 'Eyes in the sky: constitutional and regulatory approaches to domestic drone deployment', *Syracuse Law Review*, 64(1), 1–48.

Farrer, G 2008, 'The art world should not sneer at society's genuine concerns', *The Age*, 9 July, p. 11.

Faulkner, J 2011a, *The importance of being innocent: why we worry about children*, Cambridge University Press, Melbourne.

Faulkner, J 2011b, 'Vulnerability and the passing of childhood in Bill Henson: innocence in the age of mechanical reproduction', *Parrhesia*, 11, 44–55.

Feeney, K 2013, 'Sexting children charged with porn offences', *Brisbane Times*, 25 June, viewed 12 December 2014, http://www.brisbanetimes.com.au/queensland/sexting-children-charged-with-porn-offences-20130625-2oub3.html.

Ferrell, J, Hayward, K & Young, J 2008, *Cultural criminology*, Sage, London.

Fisher, S, Sauter, A, Slobodniuk, L & Young, C 2012, 'Sexting in Australia: the legal and social ramifications', viewed 12 December 2014, http://www.parliament.vic.gov.au/images/stories/committees/lawrefrom/isexting/subs/S07_-_Salvation_Army_Oasis_Hunter.pdf.

Fishman, S 1982, 'The history of childhood sexuality', *Journal of Contemporary History*, 17, 269–83.

Forde, L 2011, *Sexting: the legal implications*, CornwallStodart, viewed 12 December 2014, http://cornwalls.com.au/sharing-knowledge/legal-updates/sexting-the-legal-implications.aspx.

Foucault, M 1988, Technologies of the self, edited by LH Martin, H Gutman and PH Hutton, Tavistock Publications, London.

Foucault, M 1990, *The history of sexuality*, Penguin, London.

Fox, R 2001, 'Someone to watch over us: back to the panopticon?', *Criminal Justice*, 1(3), 251–76.

Frazer, N 1990, 'Rethinking the public sphere: a contribution to the critique of actually existing democracy', *Social Text*, 25/26, 56–80.

Fried, C & Reppucci, N 2001, 'Criminal decision making: the development of adolescent judgment, criminal responsibility, and culpability', *Law and Human Behavior*, 25, 45–61.

Furlong, A & Cartmel F 1997, *Young people and social change*, Open University Press, Berkshire.

Galfoway, L 2010, 'Thumbs down: an anti-"sexting" video ends up victim-blaming instead', *Bitch*, viewed 12 December 2014, http://askdrstephanie.com/assets/sexting.pdf.

Garland, D 1997, 'Governmentality and the problem of crime: Foucault, criminology, sociology', *Theoretical Criminology*, 1(2), 173–214.

Giddens, A 1991, *Modernity and self-identity: self and society in the late modern age*, Stanford University Press, Stanford.

Gill, R 2012, 'Media, empowermenr and the "sexualisation of culture" debates', *Sex roles*, 66, 736–45.

Gillespie, A 2010a, 'Legal definitions of child pornography', *Journal of Sexual Aggression*, 16(1), 19–32.

Gillespie, A 2010b, 'Defining child pornography: challenges for the law', *Child and Family Law Quarterly*, 22, 200–22.

Gillespie, A 2013, 'Adolescents, sexting and human rights', *Human Rights Law Review*, 13(4), 623–43.

Golan, G 2006, 'Inter-media agenda setting and global news coverage: assessing the influence of the New York Times on three network television evening news programs', *Journalism Studies*, 7(2), 323–33.

Goldstein, L 2009, 'Documenting and denial: discourses of sexual self-exploitation', *Jump Cut*, viewed 12 December 2014, http://www.ejumpcut.org/archive/jc51.2009/goldstein/.

Grahl, T 2014, 'The 6 types of social media', *Out:Think*, viewed 12 December 2014, http://outthinkgroup.com/tips/the-6-types-of-social-media.

Greenfield, P 2004, 'Inadvertent exposure to pornography on the internet', *Journal of Applied Developmental Psychology*, 25(6), 741–50.

Greer, C 2010, *Crime and media: a reader*, Routledge, London.

Gregory, R 2012, 'Submission to Victorian Law Reform Committee Inquiry into Sexting', *Women's Health West*, Law Reform Committee, Parliament of Victoria, viewed 12 December 2014, http://whwest.org.au/wp-content/uploads/2012/03/SUB_Vic-Law-Reform-Inquiry-Sexting1.pdf.

Gudelunas, D 2012, 'There's an app for that: the uses and gratifications of online social networks for gay men', *Sexuality & Culture*, 16, 347–65.

Habermas, J 1989, *The structural transformation of the public sphere: an inquiry into a category of bourgeois society*, MIT Press, Cambridge.

Hall, S 1980, Encoding / Decoding, in D Hall, D Hobson, A Lowe, and P Willis (eds). *Culture, media, language: working papers in cultural studies*, 1972–79. Hutchinson, London, pp. 128–38.

Hammarberg, T 2006, 'The human rights dimension of juvenile justice', Commissioner for Human Rights, Council of Europe, *CommDH/Speech* 12, viewed 12 December 2014, https://wcd.coe.int/ViewDoc.jsp?id=1017235.

'Handy hints' 2012, *The Geelong News*, 10 October, p. 9.

Hasinoff, A 2013, 'Sexting as media production: rethinking social media and sexuality', *New Media Society*, 15(1), 449–65.

Hayward, JO 2012, 'Hysteria over sexting: a plea for common sense approach', viewed 12 December 2014, http://works.bepress.com/cgi/viewcontent.cgi?article=1009&context=john_hayward.

Heath, S, Brooks, R, Cleaver, E & Ireland, E 2009, *An introduction in researching young people's lives*, Sage, London.

Henry, L 2010, 'Sexting: Horsham education project leads the world', *The Wimmera Mail-Times*, 22 April, viewed 12 December 2014, http://www.mailtimes.com.au/story/971377/sexting-horsham-education-project-leads-the-world/.

Herrick, C 2011, 'Aussie schools prioritising education around 'sexting': ACMA', *Computerworld*, viewed 12 December 2014, http://www.computerworld.com.au/article/393922/aussie_schools_prioritising_Education_around_sexting_acma/.

Hier, S 2008, 'Thinking beyond moral panic: risk, responsibility, and the politics of moralization', *Theoretical Criminology*, 12(2), 173–90.

Hiestand, TC 2014, 'Civil and tort liability', in Hiestand, TC & Weins, WJ (eds), *Sexting and youth*, Carolina Academic Press, Durham.

Higgins, L 2014, 'Students might face felony charges for sexting', *Detroit Free Press*, 15 October 15, 2014, viewed 12 December 2014, http://www.freep.com/story/news/local/michigan/oakland/2014/10/15/teens-face-felony-charges-sexting/17316173/.

Hill, S 2013, 'From J-Phone to Lumia 1020: a complete history of the camera phone', *Digital Trends*, viewed 12 December 2014, http://www.digitaltrends.com/mobile/camera-phone-history/.

Hills, R 2012, 'Who's afraid of Melinda Tankard Reist?', *Sydney Morning Herald*, 8 January, p. 12.

Hogg, R 1991, 'Policing and penality', *Journal of Social Justice Studies*, 4, 1–26.

Horder, J 1994, 'Rethinking non-fatal offences', *Oxford Journal of Legal Studies*, 14(3), 335–51.

Howden, S 2011, 'Cop on the cyber beat', *The Sydney Morning Herald*, 16 July, available at http://www.smh.com.au/technology/security/cop-on-the-cyber-beat-20110715-1hhxp.html.

Huges, S 2003, Hansard House of Commons Debate, 15 July 2003, column 202.

Hunt, A 1999, *Governing morals: a social history of moral regulation*, Cambridge University Press, Cambridge.

Hunt, A 2003, 'Risk and moralization in everyday life', in R Ericson & A Doyle (eds), *Risk and morality*, pp. 165–92. University of Toronto Press, Toronto.

Irigaray, L 1985, *This sex which is not one*, Cornell Press, New York.

Jackson, S 1982, *Childhood and sexuality*, Basil Blackwell, Oxford.

James, O 2005, 'He's clean bowled by a sick need for a pleasure', *Daily Telegraph*, 2 July, p. 87.

Jenkinson, P 2011, 'Giving "sexting" the cold shoulder', *YoungLife Australia*, viewed 12 December 2014, http://philipvirgilj.files.wordpress.com/2010/06/connections-july-2011-edition.pdf.

Jewkes, Y 2007, '"Killed by the internet": Cyber homicides, cyber suicides and cyber sex crimes', in Y Jewkes, (ed.), *Crime online*, Willan Publishing, Cullompton.

Jewkes, Y 2010, 'Much ado about nothing? Representations and realities of online soliciting of children', *Journal of Sexual Aggression*, 16, 5–18.

Jewkes, Y 2011a, *Media and crime*, 2nd edn, Sage, London.

Jewkes, Y 2011b, 'The media and criminological research', in P Davies, P Francis & V Jupp (eds), *Doing criminological research*, 2nd edn, Sage, London.

Jewkes, Y & Yar, M 2010, 'Introduction: the internet, cybercrime and the challenges of the twenty-first century', in Y Jewkes & M Yar (eds), *Handbook of internet crime*, Willan Publishing, Devon.

Joint Select Committee on Cyber-Safety 2011, 'High-wire act: Cyber-safety and the young', *Commonwealth of Australia*, viewed 12 December 2014, http://www.aph.gov.au/parliamentary_business/committees/house_of_representatives_committees?url=jscc/report.htm.

Jones, G & Cuneo, C 2009, 'Little girls the new sex objects – Special Investigation', *The Daily Telegraph*, 6 October, p. 2.

Karaian, L 2012, 'Lolita speaks: "Sexting," teenage girls and the law', *Crime, Media, Culture*, 8, 57–73.

Karaian, L 2014, 'Policing "sexting": responsibilization, respectability and sexual subjectivity in child protection/crime prevention responses to teenagers' digital sexual expression', *Theoretical Criminology*, 18(3), 282–99.

Katz, I, Keeley, M, Spears, B, Taddeo, C, Swirski, T & Bates, S 2014, *Research on youth exposure to, and management of, cyberbullying incidents in Australia: Synthesis report*. Social Policy Research Centre, UNSW Australia.

Keeley, M, Katz, I, Bates, S & Wong, M 2014, *Research on youth exposure to, and management of, cyberbullying incidents in Australia: Part B: Cyberbullying incidents involving Australian minors, the nature of the incidents and how they are currently being dealt with*. Social Policy Research Centre, UNSW Australia.

Kelly, L 2002, *Journeys of jeopardy: a review of research on trafficking in women and children in Europe*, IOM Migration Research Series No. 11, viewed 12 December 2014, http://www.iom.int/jahia/webdav/site/myjahiasite/shared/shared/mainsite/published_docs/serial_publications/mrs11b.pdf.

Khosravi, H 2013, 'Canadian ad campaign against sexting doesn't get teenagers', *Toronto Standard*, viewed 12 December 2014, http://torontostandard.com/the-sprawl/canadas-ad-campaign-against-sexting-doesnt-get-teenagers/.

'Kids can be charged under "sexting" laws' 2010, *The Daily Telegraph*, 19 March, p. 3.

KidsHelpline 2013, *Sexting*, viewed 12 December 2014, http://www.kidshelp.com. au/grownups/getting-help/cyberspace/sexting.php.

Kimpel, AF 2010, 'Using laws designed to protect as a weapon: prosecuting minors under child pornography laws', *New York University Review of Law & Social Change*, 34, 299–338.

Kowalski, R, Limber, S & Agaston, P 2012, *Cyberbullying: bullying in the digital age*, Wiley-Blackwell, Oxford.

Krone, T 2005, 'Does thinking make it so? Defining online child pornography possession offences', *Trends and Issues in Criminal Justice* (299), Australian Institute of Criminology, Canberra.

Labi, S 2009, 'Sydney schoolgirl, 13, in sexting investigation after sending nude photo of herself to boyfriend', *news.com.au*, viewed 12 December 2014, http://www.news.com.au/news/school-kids-in-sexting-investigation/story-fna7dq6e-1225699623818.

Law Reform Committee of Victoria 2013, *Report of the Law Reform Committee for the inquiry into sexting*, Parliament of Victoria, Parliamentary Paper No. 230, Session 2010–2013, viewed 12 December 2014, http://www.parliament.vic.gov. au/images/stories/committees/lawrefrom/isexting/LRC_Sexting_Final_Report. pdf.

Lee, M, Crofts, T, Salter, M, Milivojevic, S & McGovern, A 2013, '"Let's get sexting": risk, power, sex and criminalisation in the moral domain', *International Journal for Crime, Justice and Social Democracy*, 2(1), 35–49.

Lemert, E 1981, 'Issues in the study of deviance'. *Sociological Quarterly*, 22(2), 285–305.

Lenhart, A 2009, *Teens and sexting: how and why minor teens are sending sexually suggestive nude or nearly nude images via text messaging*, Pew Internet and American Life Project, Washington, DC.

Livingstone, S & Smith, PK 2014, 'Annual research review: Harms experienced by child users of online and mobile technologies: the nature, prevalence and management of sexual and aggressive risks in the digital age', *Journal of Child Psychology and Psychiatry*, 55(6), 635–54.

Lounsbury, K, Mitchell, K & Finkelhor, D 2011, *The true prevalence of 'sexting'*, Crimes against Children Research Centre, University of New Hampshire, viewed 12 December 2014, http://www.unh.edu/ccrc/pdf/Sexting%20Fact%20 Sheet%204_29_11.pdf.

Lupton, D 1999, *Risk*, Routledge, London.

Lyng, S 2005, 'Edgework and the risk-taking experience', in Lyng, S. (ed.), *Edgework: the sociology of risk-taking*, Routledge, New York, pp. 17–49.

Lynn, R 2010, 'Constructing parenthood in moral panics of youth, digital media and sexting', 105th Annual Meeting of the American Sociological Association, 14–17 August, Atlanta, Georgia.

McClymont K 2010, 'Prosecutor pursues first "sexting" conviction in case involving naked 13-year-girl', *Sydney Morning Herald*, 1 November, p. 1.

McDonald, D 2012, 'Policing obscenity', in P Johnson and D Dalton (eds), *Policing sex*, Routledge, London.

McGrath, H 2009, 'Young people and technology: a review of the current literature (second edition)', viewed 12 December 2014, http://www.ncab.org.au/ Assets/Files/2ndEdition_Youngpeopleandtechnology_LitReview_June202009. pdf.

MacKinnon, C 1993, *Only words*, Harvard University Press, Cambridge.

McDonald, D 2012, 'Policing obscenity', in P Johnson and D Dalton (eds), *Policing sex*, Routledge, p. 99.

McLuhan, M, & Fiore, Q with Agel, J. (1967). *The medium is the massage: an inventory of effects*. Random House, New York.

McLaughlin, J 2010, 'Crime and punishment: teen sexting in context', *Penn State Law Review*, 115, 135–81.

MacLaughlin, JH 2014, 'The first amendment' in TC Hiestand & WJ Weins (eds), *Sexting and youth*, Carolina Academic Press, Durham.

'Man fined for sex text' 2003, *The Advertiser*, 8 October, p. 13.

Mascheroni G, Ponte C, Garmendia M, Garitaonandia C & Murru MF 2010, Comparing media coverage of online risks for children in SouthWestern European countries: Italy, Portugal and Spain. *International Journal of Media and Cultural Politics* 6(1), 25–44.

Masters, R 2003, 'Sports chiefs wield $1m funding stick to enforce Warne's drugs ban', *Sydney Morning Herald*, 22 August, p. 29.

Matthews, N 1994, *Confronting rape: the feminist anti-rape movement and the state*, Routledge, London.

Matyszczyk, C 2014, 'Sexting teen convicted of child pornography', *CNET*, viewed 12 December 2014, http://www.cnet.com/au/news/sexting-teen-convicted-of-child-pornography/.

Marx, G 1995, *New Telecommunications Technologies Require New Manners*, http://www.lex-electronica.org/docs/articles_210.html (accessed 20 December 2014).

Matza, D & Sykes, G 1961, 'Juvenile delinquency and subterranean values', *American Sociological Review*, 26(5), pp. 712–19.

Mauss, M 1969, *The gift: forms and functions of exchange in archaic societies*. Translated by Ian Cunnison with an introduction by EE Evans-Pritchard. Routledge and Kegan Paul, London.

Miller, K 2012, 'A safer way to sext', *Cosmopolitan*, 9 May 2012, viewed 12 December 2014, http://www.cosmopolitan.com/sex-love/news/a10243/safe-sexting/?click=_lpTrnsprtr_18.

Mitchell, B 2001, 'Multiple wrongdoing and offence structure: a plea for consistency and fair labelling', *Modern Law Review*, 63, 393.

Mitchell, K, Finkelhor, D, Jones, L & Wolak, J 2012, 'Prevalence and characteristics of youth sexting: a national study', *Pediatrics*, 129(1), 13–20.

Monahan, K, Steinberg, L & Cauffman, E 2009, 'Affiliation with antisocial peers, susceptibility to peer influence, and antisocial behavior during the transition to adulthood', *Developmental Psychology*, 45, 1520.

Moran-Ellis, J 2012, 'Sexting, intimacy and criminal acts: translating teenage sexualities', in P Johnson & D Dalton (eds), *Policing sex*, Routledge, London, pp. 115–31.

MTV 2014, 'Sexting: what is it?', *A Thin Line*, viewed 12 December 2014, http://www.athinline.org/facts/sexting.

Nagi, A 2013, 'Sexting 101: how to send dirty messages without ugly consequences', *Cosmopolitan*, 6 March 2013, viewed 12 December 2014, http://www.cosmopolitan.com/sex-love/how-to/a4246/how-to-sext/?click=_lpTrnsprtr_14.

National Campaign to Prevent Teen and Unplanned Pregnancy 2008, *Sex and tech: results from a survey of teens and young adults*, viewed 12 December 2014, http://thenationalcampaign.org/resource/sex-and-tech.

National Center for Missing and Exploited Children 2014, *Your photo fate*, viewed 12 December 2014, http://www.netsmartz.org/RealLifeStories/YourPhotoFate.

Nelligan, K & Etheridge, M 2011, 'Facecrooks', *Weekly Times Messenger*, 25 May, p. 5.

Nelson, O 2013a, *Sexting: we're doing it wrong*, viewed 12 December 2014, http://birdeemag.com/sexting-wrong/.

Nelson, O 2013b, 'Why should girls feel ashamed', *The Age*, 22 August, viewed 12 December 2014, http://www.theage.com.au/comment/why-should-girls-feel-ashamed-20130821-2sbgk.html.

NSW Government 2009, 'Safe sexting: no such thing', viewed 12 December 2014, http://www.schools.nsw.edu.au/media/downloads/news/technology/cyber-safety/yr2009/sextingfacts.pdf.

NSW Government 2011, 'Sexting and cyber-safety: protecting your child online', viewed 12 December 2014, http://www.community.nsw.gov.au/docswr/_assets/main/documents/sexting_cyber_safety.pdf.

O'Malley, P 2010, *Crime and risk*, Sage, London.

Oliver, J 2005, 'He's clean bowled by a sick need for pleasure', *The Daily Telegraph*, 2 July, p. 87.

Ost, S 2009, *Child pornography and sexual grooming – Legal and societal responses*, Cambridge University Press, Cambridge.

Ostrager, B 2010, 'SMS. OMG! LOL! TTYL: translating the law to accommodate today's teens and the evolution from texting to sexting', *Family Court Review*, 48(4), 712–26.

Parents Protect! 2014, *Sexting*, viewed 12 December 2014, http://www.parentsprotect.co.uk/sexting.htm#.

'Parents urged to stop teens "sexting"' 2009, *AAP Bulletin Wire*, 3 May.

Parker, M 2009, 'Kids these days: teenage sexting and how the law should deal with it', viewed 12 December 2014, http://works.bepress.com/cgi/viewcontent.cgi?article=1000&context=michael_parker.

Paterson N 2012, Acting Commander, Intelligence and Covert Support Department, Victoria Police, Evidence before the Inquiry into Sexting, Law Reform Committee, Parliament of Victoria, 18 September 2012, viewed 12 December 2014, http://www.parliament.vic.gov.au/images/stories/committees/lawrefrom/isexting/transcripts/2012-09-18_Victoria_Police.pdf.

Pearson, E 2013, 'Tween sexting shock: 11-year-olds sending naked pics on phones', *The Geelong Advertiser*, 12 July, p. 1.

Peskin, M, Markham, C, Addy, R, Shegog, R, Thiel, M, and Tortolero, S 2013, 'Prevalence and patterns of sexting among ethnic minority urban high school students', *Cyberpsychology, Behaviour and Social Networking*, 16(6), 454–9.

Phippen, A 2009, 'Sharing Personal Images and Videos among Young People', *South West Grid For Learning*, available online at http://www.swgfl.org.uk/Staying-Safe/Sexting-Survey. Last accessed 24 October 2014.

—— (2012), *Sexting: An Exploration of Practices, Attitudes and Influences*, Report for the NSPCC, available online at http://www.nspcc.org.uk/Inform/resourcesfor-professionals/sexualabuse/sexting_wda93252.html. Last accessed 24 January 2014.

Pickering, S 2008, 'The new criminals: refugees and asylum seekers', in Anthony, T & Cunneen, C (eds), *The critical criminology companion*, Hawkins Press, Sydney, pp. 169–79.

Podlas, K 2011, 'The "legal epidemiology" of the teen sexting epidemic: how the media influenced a legislative outbreak', *Pittsburgh Journal of Technology Law and Policy*, 12, viewed 12 December 2014, http://tlp.law.pitt.edu/ojs/index. php/tlp/article/view/91/98.

Podlas, K 2014, 'Media Activity and Impact', in TC Hiestand & WJ Weins (eds), *Sexting and youth*, Carolina Academic Press, Durham, pp. 123–51.

Porter, L 2008, 'Malice in wonderland', *Sunday Age*, 10 August, p. 1018.

Potter, RH & Potter, LA 2001, 'The internet, cyberporn, and sexual exploitation of children: media moral panics and urban myths for middle-class parents?', *Sexuality and Culture*, 5(3), 31–48.

Powell, A 2010, 'Configuring consent: emerging technologies, unauthorised images and sexual assault', *Australian and New Zealand Journal of Criminology*, 43(1), 76–90.

Powell, A 2007, 'Sexual pressure and young people's negotiation of consent', ACSSA Newsletter No. 14 June 2007, pp. 8–16. http://www.aifs.gov.au/acssa/ pubs/newsletter/acssa_news14.pdf.

Pratt, J 2000, 'Sex crimes and the new punitiveness', *Behavioral Sciences and the Law*, 18(2–3), 135–51.

Pritchard, J 2008, 'WA: 10 per cent of kids cyber-bullied: WA survey', *AAP General News Wire*, 22 October.

Pyyhtinen, O 2014, *The gift and its paradoxes: beyond mauss*, Ashgate.

Ratcliffe, J, Wallack, L, Fagnani, F & Rodwin, V 1984, 'Perspectives on prevention: health promotion vs health protection', in J de Kervasdoue, J Kimberley & G Rodwin (eds), *The end of an illusion: the future of health policy in western industrialized nations*, University of California Press, California.

Ray, R 2008, The Role of the Attorney-General: an Australian Perspective, Law Council of Australia, viewed 12 December 2014, http://www.lawcouncil.asn.au/ lawcouncil/images/LCA-PDF/speeches/20081013TheRoleoftheAttorney.pdf.

Renold, E & Ringrose, J 2011, 'Schizoid subjectivities?: re-theorising teen-girl's sexual cultures in an era of "sexualisation"', *Journal of Sociology*, 47(4), 389–409.

Richards, R & Calvert, C 2009, 'When sex and cell phones collide: inside the prosecution of a teen sexting case', *Hastings Communications and Entertainment Law Journal*, 32(1), 1–40.

Ringrose, J 2010, 'Sluts, whores, fat slags and Playboy bunnies: teen girls' negotiations of "sexy" on social networking sites and at school', in C Jackson, C Paechter & E Renold (eds), *Girls and education 3–16*, Open University Press, Maidenhead.

Ringrose, J 2012, 'When it comes to 'sexting' the risks are greater to girls', *IOE London Blog*, web log post, 16 May, viewed 12 December 2014, http://ioelondonblog.wordpress.com/2012/05/16/when-it-comes-to-sexting-.

Ringrose, J & Renold, E 2012a, 'Slut-shaming, girl power and "sexualisation": thinking through the politics of the international SlutWalks with teen girls', *Gender and Education*, 24(3), 333–43.

Ringrose, J & Renold, E 2012b, 'Teen girls, working class femininity and resistance: re-theorizing fantasy and desire in educational contexts of heterosexualized violence', *International Journal of Inclusive Education*, 16(4), 461–77.

Ringrose, J, Gill, R, Livingstone, S & Harvey, L 2012, *A qualitative study of children, young people and 'sexting'*, NSPCC, London.

Ringrose, J, Harvey, L, Gill, R & Livingstone, S 2013, 'Teen girls, sexual double standards and "sexting": gendered value in digital image exchange', *Feminist Theory*, 14(3), 305–23.

Rosenberg, E 2011, 'In Weiner's wake, a brief history of the word "sexting"', *The Wire*, viewed 12 December 2014, http://www.thewire.com/national/2011/06/brief-history-sexting/38668/.

Rowe, M 2007, 'Rendering visible the invisible: police discretion, professionalism and decision-making', *Policing and Society*, 17(3), 279–94.

Ryan, E 2010, 'Sexting: how the state can prevent a moment of indiscretion from leading to a lifetime of unintended consequences for minors and young adults', *Iowa Law Review*, 96, 357–83.

Salter, M & Crofts, T 2015, 'Revenge pornography', in Lynn Comella & Shira Tarrant (eds), *New views on pornography: sexuality, politics, and the law*, Praeger, Westport, pp. 233–53.

Salter, M, Crofts, T & Lee, M 2013, 'Beyond criminalisation and responsibilisation: sexting, gender and young people', *Current Issues in Criminal Justice*, 24(3), 301–16.

Scott S, Jackson S and Backett-Milburn K (1998) Swings and roundabouts: risk anxiety and the everyday worlds of children. *Sociology* 32(4), 689–705.

SECASA 2012, 'Respect me. Don't seXt me', viewed 12 December 2014, http://www.secasa.com.au/assets/Documents/Sextingpostcard.pdf.

Sennett, R 1977, *The fall of public man*, London, Penguin.

Sentencing Advisory Council 2012, *Sentencing children and young people in Victoria*, viewed 12 December 2014, http://www.sentencingcouncil.vic.gov.au/sites/default/files/publication-documents/Sentencing%20Children%20and%20Young%20People%20in%20Victoria.pdf.

'Sex life of teens an eye opener' 2007, *The Mercury*, 27 January, p. 3.

'Sex text cop's rank cut' 2007, *Sunday Territorian*, 2 September, p. 1.

Shafron-Perez, S 2009, 'Average teenager or sex offender: solutions to legal dilemma caused by sexting', *The John Marshal Journal of Computer & Information Law*, 26, 431–53.

Shoveller, JA & Johnson, JL 2006, 'Risky groups, risky behaviour, and risky persons: dominating discourses on youth sexual health', *Critical Public Health*, 16, 47–60.

Simester, AP & Sullivan, GR 2007, *Criminal law: theory and doctrine*, 3rd edn, Hart, Oxford.

Simpkins, L 2010, Commonwealth, *Parliamentary Debates*, House of Representatives, 9 March 2010, 2046.

Simpson, B 2013, 'Challenging childhood, challenging children: children's rights and sexting', *Sexualities*, 16(5–6), 690–709.

Sinnerton, J 2009, 'Childhood innocence caught in a sinister web – Parents get the call to educate naive teens about the dark side of technology', *The Sunday Mail*, 24 May, p. 50.

Slane, A 2010, 'From scanning to sexting: the scope of protection of dignity-based privacy in Canadian child pornography law', *Osgoode Hall Law Journal*, 48, 543–93.

Slipper, P 2004, Commonwealth, *Parliamentary Debates*, House of Representatives, 4 August 2004, 32035–36.

Sontag, S 1977, *On photography*, Penguin, London.

South Eastern Centre against Sexual Assault 2012, 'Submission no. 516', Law Reform Committee, Parliament of Victoria, viewed 12 December 2014, http://www.parliament.vic.gov.au/images/stories/committees/lawrefrom/isexting/subs/S16_-_SECASA.pdf.

Squires, R 2009, 'Mobile tabs on tends', *The Sunday Telegraph*, 27 September, p. 32.

Stanko, E 1990, *Everyday violence: how women and men experience sexual and physical danger*, Pandora, New York.

Steinberg, L & Scott, E 2003, 'Less guilty by reason of adolescence: developmental immaturity, diminished responsibility, and the juvenile death penalty', *American Psychologist*, 58, 1009–18.

Strassberg, D., McKinnon, R., Sustaíta, M., and Rullo, J. 2013, 'Sexting by high school students: an exploratory and descriptive study', *Archives of Sexual Behaviour*, 42(1), 15–21.

Strauss, A & Corbin J 1998, *Basics of qualitative research: techniques and procedures for developing grounded theory*. Thousand Oaks, California, Sage Publications.

Submission No 3 2013, Law Reform Committee, Parliament of Victoria, viewed 12 December 2014, http://www.parliament.vic.gov.au/images/stories/committees/lawrefrom/isexting/subs/S03_-_Name_Withheld.pdf.

Surette, R 2010, *Media, crime and criminal justice: images, realities and policies*, Wadsworth, Belmont.

Svantesson, D 2011, '"Sexting" and the law: 15 minutes of fame, and a lifetime of shame', *Masaryk University Journal of Law and Technology*, 5(2), 289–303.

Tallon, K, Choi, A, Keeley, M, Elliott, J & Maher, D 2012, 'New Voices/New Laws: School-age young people in New South Wales speak out about the criminal laws that apply to their online behaviour', National Children's and Youth Law Centre and Legal Aid NSW, viewed 12 December 2014, http://www.lawstuff.org.au/__data/assets/pdf_file/0009/15030/New-Voices-Law-Reform-Report.pdf.

Taylor, I 1999, *Crime in context: a critical criminology of market societies*, Polity Press, Cambridge.

Taylor, M & Quayle, E 2003, *Child pornography: an internet crime*, Brunner-Routledge, Hove.

Taylor, M, Holland, G & Quayle, E 2001, 'Typology of Paedophile Picture Collections', *Police Journal*, 74(97).

'Teen "Sexting" out of control' 2009, News.com.au 2 February 2012, viewed 12 December 2014, http://www.news.com.au/news/teen-sexting-out-of-control/story-fna7dq6e-1111118730003.

Temple, J, Paul, J, van den Berg, P, Lee, V, McElhany, A & Temple, B 2012, 'Teen sexting and its association with sexual behaviors', *Archives of Pediatrics & Adolescent Medicine*, 166(9), 828–33.

The Education Shop 2015, *Photograph DVD-ROM*, viewed 11 January 2015, http://www.theeducationshop.com.au/shop/product.asp?pID=2390.

ThinkUKnow 2010, *Megan's story*, viewed 12 December 2014, http://www.thinkuknow.org.au/site/megan.asp.

ThinkUKnow 2014a, *Sexting*, viewed 12 December 2014, http://www.thinkuknow.org.au/kids/sexting.asp.

ThinkUKnow 2014b, *How to stay in control – mobiles*, viewed 12 December 2014, http://www.thinkuknow.org.au/site/fun_mobiles.asp.

ThinkUKnow 2014c, *Tools and resources*, viewed 12 December 2014, http://www.thinkuknow.org.au/site/tools.asp.

ThinkUKnow UK 2014, *Sex. Relationships. The internet*, viewed 12 December 2014, http://www.thinkuknow.co.uk/14_plus/.

Tin, J 2011, 'Kids branded for a lifetime – Lewd texts lead to sex crime list'. *The Sunday Mail*, 9 October, p. 7.

Tomazin, F 2013, 'New Victorian law to crack down on malicious sexting', *The Age*, 15 December 2013, viewed 12 December 2014, http://www.theage.com.au/victoria/new-victorian-law-to-crack-down-on-malicious-sexting-20131214-2ze9i.html.

United Nations Committee on the Rights of the Child, *General Comment No 10: children's rights in juvenile justice*, 44th sess, UN Doc CRC/C/GC/10 (25 April 2007).

United Nations *Standard Minimum Rules for the Administration of Juvenile Justice*, 96th plen mtg, UN Doc A/RES/40/33 (29 November 1985).

Vanderbosch, H, Simulioniene, R, Marczak, M, Vermeulen, A & Bonetti, L 2013, 'The role of the media', in PK Smith & G Steffgen (eds), *Cyberbullying through the new media: findings from an international network*, Psychology Press, Florence.

Ventre, K & Doukas, D 2012, 'The sext files: Christian lobby wants tougher laws to protect children', *Crikey*, 10 October, viewed 12 December 2014, http://www.crikey.com.au/2012/10/10/the-sext-files-christian-lobby-wants-tougher-laws-to-protect-children/?wpmp_switcher=mobile.

Victoria Legal Aid 2012, 'Submission No. 58', Law Reform Committee, Parliament of Victoria, viewed 12 December 2014, http://www.parliament.vic.gov.au/images/stories/committees/lawrefrom/isexting/subs/S58_-_Victoria_Legal_Aid.pdf.

Victoria Police 2012, Victoria Police Manual, Procedures and Guidelines, Disposition of Offenders.

Viellaris, R 2010, 'Tougher laws on sexting – Teens may be caught in porn crime swoop', *The Courier-Mail*, 9 May, p. 7.

Virilio, P 1986, *Speed and politics: an essay on dromology*, Semiotext(e), New York.

Walker, S, Sanci, L & Temple-Smith, M 2011, 'Sexting and young people: experts' views', *Youth Studies Australia*, 30(4), 8–16, viewed 12 December 2014, http://journals.sfu.ca/ysa/index.php/YSA/article/viewFile/129/145.

Wartella, E & Jennings, N 2000, 'Children and computers: new technology – old concerns', *The Future of Children – Children and Computer Technology*, 10(2), 31–43.

Wastler, S 2010, 'The harm in "sexting": analyzing the constitutionality of child pornography statutes that prohibit the voluntary production, possession, and dissemination of sexually explicit images by teenagers', *Harvard Journal of Law and Gender*, 33, 687–702.

Weins, WJ 2014, 'Concepts and contexts', in TC Hiestand & WJ Weins (eds), *Sexting and youth: a multidisciplinary examination of research, theory and law*, Carolina Academic Press, Durham, pp. 3–32.

Weins, WJ & Todd, HC 2009, 'Sexting, statutes, and saved by the bell: introducing a lesser juvenile charge with an "aggravating factors" framework', *Tennessee Law Review*, 77, 1–56.

Weisskirch, R & Delevi, R 2011, '"Sexting" and adult romantic attachment', *Computers in Human Behavior*, 27, 1697–701.

Western Australian Police Force 2012, 'Submission No. S44', Law Reform Committee, Parliament of Victoria viewed 12 December 2014, http://www.parliament.vic.gov.au/images/stories/committees/lawrefrom/isexting/subs/S44_-_Office_of_Commissioner_of_Police_WA.pdf.

Williams, K 2012, *Textbook on criminology*, 7th edn, Oxford University Press, Oxford.

Wilson, W 2007, 'What's wrong with murder?', *Criminal Law and Philosophy*, 1, 157–77.

Witzleb, N 2009, 'Giller v Procopets: Australia's privacy protection shows signs of improvement', *Torts Law Journal*, 17, 121–9.

Wolak, J & Finkelhor, D 2011, 'Sexting: a typology' crimes against children research centre, University of Hampshire, viewed on 12 December 2014, http://www.unh.edu/ccrc/pdf/CV231_Sexting%20Typology%20Bulletin_4-6-11_revised.pdf.

Wolak, J, Finkelhor, D & Mitchell, K 2012, 'How often are teens arrested for sexting? Data from a national sample of police cases', *Pediatrics*, 129(1), 4–12.

'Your calls' 2003, *Illawarra Mercury*, 12 August, p. 15.

Index

GPSR Compliance
The European Union's (EU) General Product Safety Regulation (GPSR) is a set
of rules that requires consumer products to be safe and our obligations to
ensure this.

If you have any concerns about our products, you can contact us on

ProductSafety@springernature.com

In case Publisher is established outside the EU, the EU authorized
representative is:

Springer Nature Customer Service Center GmbH
Europaplatz 3
69115 Heidelberg, Germany